Money Stock Control
and Inflation Targeting in Germany

Contributions to Economics

Further volumes of this series can be found at our homepage
http://www.springer.de/cgi-bin/search_book.pl?series=1262

Frank Riedel
Imperfect Information and Investor Heterogeneity in the Bond Market
2000. ISBN 3-7908-1247-1

Kirsten Ralf
Business Cycles
2000. ISBN 3-7908-1245-5

Michele Bagella/
Leonardo Becchetti (Eds.)
The Competitive Advantage of Industrial Districts
2000. ISBN 3-7908-1254-4

Frank Bohn
Monetary Union and Fiscal Stability
2000. ISBN 3-7908-1266-8

Jaime Behar
Cooperation and Competition in a Common Market
2000. ISBN 3-7908-1280-3

Michael Malakellis
Integrated Macro-Micro-Modelling Under Rational Expectations
2000. ISBN 3-7908-1274-9

Stefan Baumgärtner
Ambivalent Joint Production and the Natural Environment
2000. ISBN 3-7908-1290-0

Henri Capron, Wim Meeusen (Eds.)
The National Innovation System of Belgium
2000. ISBN 3-7908-1308-7

Tobias Miarka
Financial Intermediation and Deregulation
2000. ISBN 3-7908-1307-9

Chisato Yoshida
Illegal Immigration and Economic Welfare
2000. ISBN 3-7908-1315-X

Nikolaus Thumm
Intellectual Property Rights
2000. ISBN 3-7908-1329-X

Max Keilbach
Spatial Knowledge Spillovers and the Dynamics of Agglomeration and Regional Growth
2000. ISBN 3-7908-1321-4

Alexander Karmann (Ed.)
Financial Structure and Stability
2000. ISBN 3-7908-1332-X

Joos P. A. van Vugt/Jan M. Peet (Eds.)
Social Security and Solidarity in the European Union
2000. ISBN 3-7908-1334-6

Johannes Bröcker/Hayo Herrmann (Eds.)
Spatial Change and Interregional Flows in the Integrating Europe
2001. ISBN 3-7908-1344-3

Kirstin Hubrich
Cointegration Analysis in a German Monetary System
2001. ISBN 3-7908-1352-4

Nico Heerink et al. (Eds.)
Economic Policy and Sustainable Land Use
2001. ISBN 3-7908-1351-6

Friedel Bolle/Michael Carlberg (Eds.)
Advances in Behavioral Economics
2001. ISBN 3-7908-1358-3

Volker Grossmann
Inequality, Economic Growth, and Technological Change
2001. ISBN 3-7908-1364-8

Thomas Riechmann
Learning in Economics
2001. ISBN 3-7908-1384-2

Nicole Pohl
Mobility in Space and Time
2001. ISBN 3-7908-1380-X

Claus Brand

Money Stock Control and Inflation Targeting in Germany

A State Space Modelling Approach to the Bundesbank's Operating Procedures and Intermediate Strategy

With 24 Figures and 26 Tables

Springer-Verlag Berlin Heidelberg GmbH

Series Editors
Werner A. Müller
Martina Bihn

Author
Dr. Claus Brand
European Central Bank
Kaiserstraße 29
60311 Frankfurt a.M.
Germany
E-mail: claus.brand@ecb.int

This book was submitted as a doctoral dissertation
to the Universität GH Essen, Germany, in 1999

ISSN 1431-1933
ISBN 978-3-7908-1393-7
Cataloging-in-Publication Data applied for
Die Deutsche Bibliothek – CIP-Einheitsaufnahme
Brand, Claus: Money stock control and inflation targeting in Germany: a state space modelling approach to the Bundesbank's operating procedures and intermediate strategy; with 26 tables / Claus Brand. – Heidelberg; New York: Physica-Verl., 2001
(Contributions to economics)
Zugl.: Essen, Univ., Diss.
ISBN 978-3-7908-1393-7 ISBN 978-3-642-57601-0 (eBook)
DOI 10.1007/978-3-642-57601-0

Softcover Design: Erich Kirchner, Heidelberg

SPIN 10797196 88/2202-5 4 3 2 1 0 – Printed on acid-free paper

Contents

1. Introduction ... 1
1.1 Intermediate strategies for monetary policy ... 1
1.2 The role of the Bundesbank ... 3
1.3 The methodological framework ... 4

2. Measuring monetary policy: Operating procedures and intermediate strategies ... 7
2.1 The conduct of monetary policy in Germany ... 7
2.1.1 The practice of monetary targeting ... 7
2.1.2 The development of instruments for monetary control ... 19
2.2 Operating procedures and money supply ... 30
2.3 A note on the identifiability of money demand ... 32
2.3.1 The identification problem ... 32
2.3.2 Money demand and monetary policy rules ... 33
2.3.3 Tracing the supply side using bank reserves? ... 34
2.4 A note on the identifiability of autonomous monetary policy actions ... 35
2.4.1 Common identification problems in *VAR*s ... 35
2.4.2 Identifying monetary policy regimes ... 37
2.4.3 Narrative approaches ... 39
2.4.4 Unresolved issues ... 39
2.5 Evidence from recent empirical analyses of German monetary policy ... 40
2.5.1 Was there no role for monetary aggregates in Germany? 40
2.5.2 Did the Bundesbank pursue a Lombard rate regime? .. 41

3. Theoretical framework ... 45
3.1 Basic considerations ... 45
3.2 Interest rate operating procedure (from 1985 on) ... 47
3.3 An alternative approach: reserves targeting ... 49
3.4 Discount window borrowing procedure (1975–1984) ... 51
3.5 Concluding remarks ... 52

4. Analysis of time series using linear state space models 53
4.1 Basic concepts 53
4.1.1 Common approaches to multivariate time series analysis 53
4.1.2 The system theoretic approach 54
4.1.3 Filtering and smoothing 55
4.2 The linear state space model 55
4.3 Specific properties of the linear model 58
4.3.1 Innovation state space representation 58
4.3.2 Linear state space models and time series models 59
4.3.3 Minimality 64
4.4 Signal extraction using the Kalman filter 67
4.4.1 Filtered forecasts 67
4.4.2 Smoothed forecasts 70
4.4.3 The use of the Kalman filter in econometrics 70
4.5 Structural analysis 71
4.5.1 Impulse–responses to orthogonal innovations 71
4.5.2 Impulse–responses to non–orthogonal innovations using a Wold–ordering scheme 72
4.5.3 Impulse–responses to non–orthogonal innovations: Beyond the Wold–ordering scheme 74
4.5.4 The forecast error variance decomposition 76
4.5.5 Distribution of impulse–response functions 77
4.6 Model selection and estimation 79
4.6.1 The model building algorithm 79
4.6.2 Salient features of the algorithm as compared with *VARs* 83
4.6.3 Model specification tests 85
4.7 Modelling nonstationary time series and common stochastic trends 88
4.7.1 Detrending and common trend representation in econometrics 88
4.7.2 Modelling trend and cycle 90
4.7.3 A useful generalisation for cointegrated time series 95
4.7.4 Properties of the decomposition into permanent and transitory components 96

5. Empirical implementation and results 101
5.1 Is a multiplier approach adequate to model German money supply? 101
5.1.1 Data 101
5.1.2 Results 102
5.2 Monetary targeting and the business cycle 117
5.2.1 Data 117
5.2.2 Results 118
5.3 A quantity theory based approach to inflation targeting 126
5.3.1 Money stock control and inflation targeting 126

5.3.2 The P^* approach 128
5.3.3 Data and results 129

6. Conclusions 141
6.1 Methodological remarks 141
6.2 Money stock control and the day–to–day conduct of monetary policy 142
6.3 Money stock control and inflation targeting in Germany 143
6.4 Prospects for the ECB's monetary policy strategy 144

List of figures 147

List of tables 149

Bibliography 151

A. GAUSS–programs 157
A.1 Estimation of balanced state space model 157
A.2 Obtaining in–sample forecasts using the Kalman filter 166
A.3 Calculation of impulse–responses 168
A.4 Calculation of forecast–error variance decompositions 169
A.5 Decomposition of Error Variance Covariance-Matrix Δ 170
A.6 Aoki C-Test for model specification 171

List of figures

2.1 Inflation and the development of the German overnight money market rate (monthly: 1974.01 - 1997.04; dotted line: overnight rate; solid line: annual change in consumer price index.) 13
2.2 Development of M3 (monthly: 1974.01 - 1997.04). 14
2.3 Development of West German GDP – (quarterly, in prices of 1991, 1974.01 - 1990.04). 15
2.4 Development of GDP for unified Germany – (quarterly, in prices of 1991, 1991.01–1998.01). 16
2.5 Development of the German Lombard, discount and overnight money market rate 21
2.6 Development of Lombard and discount loans and credit via *REPO*s 24

4.1 Graphical representation of model (4.3)–(4.4) 58
4.2 Graphical representation of system (4.10), (4.11) in innovation form. 59
4.3 The Kalman filter 69

5.1 Impulse–responses from money market model: 1991.01–1997.04 . . . 107
5.2 Forecast error variance decomposition from money market model: 1991.01–1997.04. 108
5.3 Impulse–responses from money market model: 1985.02–1990.05 . . . 111
5.4 Forecast error variance decomposition from money market model: 1985.01–1990.05 112
5.5 Impulse–responses from money market model: 1975.01–1985.01 . . . 115
5.6 Forecast error variance decomposition from money market model: 1975.01–1985.01 116
5.7 Impulse–responses from general model: 1990.05–1997.04 120
5.8 Impulse–responses from general model: 1990.05–1997.04 121
5.9 Impulse–responses from general model: 1975.01–1985.01 124
5.10 Impulse–responses from general model: 1975.01–1985.01 125
5.11 Capacity utilisation: 1975.I–1997.IV. 131
5.12 Velocity of German M3: 1975.I–1997.IV. 132
5.13 GDP deflator and P^*: 1975.I–1997.IV. 133
5.14 Impulse-responses for price gap and overnight rate from state space representation: 1975.I–1997.IV. 138
5.15 Impulse-responses for price gap and overnight rate from VAR representation: 1975.I–1997.IV. 139

List of tables

2.1 Monetary targets of the Deutsche Bundesbank 11

3.1 Interaction among the variables under an interest rate rule 49
3.2 Interaction among the variables under a reserves targeting procedure 51
3.3 Interaction among the variables under the discount borrowing rule 52

5.1 Singular values of trend part for small model (1991.01–1997.04) .. 103
5.2 Ratios of singular values of trend part for small model (1991.01–1997.04) 104
5.3 Residual diagnostics: Trend part of model for subperiod 1991.01–1997.04 104
5.4 Singular values of cyclical part for small model (1991.01–1997.04). 104
5.5 Ratios of singular values of cyclical part for small model (1991.01–1997.04) 105
5.6 Residual diagnostics: Joint model for subperiod 1991.01–1997.04.. 105
5.7 Model parameter estimates (1991.01–1997.04) 106
5.8 Model parameter estimates (1985.02–1990.05) 109
5.9 Residual diagnostics for subperiod 1985.02–1990.05 110
5.10 Model parameter estimates (1975.01–1985.01) 113
5.11 Residual diagnostics for subperiod 1975.01–1985.01 114
5.12 Model parameter estimates (1990.06–1997.04) 119
5.13 Residual diagnostics for subperiod 1990.06–1997.04 119
5.14 Forecast error decomposition: 1990.06–1997.04 122
5.15 Model parameter estimates (1975.01–1985.01) 123
5.16 Residual diagnostics for subperiod 1975.01–1985.01 123
5.17 Forecast error decomposition: 1975.01–1985.01 126
5.18 Parameter estimates and residual diagnostics: State space implementation of P^*–model for West–Germany (1975.I–1990.IV) 134
5.19 Parameter estimates and residual diagnostics: State space implementation of P^*–model for unified Germany (1975.I–1997.IV) 135
5.20 Variance decomposition from state space implementation of P^*–model 135
5.21 Parameter estimates and residual diagnostics: State space implementation of P^*–model for unified Germany (1975.I–1997.IV) 137
5.22 Variance decomposition from Bundesbank-reaction-function. 137

1. Introduction

1.1 Intermediate strategies for monetary policy

The launch of a single European currency in January 1999 has been sparking a heated debate over what strategy the European Central Bank's policy should be based on so as to distribute and maintain monetary stability in Europe. In order to pass the Bundesbank's reputation as a tough inflation fighter on to the European Central Bank there have been strong efforts to make the ECB a close copy of the Bundesbank. It might be surmised that there will be a lot of similarities in its intermediate strategies. Among other indicators, the ECB's policy will be based on the growth rate of a broad monetary aggregate consistent with its definition of price stability. As a key instrument in the new central bank's instruments, *REPO* operations will constitute the main refinancing source of private banks and, in addition, minimum reserve requirements have been introduced to facilitate the authority's command over the banking sector's liquidity by means of stabilising the demand for central bank money.

After having introduced monetary targeting in the 1970s, in the 1980s, the Bank of England and the Fed soon abandoned it again, because of distortions from financial innovations and currency substitution. But the Bundesbank strongly defended its intermediate strategy of monetary targeting and advocated its implementation in the European System of Central Banks.

The Fed announced a target for different monetary and credit aggregates for the first time in spring 1975 (see Bernanke and Mishkin (1992)). It targeted the interest rate in the interbank money market in order to meet these monetary targets but allowed fluctuations in the monetary base. On 6 October 1979 the Fed's Chairman Paul Volcker announced a more pronounced policy of monetary targeting: Henceforth, the Fed targeted the monetary base using a "nonborrowed reserves procedure": it targeted the amount of central bank credit excluding discount loans. Due to high and volatile interest rates in the money market induced by this operating procedure, it was abandoned in 1982 and the Fed began a gradual process of backing away from monetary targeting. Targets for monetary growth were dropped and, in February

1993, Fed Chairman Alan Greenspan proclaimed that the Fed would give less weight to monetary aggregates to guide itself (see Blinder (1998, pp. 26–29))[1].

From 1976 through 1990, the Bank of England based its policy on monetary growth rates using different aggregates, but finally abandoned this strategy because of invariable failures to meet its targets. Apart from the Swiss National Bank, the Bundesbank was by then the sole remaining monetary targeter.

However, it might be conjectured that even in Germany monetary targets played only a weak role throughout the past decades for at least two reasons. Firstly, the record to meet the targets has been poor. Secondly, from the empirical point of view it might be doubted that there was a reliable relationship between the monetary aggregates and inflation and output.

For this reason it might be doubted that the Bundesbank placed great emphasis on monetary targeting, and one might wonder why it advocated monetary targeting as a rule for the European Central Bank's future policy. In October 1998 the governing council of the ECB took the decision to follow a two pillar strategy. It announced that monetary policy will aim at maintaining price stability defined as an increase in the Harmonised Index of Consumer Prices of below 2% per annum. In order to achieve this objective it will base its monetary policy decisions on two pillars, namely a prominent role for money and a broad assessment of the outlook for price stability (see ECB, Monthly Bulletin, January 1999). Thereby the prominent role for money is signalled by a reference value of monetary growth for the broad monetary aggregate M3 [2] which is consistent with its definition of price stability. However, in contrast to the Bundesbank's officially stated strategy, the ECB's reference value for money growth does not constitute an intermediate target. In particular, it does not constitute commitment on the part of the ECB to mechanically correct deviations of money growth from the reference value. It is mainly reflecting the ECB's view that inflation is ultimately a monetary phenomenon

---

[1] Quite interestingly, speaking of the "death of monetarism" Blinder (1998, p. 28) who had practical experience as vice–chairman of the Federal Reserve Board interprets this change as an overt dismissal of *any* monetarist approach to monetary policy. He envisages monetary policy in terms of setting interest rates to target demand, output gaps and, thereby, inflation. In the light of his documentation the fact that monetary aggregates were relinquished as instruments in 1982 marked the jettisoning of monetarism.

[2] M3 as observed by the ECB consists of "currency in circulation (net) plus certain liabilities of MFIs" (i.e. the Monetary Financial Institutions) "resident in the euro area and in the case of deposits, the liabilities of some institutions that are part of central government (such as Post Offices and Treasuries). These liabilities included in M3 are: overnight deposits; deposits with an agreed maturity of up to two years; deposits redeemable at notice up to three months; repurchase agreements; dept securities issued with a maturity of up to two years (net). Only such positions vis-à-vis euro area residents other than MFIs and central government are included in M3" (see ECB Press Release as of 14 December 1998).

and that the analysis of monetary developments constitutes indispensable information for the conduct of monetary policy.

To reconcile the potential achievements of a policy relying on monetary analysis, it is of crucial importance how the Bundesbank's policy might be assessed in hindsight, because it might be regarded as the one of the most successful central banks in the world in terms of achieving and maintaining low inflation rates.

1.2 The role of the Bundesbank

Recently, the role for monetary targeting in Germany has been analysed by Clarida and Gertler (1996) and Bernanke and Mihov (1997). They provide a great step towards understanding the conduct of German monetary policy and might help to reach agreement with respect to the controversy on European monetary policy. They conclude that the Bundesbank targeted inflation rather than monetary aggregates. In order to model the conduct of day–to–day policy, Clarida and Gertler (1996) assume that the Bundesbank stabilised overnight interest rates in the money market, whereas Bernanke and Blinder (1997) assume a Lombard rate regime. There are some objections to these approaches. Firstly, Clarida and Gertler (1996) do not in fact model demand and supply in the German money market, and hence, it is not quite clear in how far the Bundesbank did accommodate demand shocks in order to smooth interest rates. Secondly, Bernanke and Mihov (1997) do present an explicit model of the German reserves market. But they do not include a broad monetary aggregate into the reserves market model, so that it is impossible to infer how money demand shocks are transmitted to this market. It might be objected that they fail to accurately identify demand and supply in the money market and, hence, monetary policy. Moreover, their assumption that throughout the past decades the Bundesbank conducted its day–to–day policy in terms of targeting the Lombard rate inappropriately reflects the evolution that took place in the Bundesbank's policy instruments since the 1980s.

As in most industrial countries, from the beginning of the 1980s, the Bundesbank imposed restrictions on the recourse by banks to conventional open ended central bank lending facilities (see Kasman (1992)). The Lombard rate was raised to penal levels and tended to serve as an upper limit for money market rates. There was increasing use of flexible money market operations and other fine–tuning instruments. The burden of reserve requirements had been lowered. Changes in reserve ratios as a means of making adjustments in banks' reserve positions were limited. This specific development is well reflected in the current shape of the ECB's money market instruments.

In recent years the Bundesbank stated that the achievement of its monetary policy objectives was mainly concerned with stabilising the overnight money market interest rate, the *Tagesgeldsatz* (see Deutsche Bundesbank (1994, p. 62)). At the beginning of the 1980s the Bundesbank shifted gradually away from a policy of discount window borrowing, and attached more importance to open market operations. A reason for this might be that, with the former instruments at hand, increases of short–term interest rates to the extent necessary to counter a build–up of inflation could be delayed. This development is being reviewed in Chapter 2.

The question therefore arises how different operating procedures during certain sub–periods served to meet the Bundesbank's intermediate goal of stabilising the growth of the money stock in the economy. The assessment of this relationship is one of the main purposes of this study. Therefore, in Chapter 3 a model of the German money market is developed that allows the identification of supply and demand shocks. With an empirical implementation of this model at hand, it will be possible to determine whether bank reserves were more demand or supply determined, and – in the case of an interest rule period – in how far money demand shocks have been offset by the Bundesbank, so that they did not have any impact on interest rates. This requirement is supposed to be crucial with respect to the identifiability of empirical money demand equations as already pointed out by Gordon (1984) and Cooley and LeRoy (1981).

Above all, it is shown whether a liquidity effect is detectable, and whether, in the case of changes in the stance of monetary policy, effects on bank liquidity and the money stock are observable. Empirical results (Chapter 5) suggest that in order to pursue its intermediate strategy, the Bundesbank had been stabilising overnight money market rates. This is in sharp contrast to a money multiplier approach to the money supply process.

Furthermore, in order to draw conclusions about the importance of monetary targeting relative to targeting inflation and output in the central bank's reaction function, the Bundesbank's policy when faced with changes in economic activity and inflationary pressure is analysed in a more general setting. For the same purpose, a model of monetary policy is additionally presented that mimics the Bundesbank's officially stated implementation of monetary targets as closely as possible. The results suggest quite different conclusions than those drawn by Bernanke and Mihov (1997) and Clarida and Gertler (1996).

1.3 The methodological framework

Some remarks on the econometric method used in this context are to be made here. The methodology presented in Chapter 4 follows closely Masanao Aoki's (1990) state space modelling approach for multivariate time series. Impulse–response functions subject to different structural identification schemes are used. Hence, a further purpose of this study is to assess the power and limitations of this relatively unknown modelling technique. In contrast to the cointegration literature, Aoki's approach allows for a decomposition of non-stationary time series into permanent and cyclical components – so as to analyse long-run and short-run dynamics – without imposing unit roots. It is shown that state space models should offer a more parsimonious representation of time series than vector autoregressions. They may thus overcome various difficulties arising in the context of conventional *VAR* models, such as inaccuracy of coefficient estimates due to multicollinearity, and arbitrariness with respect to the final model choice, since selection criteria tend to be flat.

Both on the theoretical and on the applied level, this study provides a conclusive comparison between *VAR* modelling and the system theoretic approach. The application should significantly contribute to extend practical experience with this specific approach which is yet widely unknown and only barely accepted among econometricians.

The approach has been fiercely criticised by econometricians for its lack of statistical foundations. In order to bridge this gap, in this study, statistical tests aimed at facilitating model selection that have been introduced only recently are applied. Up to date, dynamic multipliers from linear state space models have been displayed without error bounds. Therefore, in order to illustrate the efficiency of the modelling technique and to compare it with *VAR*s, we present confidence bounds for impulse–responses based on resampling techniques.

2. Measuring monetary policy: Operating procedures and intermediate strategies

2.1 The conduct of monetary policy in Germany

2.1.1 The practice of monetary targeting

> *"If we consider one kingdom by itself, it is evident, that the greater or less plenty of money is of no consequence;"[...]"It seems a maxim almost self evident, that the prices of every thing depend on the proportion between commodities and money, and that any considerable alteration on either has the same effect, either of heightening or lowering the price. Encrease the commodities, they become cheaper; encrease the money, they rise in their value. As, on the other hand, a diminution of the former, and that of the latter, have contrary tendencies." [...]"It is also evident, that the prices do not so much depend on the absolute quantity of commodities and that of money, which are in a nation, as on that of the commodities, which come or may come to market, and of the money which circulates."*
> DAVID HUME (1752)

The monetarist approach to monetary policy. In 1974, when German monetary policy was freed from the exchange rate constraints of the Bretton Woods era, the Bundesbank implemented a policy of monetary targeting. An annual monetary target for 1975 was pre–announced in December 1974. The policy had been maintained until January 1999 when the ECB took over the responsibility for monetary policy in Europe. The Bundesbank's strategy reflected its adoption of the monetarist view to consider inflation as a monetary phenomenon. For that reason, controlling the money stock was thought to be appropriate to achieve its statutory goal of price stability. It started with targeting a point in money growth and from 1979 targeted money within a projected range. Thereby, in 1988, the Bundesbank shifted from "central bank money" to M3[1].

The use of a broad monetary aggregate as an indicator as well as an intermediate variable for monetary policy reflected two important assumptions. Firstly, the Bundesbank stated that it could control $M3$ with sufficient precision. Secondly, the strategy rested on the assumption that there is a well–understood and empirically reliable relationship with the final goal of price stability. $M3$ was considered to show a fairly stable positive relationship with nominal GDP and a negative relationship with interest rates. In the long–run a connection between the growth rate of the aggregate and changes in the price level was thought to be empirically proven. In this respect, $M3$ was thought to be superior to other indicators such as interest rates or interest rate spreads and credit aggregates (see Deutsche Bundesbank (1995, pp. 68–80)).

Setting the monetary target. When implementing its annual monetary targets, the Bundesbank primarily took into account envisaged growth rates in prices and the forecasted increase in potential output. Hence, there was always underlying an explicitly stated goal for inflation that the annual growth rate of the designated monetary aggregate was derived from.

The targeting procedure rested on the quantity theoretic link between money and prices: it was assumed that price stability can only be achieved if the money stock expands at a pace that is in line with real economic growth. Theoretically, the concept draws on the quantity theory originated from David Hume's 18th–century essay "Of money", from which we quoted at the beginning of this section. Consider the following identity:

$$P_t Y_t = M_t V_t,$$

where P_t represents the price level at time t, Y_t real aggregate output, M_t the nominal money stock of, say, $M3$, and V_t its velocity. Assuming that V_t

[1] M3 as defined by the Bundesbank consisted of currency and sight deposits held by domestic non–banks with domestic credit institutions, time deposits for less than four years held by domestic non–banks with domestic credit institutions, and savings deposits at three months' notice held by domestic non–banks with domestic credit institutions (see Deutsche Bundesbank (1995, p. 72)). "Central bank money" as defined by the Deutsche Bundesbank (1995, p. 84) comprised currency in circulation in the hands of non–banks and the required minimum reserves (other than minimum–reserve–carrying bank debt securities) calculated at constant reserve ratios as at January 1974. Thereby currency was accounted at its full weight and bank deposits were included in accordance with the historical reserve ratios assigned to individual money stock components reflecting their differing degree of liquidity. Thereby a ratio of 16.6% for sight deposits, 12.4 % for time deposits and 8.1% for savings deposits was applied. The components included in this money stock largely coincided with M3. In contrast to M3, savings deposits at over three months', but less than four years', notice and bank savings bonds with maturity of less than four years were additionally included in the "central bank money" stock.

is stable, or at least forecastable, this identity results in the quantity theory of money[2]. Reading the equation from the right hand side to the left, a link between money and nominal income would be established. Transforming the quantity equation into percentage changes, where $\dot{m}_t$, $\dot{y}_t$, $\dot{p}_t$, $\dot{v}_t$ denote these changes, and solving for $\dot{m}_t$,

$$\dot{m}_t = \dot{p}_t + \dot{y}_t - \dot{v}_t$$

is derived. Because actual real output depends on the degree λ of capacity utilisation, $Y_t = \lambda_t \bar{Y}_t$, where $\bar{Y}_t$ represents real potential output,

$$\dot{y}_t = \dot{\lambda}_t + \dot{\bar{y}}_t.$$

The change in velocity might be decomposed into changes caused by a (changes in the) long–term trend $\dot{v}_t^T$ and a cyclical trend $\dot{v}_t^C$, so that:

$$\dot{v}_t = \dot{v}_t^T + \dot{v}_t^C.$$

Therefore,

$$\dot{m}_t = \dot{\lambda}_t + \dot{\bar{y}}_t + \dot{p}_t - \dot{v}_t^T - \dot{v}_t^C.$$

This equation can be modified assuming that the cyclical component in velocity has the same behaviour as the cyclical component of production so that $\dot{\lambda}_t - \dot{v}_t^C = 0$.

The monetary target $\dot{m}_t^*$ was derived so as to achieve a level of an "unavoidable" or "normative" (see Deutsche Bundesbank (1995, pp. 83–85)) price increase $\dot{p}_t^*$. Substituting accordingly the rule for setting growth rates in $M3$ was given by:

$$\dot{m}_t^* = \dot{\bar{y}}_t + \dot{p}_t^* - \dot{v}_t^T.$$

From these benchmark figures – the growth rate of production potential, the "normative" price increase and the trend decline in velocity – the average annual growth rate of the money stock was derived.

The term "unavoidable" or "normative" price level is misleading in this context. Firstly, the concept reflected the widely shared assumption that official price indices overstated the true inflation rate because they tend to undercompensate for the improvements in the quality of goods. Secondly, the Bundesbank took account of the consideration that price decisions which have already entered into the decisions of economic agents can only gradually

[2] In the equation V_t could be substituted by $\bar{V}_t$, where $\bar{V}_t = P_tY_t/M_t$. Assuming that money demand negatively depends on an interest rate i_t and positively on real income Y_t, equilibrium velocity $\bar{V}_t$ can be written $\bar{V}_t = Y_t/m(i_t, Y_t)$, where m denotes the demand for real money balances. If this demand function is stable, the money stock can be controlled by setting interest rates, and furthermore, the quantity theory of money establishes a stable relationship between money and prices. An additional amount of money will result in a rising price level if not accommodated by an equivalent supply of commodities, supposed that velocity does not change fundamentally.

be eliminated. Nevertheless, if price increases were forecasted at a level which seemed intolerable for the Bundesbank, $\dot{p}_t^*$ was invariably set below that level.

The Bundesbank used long–term variables, because it did not intend to fine–tune the economy. Instead, the ultimate goal was price stability and the financing of economic growth (see Deutsche Bundesbank (1995, p. 85)). The strategy implied a considerable stabilisation of macroeconomic activity. If real GDP was forecasted to grow at a lower rate than real potential output, the Bundesbank would nevertheless have allowed $M3$ to grow at a rate consistent with the *trend* in potential output. In the case of a recession, the strategy induced an injection of liquidity so as to prevent a coincident decline in the money stock and in production. Therefore, the Bundesbank allowed ample liquidity to flow into the economy as long as a negative output gap prevailed. If, on the other hand, the economy was booming, thereby pushing real GDP above potential output growth, a more restrictive policy stance was induced: in this case $M3$ was only allowed to grow in line with the trend in GDP and not with its actual movements.

Monetary targets and the scope for discretion. In 1974, the Bundesbank first started targeting a point in money growth and, from 1979 on, set the monetary growth rates in terms of a target range. By setting varying ranges – or "corridors" – it took account of the extent of uncertainty to which the development of the money stock was influenced by exogenous circumstances. At times when it intended to tighten monetary policy, the target range was narrowed (see Deutsche Bundesbank (1995, p. 87)).

Both the inflation and the monetary goals were set quite moderately, so as to accommodate shocks to the economic system. Even in its official statements the Bundesbank never regarded its annual targets as the sole guideline for the conduct of its policy. It always stressed that domestic and external factors had to be taken into account (see Deutsche Bundesbank (1995, pp. 88–91)) as well. Even though floating exchange rates considerably broadened the scope for monetary policy, especially long term interest rates became increasingly determined on international financial markets. Developments in U.S. interest rates and in the DM–$–exchange rate played a prominent role in the conduct of German monetary policy. Whenever the DM appreciated against the US–$, as it was the case in 1978 and during the years 1986–1987, the Bundesbank could afford an expansionary policy stance and allowed the money stock to overshoot the target without failing to meet its inflation target. The flexibility in its behaviour to set inflation and monetary targets was especially pronounced during the two oil price shocks in 1974 and 1981.

Hence, the Bundesbank conducted its officially stated policy in a flexible way. As reflected in Table 2.1, during the period 1975–1997 it failed to meet its monetary targets in 11 out of 23 cases. The Bundesbank was always aware of the long and variable lags in the transmission of monetary policy. It always took account of the fact that, in the medium term, prices may deviate from

The record of meeting monetary and inflation targets					
Year	Target: % growth of money	Actual % growth (rounded figures)	Monetary target achieved	Inflation target	Actual inflation rates
1975	ca. 8	10	no	5–6	7.1
1976	8	9	no	4–5	5.0
1977	8	9	no	≤ 4	4.3
1978	8	11	no	3	3.7
1979	6-9	6	yes	3	4.0
1980	5-8	5	yes	$3\frac{1}{2} - 4$	5.4
1981	4-7	4	yes	$3\frac{1}{2}$	6.3
1982	4-7	6	yes	$3\frac{1}{2}$	5.2
1983	4-7	7	yes	3	3.3
1984	4-6	5	yes	2	2.4
1985	3-5	5	yes	2	2.1
1986	3,5-5,5	8	no	2	−0.1
1987	3-6	8	no	2	0.2
1988	3-6	7	no	2	1.3
1989	ca. 5	5	yes	ca. 2	2.8
1990	4-6	6	yes	2	2.7
1991	3-5	5	yes	2	3.6
1992	3,5-5,5	9	no	2	5.1
1993	4,5-6,5	7	no	2	4.5
1994	4-6	6	yes	2	2.7
1995	4-6	3	no	2	1.8
1996	4-7	8,6	no	2	1.5
1997	3,5-6,5	5	yes	$1\frac{1}{2}$–2	1.8

Table 2.1. Monetary targets of the Deutsche Bundesbank

the path mapped out by monetary growth. It was assumed, that money leads inflation only in the long–run, whereas in the short–run inflation itself is determined by own lags, import prices, the exchange rate, wages, value added taxes and fiscal effects (see Deutsche Bundesbank (1992, p. 26)).

Due to its poor success in terms of meeting its announced growth rates either in the Central Bank Money stock or $M3$ it has often been argued that the Bundesbank had made its monetary targets subservient to its inflation targets. Clarida and Gertler (1996) and Bernanke and Mihov (1997) state that it would be more appropriate to describe the German central bank as a *direct inflation targeter*. They argue that excess money growth sometimes coincided with meeting the inflation goal. They criticise that, if the Bundesbank's behaviour indeed reflected a policy of monetary targeting, it should have allowed policy to respond to deviations of money growth from target, even if inflation was on target. This criticism clearly highlights the difficulties surrounding the controversy to what extent monetary policy in Germany was guided by quantity theory considerations.

A brief historical review on the data. Obviously there was a considerable degree of discretion in the conduct of its policy. If the Bundesbank failed to meet an annual target, it simply set the new corridor according to the actual amount of money in the economy, so that monetary developments were accommodated. It is difficult to deduce from the Bundesbank's performance at meeting its objectives when monetary policy in Germany was more contractionary or more expansionary. One should be careful to identify changes in the target aggregate with changes in the stance of monetary policy. As indicated in the introduction, changes brought about by financial innovations, currency substitution and deregulation make it impossible to use money growth rates as a measure of the direction of policy. Above all, it might be argued that developments in a broad monetary aggregate like $M3$ reflect changes in money demand rather than in the policy stance. Only tentative inference is therefore to be drawn on this basis.

Due to the oil price shock of the 1970's, inflation climbed above 7% by the end of 1974 (see Figure 2.1), when the Bundesbank embarked on monetary targeting. A severe economic downturn occurred and the Bundesbank permitted money growth and inflation to overshoot their targets. Figures 2.3 and 2.4 show the development of German GDP from 1974–1998. Recovery took place in the late 1970s and, at the beginning of the 1980s, in response to extraordinary high interest rates in the United States, German rates rose from 3 % in 1978 to 12% in 1981. Inflation was permitted to overshoot, but monetary targets were met. Economic activity slowed down. The years from 1983 until German unification in 1990 were characterised by a weak economy, decreasing inflation and interest rates. In the years 1986–1988 monetary targets were not met[3]. Economic recovery took place from 1989 on and merged with the demand boom triggered by German unification, reinforced by fiscal expansion in 1990. On the eve of unification, the West German economy was already approaching capacity output. The achievement of monetary targets was mixed in the following years, and inflation at 4% at the beginning of the 1990's was generally above the target value. The Bundesbank aggressively tightened monetary policy. As it is known, this had a disastrous effect on the European monetary system. Obviously European central banks were reluctant to adopt the high level of German interest rates without need to bring down inflation further and thereby risking even more unemployment.

From 1993 on, the Bundesbank began to slightly ease interest rates in response to rising unemployment and decreasing inflation. This policy was maintained until 1999. It was accompanied by a convergence of interest rates throughout Europe, as European Monetary Union approached, and it has been pursued by the European Central Bank.

[3] During this period the DM depreciated against the US–$, thereby facilitating a more expansionary policy stance and interest rate reductions without inducing inflation. The inflation target was easily met during these years.

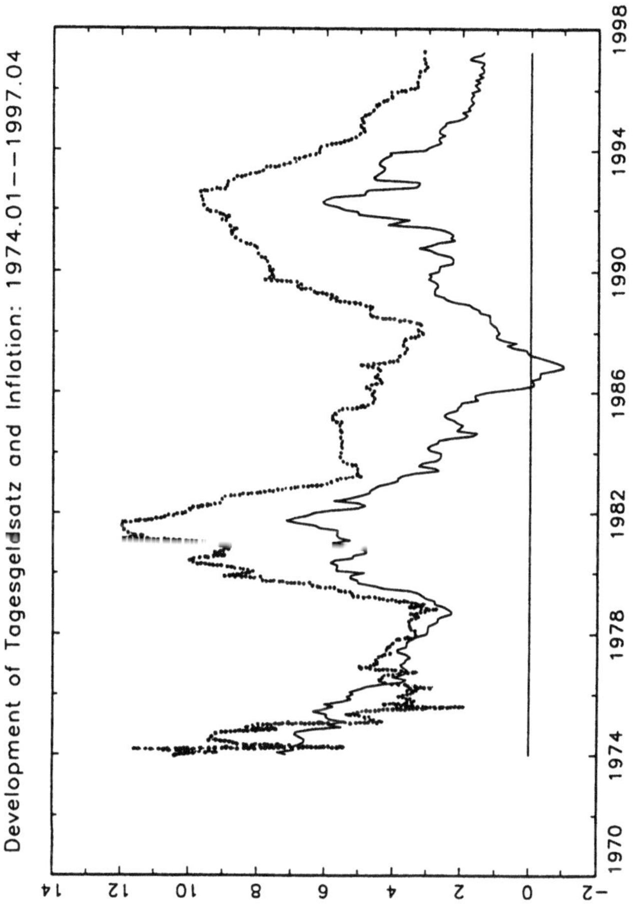

Fig. 2.1. Inflation and the development of the German overnight money market rate (monthly: 1974.01 – 1997.04; dotted line: overnight rate; solid line: annual change in consumer price index.)

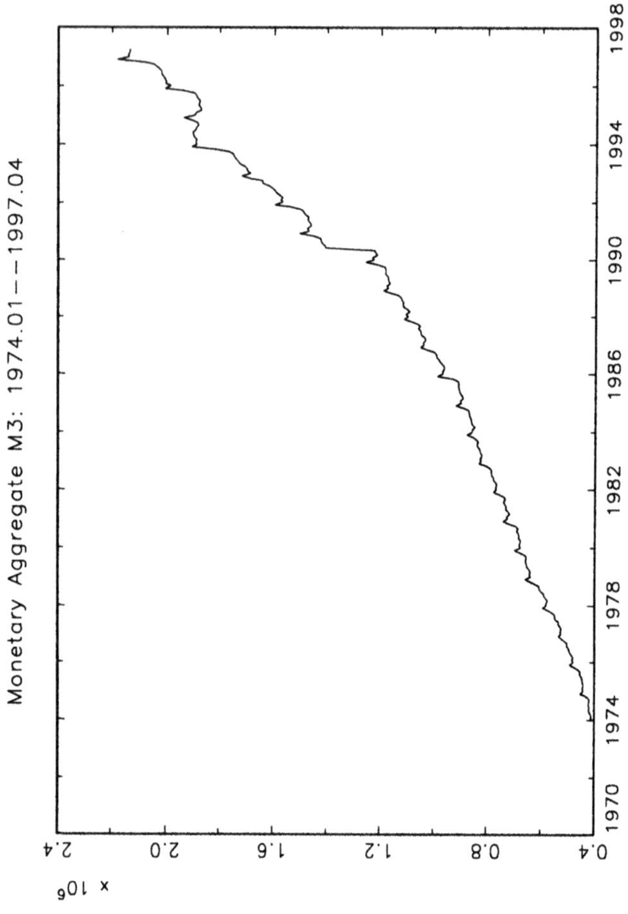

Fig. 2.2. Development of M3 (monthly: 1974.01 – 1997.04).

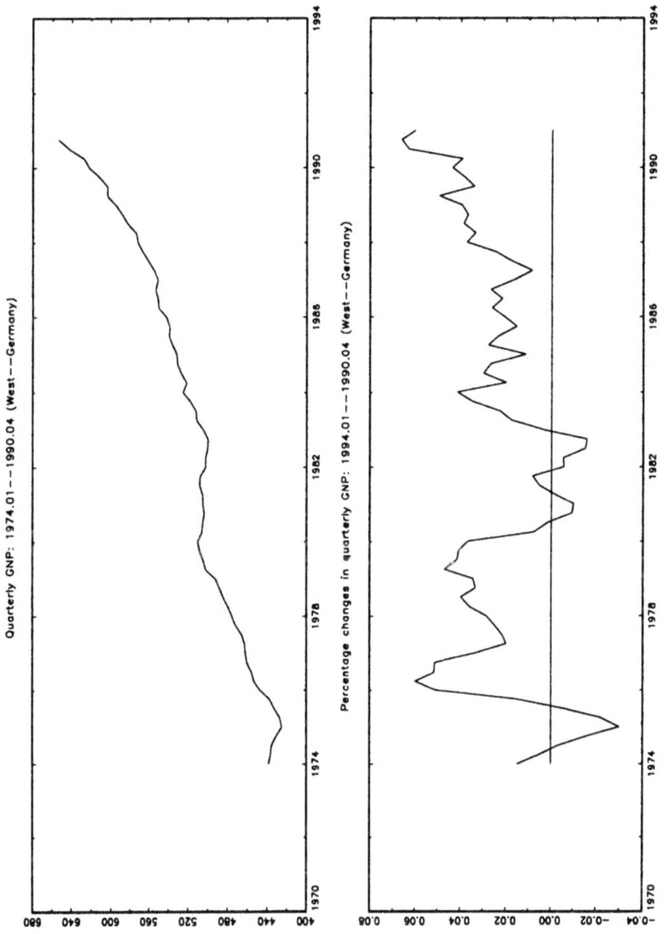

Fig. 2.3. Development of West German GDP – (quarterly, in prices of 1991, 1974.01 – 1990.04).

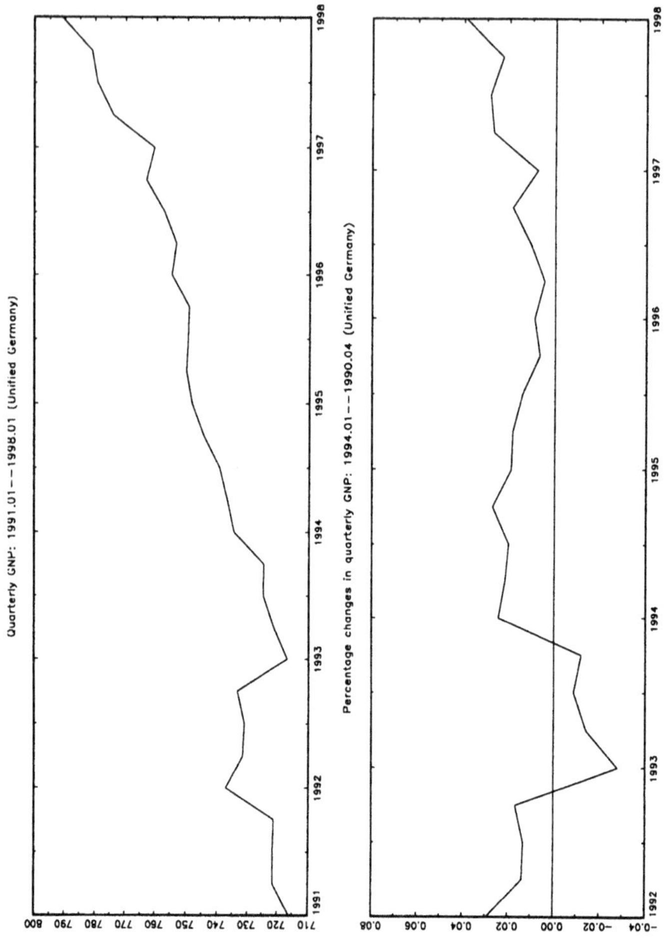

Fig. 2.4. Development of GDP for unified Germany – (quarterly, in prices of 1991, 1991.01–1998.01).

The Bundesbank stuck to a policy of constantly lowering interest rates despite the failure to meet its monetary targets in recent years and despite hesitant economic recovery in 1998. A reason for this might be that, despite economic growth, unemployment in Germany has been steadily rising as a result of labour market rigidities and high non–wage labour costs arising from the costly social security, health care and retirement system for Germany's ageing population.

When the new European currency was launched in January 1999, Euro–zone interest rates had converged at historically low levels. Inflation rates in terms of consumer price indices dropped below 1 % and economic growth in Germany as well as in the Euro–zone had weakened considerably.

The choice of the appropriate aggregate. The choice of the target aggregate was motivated by considerations of the link between the respective aggregate and the macroeconomic variables of interest. It is a prerequisite that there be a predictable relationship with nominal GDP and prices. In addition, it should be controllable by the central bank's policy instruments. It is thus crucial to assess both of these issues.

Until 1987, the choice fell on "Central bank money". However, the heavy weight of currency in circulation in this money stock was considered unsatisfactory. Because currency in circulation responded sharply to movements in interest rates, its heavy weight implied that the Central bank money stock over– or understated the trend of monetary expansion. In addition to that, the minimum reserve ratios increasingly deviated from those applied in the definition of Central bank money. Therefore, the correlation between the money target and the ongoing provision of central bank money increasingly weakened. In 1987 Central bank money was replaced by $M3$. Movements in both aggregates had been very similar over the long–run. Because $M3$ became increasingly plagued by financial innovations and currency substitution, in recent years the Bundesbank also observed M3E[4].

There was always a debate going on in Germany as to whether there were other monetary aggregates having a more stable relationship with output and prices (see, for example, Gaab (1996)). On top of that, there were theoretical reservations with respect to M3. Given a quantity theoretic approach to inflation, it is desirable to target a transaction–equivalent monetary aggregate. However, there are assets of higher liquidity that are not contained in M3, whereas on the other hand M3 contains components of a relatively low liquidity. Furthermore, the use of official monetary aggregates is theoretically unsatisfactory in the light of a demand–for–money theory (see Barnett, Fisher and Serletis (1992)). Simple sum aggregates do not accurately measure the

[4] M3E: "M3 Extended" comprised $M3$, Euro–deposits, short–term bank debt securities and certificates of domestic and foreign money market funds in the hands of domestic non–banks (less the bank deposits and short–term bank debt securities in the hands of domestic money market funds (see Deutsche Bundesbank (1995, p. 72)).

actual quantities of the monetary products that optimising economic agents select in the aggregate. Since the relative prices of the aggregated components fluctuate over time, their respective quantities of different liquidity will do so as well. However, in a simple–sum aggregate, this will not change the "moneyness" or transaction–equivalence of the aggregate. The form of aggregation implies that all components are perfect substitutes. If this were indeed the case, then optimising agents should simply resort to the component yielding the highest interest rate.

It has always been debated whether there are other monetary aggregates having a more stable relationship with output and prices. Despite changes in velocity of M3 apparently brought about by financial innovations, and the obvious failure to meet the target in recent years, the Bundesbank stuck to its strategy. Moreover, monetary targeting has been questioned with respect to building up the European Central Bank. The ECB so far decided that it will guide itself by a "reference value for monetary growth" (see ECB Press Conference as of 1 December 1998), playing – among other indicators – a "prominent role in the governing councils monetary policy assessment". That reference value will be applied to M3[5] and its growth rate was set by an annual rate of 4.5%.

Apart from its policy of monetary targeting, the Bundesbank stated that the achievement of its policy objectives primarily depends on the management of the day–to–day rate in the interbank money market, the *Tagesgeldsatz* (see Deutsche Bundesbank (1995, pp. 91–96)). Throughout the past decades, a considerable evolution took place in its operating instruments that served to gain more direct and flexible influence on this market. In managing the reserve position of the banking system, the Bundesbank pursued short–run operating objectives. They served to link short–term money market conditions with the intermediate goal in M3 so as to meet the ultimate objective of price stability. Additionally, they were used as a device to signal monetary policy intentions to market participants. Ideally, the Bundesbank should have had tight control over money market conditions. The Bundesbank called this strategy "indirect monetary targeting" (Deutsche Bundesbank (1995)). The Bundesbank finally stated that its achievement of monetary policy objectives was also concerned with stabilising the overnight money market interest rate (see Deutsche Bundesbank (1994, p. 62)).

The design of the European Central Bank's money market instruments has largely been drawn on that of the Bundesbank. *REPO* operations provided under an auction procedure are constituting the main refinancing source of the commercial banking sector and along with minimum reserve requirements are now salient features of the ECB's tools.

It should therefore be worthwhile to consider how these instruments served the purposes of monetary policy in Germany.

[5] For the ECB's definition of M3, see Chapter 1.

2.1.2 The development of instruments for monetary control

There was a wide range of interest rate and liquidity policy instruments available to the Bundesbank to enable it to discharge its duties. The extent to which a specific instrument was used to influence money market conditions varied over time. As interest rate policy it was setting conventional administered interest rates (Lombard and discount rates) and the *REPO* rate, the rate applied to security repurchase agreements. As liquidity policy instruments the Bundesbank limited both qualitatively and quantitatively the access to rediscount Lombard and discount loans. In order to discourage undesirable inflows of funds, say, from abroad, the Bundesbank at times resorted to "moral suasion" as well (see Deutsche Bundesbank (1995, pp. 98–99)).

During the past decades, a considerable evolution took place in the Bundesbank's money market instruments. Interest rates of conventional open-ended central bank lending facilities were raised to penal level and served as an upper limit for money market rates. During the 1970s the central bank relied on a system of administered interest rates to implement its policy. Banks' marginal reserve demand had been largely met through central bank credit facilities, often at levels below market interest rates. Since the 1980s there had been increasing use of money market operations and other fine–tuning instruments. They were mainly used to neutralise fluctuations in bank liquidity and to influence money market rates in accordance with current monetary policy requirements. It was at the beginning of the 1980s that the Bundesbank shifted gradually away from a policy of discount window borrowing and placed more importance on open market operations. The burden of reserve requirements had been lowered considerably. Changes in reserve ratios as a means of making adjustments in banks' reserve positions were limited. A reason for this development may be that, with the former instruments at hand, there was a bias towards delaying increases of short–term interest rates to the extent necessary to counter a build–up of inflation.

Domestic components in the German money market consisted almost entirely of Bundesbank loans to domestic banks. Among these loans the traditional discount credit was the most important source of central bank money until the beginning of the 1980s. Open market paper government securities and treasury bills made up only a very small fraction of its assets. This is due to Article 20 of the Bundesbank Act, the *Bundesbankgesetz*, which rules out financing of government deficits by the central bank (see Deutsche Bundesbank (1995, p. 149)). For this reason, outright open market operations played only a minor role in the conduct of monetary policy.

The use of conventional discount credit facilities. To grant discount loans, the Bundesbank discounted foreign and domestic commercial bills and prime bankers' acceptances. They had a fixed maturity up to 90 days and could not be repaid before maturity. It constituted a credit facility to be drawn on the initiative of banks, if necessary, at charges known in advance and normally subject only to infrequent changes. However, the total amount of rediscount credit available to banks could be limited by laying down overall rediscount quotas. Discount window lending provided an ongoing source of subsidised funds to meet a portion of lasting reserve demand. In Germany, this facility had been particularly large in comparison with other industrialised countries (see Kasman (1992, p. 16)). It accounted for about one quarter of central bank assets. Discount loans served as a source basis for refinancing. Since 1978, German banks had been fully using their contingencies most of the time. The Bundesbank did not use moral suasion so as to discourage banks from using their discount quotas fully. Consequently, changes in quotas directly changed banks' reserves. Unused discount facilities increased only at times when expected interest rates decreased. In periods of a glut of liquidity the call rate could fall below the discount rate, because banks could reduce the amount of discount credit they had taken only as the bill fell due.

Discount window lending did not accommodate banks' unanticipated reserve needs. With the Lombard lending facility, the Bundesbank provided an additional line of credit (at a significantly higher interest rate than the discount rate) to meet unexpected short–term liquidity demand. It granted loans at interest against the collateral of certain Security Dept Register Claims (*Schuldbuchforderungen*). As in the case of the discount loans it could be drawn on by the initiative of banks, if needed, at charges known and subject to infrequent changes but at penal level. Its main purpose was to serve as last–resort assistance at times of financial stress and to facilitate monetary restraint. The Lombard rate was therefore always held above the discount rate. Normally, it formed an upper limit to fluctuations in the day–to–day rate, because no bank should have paid higher rates in the interbank market than it had to for the recourse to Lombard credit. Though without official commitment, Lombard loans represented an access to open–ended lines of credit for temporary liquidity needs at the banks' discretion.

This was in contrast to policy practices in the United States. Discount window lending is provided at subsidised rates and only in accordance with administrative discretion. The Fed hereby intends to discourage banks from the use of subsidised credit.

In Germany, Lombard credit was collateralised with trade bills, securities and treasury bills and – in contrast to discount credits – could be repaid at any time. Maturity was up to 3 months at maximum. Even though Lombard lending was never used for meeting lasting reserve needs, it in fact often served to accommodate the system's residual need for reserves. It was thus a key instrument to achieve the smoothing of interest rates in the overnight money market. Since discount contingencies served to keep the discount rate below the call rate, the discount rate served as floor and – most of the time – the Lombard rate as ceiling for money market rates. This can be observed in Figure 2.5.

Money market rates rose above the Lombard rate only at times of extraordinary financial stress. In 1985 the Bundesbank stated that the Lom-

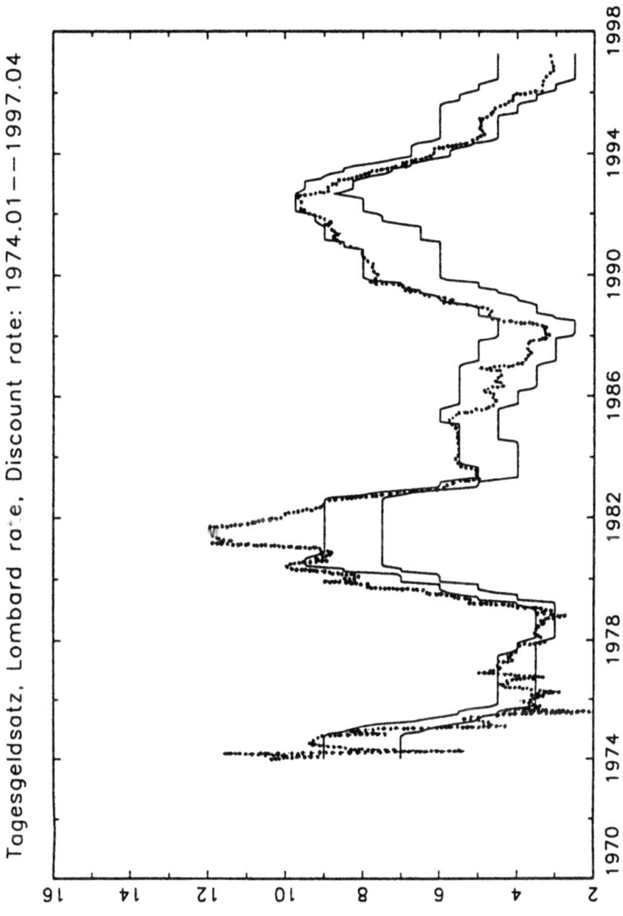

Fig. 2.5. Development of the German Lombard (upper solid line), discount (lower solid line) and overnight money market rate (dotted line): monthly, 1974.01 - 1998.01

bard rate was then the "centre of gravitation" for money market rates (see Bundesbank (1985, p. 51)) . It generally had a greater significance for interest rate trends in the money market. Depending on the banks' need for liquidity they tended to move above or below the Lombard rate. At times of unusual reserve ease the market rate could move lower if the banks had little outstanding Lombard credit to repay. In this situation the discount rate could check the fall to the extent that utilisation of discount quotas decreased. The day–to–day rate moved above the Lombard rate and became considerably more volatile in the period after 1978 when the Bundesbank engaged in monetary restriction. As can been seen from Figure 2.5 it settled above the rate for special Lombard lending facilities: at times of monetary tightening, the Bundesbank restricted or even suspended Lombard lending and instead introduced special Lombard lending facilities. This was the case in 1974 when the Bundesbank tried to curb inflation arising from the oil price shock, and the periods of international financial strain through 6/1979–2/1980 and 2/1981–5/1982. Discount quotas as well as Special Lombard rates considerably higher than the usual rate were imposed so as to restrict the banking sector's access to central bank money. As a result, contingencies amounted up to 15–20% of discount quotas. Note that in 2/1981 the special Lombard rate was 12%, and in March 1981 Lombard lending was totally suspended and reintroduced only in May 1982. A progressive lowering of interest rates on Special Lombard loans underpinned the subsequent progressive decline in market rates, and a close relationship between the rate on ordinary Lombard facilities and the day–to–day money market rate re–emerged when these facilities were reopened. From that time on, there were no more restrictions on Lombard lending.

The Bundesbank stated that changes in the amount of Lombard loans and discount quotas did not reflect changes in the stance of monetary policy, because they were predominantly of compensatory nature to "technically" adjust bank liquidity. It was rather the discount and the Lombard rate, the refinancing costs, that were used to exert influence on the monetary base. (see Deutsche Bundesbank (1995, pp. 105–107)). Thus, the *size* of loans should *not* be interpreted as a signal of the stance of monetary policy. The reason for this is that quotas have been reduced (or increased) to counter movements in the supply of bank reserves from other sources. Especially in the case of foreign exchange market interventions, the Bundesbank changed discount and Lombard contingencies to be able to successfully sterilise effects on the monetary base. Thus, currency crises usually coincided with changes in contingencies. Free liquidity reserves existed up to a considerable amount only in the 1970s – they have been gradually reduced in the course of the developments of alternative refinancing and fine tuning instruments. Traditional rediscounting was supplanted as the normal instrument for meeting banks' reserve needs. It was granted on concessional terms in limited amounts and had little impact on interest rates in the interbank money market.

The development of fine tuning instruments in the 1980s. As a more flexible instrument for short-term liquidity management in the 1980s, the Bundesbank introduced *security repurchase agreements* (*REPO*s). They were loans to commercial banks using a bank's commercial bills and securities as collateral – as in the case of discount credit. The maturity of *REPO*s was 3 days to 63, the majority extending over a month. In the period from 1973 to 1982 the Bundesbank published special market-related rates at which it was prepared to purchase bills eligible for rediscounting from banks under repurchase agreements outside banks' discount quotas at various times. Maturity was 10 or 20 days. Since 1982, they have been used more extensively. They were employed to smooth the development of bank reserves arising from large annual transfers of Bundesbank profits to the government and to absorb reserves potentially building up from a reduction in reserve requirements and increases in discount contingencies. It was not until June 1979 that the Bundesbank engaged in *reversed security transactions.* The official term "Open market operations with repurchase agreements"(Deutsche Bundesbank (1995, p. 113)) is misleading in this context since the Bundesbank did not in fact sell or repurchase assets in these operations. They constitute a purchase of securities under a contract providing for their resale at a specified price on a given future date. These reversed transactions in domestic securities for regulating money market developments had been increased ever since the beginning of the 1980s. At the beginning of the 1990s, they had become the principal instrument to serve the central banks' purpose. Purchase and resale transactions were used to supply reserves in very flexible ways, while sale and repurchase agreements could serve to absorb reserves.

Periodic reversed security transactions were offered under an auction procedure, usually taking place once a week. They constituted the principal instrument for supplying banks' foreseeable reserve needs and for smoothing short-term interest rates. They replaced Lombard and discount loans as the main refinancing facility. *REPO*s were geared to covering the prospective reserve requirements of the banking system for a month or two in advance, so that the banks' needs for different sources of central bank credit remained limited.

Figure 2.6 shows the development of the (relative) quantities that these respective refinancing facilities amounted to over time. Whereas in the 1970s discount and Lombard loans amounted to roughly 95% of the commercial banks' refinancing facilities, this figure dropped to approximately 30% in 1994, whereas at the same time the *REPO*s made up 69.7% (see Deutsche Bundesbank (1995, p. 109)).

Two different auction procedures were used to supply credit through repurchase operations. They differed in the extent to which they permitted bids to influence the rate applied. Consequently, depending on the procedure, the Bundesbank at times aimed to exert more or less influence on the rate, and was sometimes willing to accept rates more influenced by market forces. Both

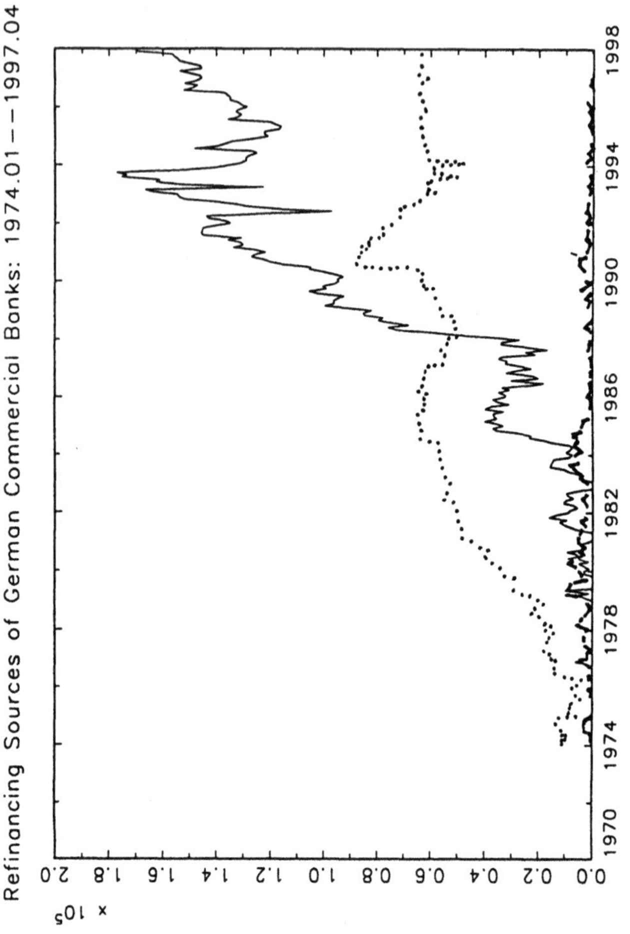

Fig. 2.6. Development of Lombard and discount loans (dashed and dotted line respectively) and credit via *REPO*s (solid line): monthly, 1974.01 – 1998.01.

procedures allowed the Bundesbank to exert tight control over the amount of reserves supplied, as well as over the timing and duration of operations.

The two different tender procedures were the "fixed–rate tender" (*Mengentender*) and the "variable rate tender"(*Zinstender*). In the first case, the banks quoted amounts they were willing to buy at a rate fixed (the *Wertpapierpensionssatz*) by the Bundesbank in advance. Individual bids for amounts of above DM 1 million were scaled down using a uniform allotment ratio. This was the most commonly used procedure. It was used to exert a more direct influence on money market rates. Especially at times of uncertainty concerning the stance of monetary policy, the use of this procedure had a signalling and stabilising effect on the money market. The *Zinstender* related the rate and amount applied more to market conditions. In this case, banks had to submit both amounts and prices. Banks were allowed to submit amounts ranked by different interest rates. Two different auction procedures were then used to allot the total amount of credit. In the context of the Dutch–style auction exclusively used until autumn 1988, the Bundesbank at first announced a minimum rate. Loans were then granted at a standardised rate. In the case of the US–style auction, the banks may have had to pay the rate they indicated in the bid: bids at or above the *Wertpapierpensionssatz*, the rate applied by the Bundesbank, were fully granted, whilst those below the rate were again individually scaled down. In order to prevent commercial banks from making arrangements with respect to quoted rates, bids could be quoted in 0.01% steps. In contrast to the volume tender, the interest tender procedure seemed to be aimed more at preserving a degree of uncertainty about the terms on which banks' future liquidity needs would have been met. With this operating instrument at hand, the Bundesbank had more direct and flexible control over money market conditions. It was no longer committed to previously published interest rates.

The most important advantage compared to traditional lending facilities was that they were granted on the initiative of the central bank: It set the amount, the timing and the duration of the contract and autonomously decided whether to renew it or to let it unwind upon maturity.

The final establishment of *REPO*s as the main policy tool occurred in February 1985. A structural change in the relationship between the overnight rate and the day–to–day rate took place. Until then, movements in the overnight rate were tied to the Lombard rate. In February 1985, the Bundesbank re–established the function of the Lombard credit as a last–resort assistance at times of financial stress by raising the Lombard rate to a level above that used in its *REPO* operations, and began to use these market operations to supply reserves more liberally. This can be seen in Figure 2.5. It freed money market rates throughout the maturity spectrum from dependence on the Lombard rate, permitting them to move more flexibly to changes in rates applied in the *REPO*s. In the beginning, they took place three times a month; since December 1993, at least four times, eventually more often and with different maturity, so as to prevent the banks' bids being influenced by longer–term interest expectations. In an effort to offset massive inflows of foreign exchange, *REPO*s have sometimes been suspended. This was the case for example during the EMS–crises of autumn 1992 and 1993. The effect is clearly visible in Figure 2.6. Eventually it was supported by raising minimum reserve requirements and reducing discount quotas[6].

At times, the Bundesbank engaged in especially short–term reversed transactions and provided credit with maturity of 2 to 10 days settled in one day (*Schnelltender*). To preclude excessive liquidity in the money market that might cause the day–to–day rate to fall below the discount rate, the Bundesbank offered banks treasury bills with short–term maturity of usually three days to outlet surplus funds. Their maturity was one to three days – and might have appropriately served as a "lower limit", or *Auffanglinie*, for the overnight rate, as the Bundesbank put it. That is, under normal circumstances the rate applied placed a floor to fluctuations in the *Tagesgeldsatz.* Because of the maturity of discount credits, this was not always possible with the discount rate. Since 1985, the overnight rate effectively fluctuated within the channel set by the Lombard rate and the short–term treasury bill rate.

In order to encourage exports of funds by banks, the Bundesbank also used swap transactions in the foreign exchange market. The Bundesbank bought (sold) foreign exchange spot and at the same time sold (bought) back forward, where the swap rate is equivalent to an interest rate. The Bundesbank also concluded foreign exchange transactions under repurchase agreements (for a more detailed exposition, see Deutsche Bundesbank (1995, pp. 133–135)).

In order to fine–tune the money market, it also took advantage of the statutory requirement (§ 17 of the Bundesbank Act) that until 1994 Federal authorities had to deposit their liquid funds with the Bundesbank. In order to influence money market conditions on a short–term basis, these public sector balances had been shifted into the money market or withdrawn from it.

An exception from the use of *REPO*s as a main policy tool was made in 1990, the year of German unification. A wide range of financial assets became available to East Germans as West German banks moved into the East. In order to participate in open market operations, however, East German banks needed access to high quality trade bills and securities. Since they did not have

[6] Obviously, the Bundesbank's success at sterilising interventions was mixed. As von Hagen (1989) argues, intervention was especially difficult when the DM's position in both the US–$ market and the market of EMS currencies was strong. The Bundesbank was then unable to buy EMS currencies and sell them on the US–$ market, as it frequently occurred in the 1980s. If offsetting intervention did not work, then sterilisation was imperfect and interventions could have a lasting effect on the monetary base. Consequently, an overshooting of M3 after intervention periods can be observed. The observed correlation in movements in the DM–$ rate and the performance in meeting monetary targets might as well be given the interpretation that the Bundesbank eases monetary policy in the case of a depreciation of the DM. This view was adopted in Trehan (1989).

such securities, they suffered a competitive disadvantage and the Bundesbank granted them higher discount quotas and the permission to discount bills and securities of lower quality[7]. Minimum reserve requirements were introduced in East Germany in August 1990. After some time qualitative requirements for their papers were tightened (see the respective monthly reports of the Bundesbank).

Minimum reserve requirements. In order to successfully implement monetary policy, the Bundesbank relied on reserve requirements as a key instrument. Banks were obliged to hold a certain amount of non–interest bearing reserve deposits with the central bank. The ratios of reserve requirements were linked to certain categories and the respective volume of bank liabilities (see Deutsche Bundesbank (1995, pp. 121–131)). The higher the liquidity of liabilities, the higher was the respective reserve ratio. Since March 1978 central bank deposits held by commercial banks for clearing purposes and currency deposited outside the central bank could be counted towards reserve requirements. In August 1995 this deductability was abolished. The reserve maintenance period was one month and reserve holdings were permitted to be averaged over the reserve period thus providing an element of flexibility in the early part of the period. Reserve demand was influenced by a combination of lagged and contemporaneous reserves accounting. Reserve requirements were calculated according to the average of banks' liabilities at the "*Bankwochenstichtage*" (the 23rd, the last day of the preceding month, the 7th and 15th of the current month) or according to the levels at the close of all business and non–business days from the 16th of the preceding month to the 15th of the current month. Requirements were announced on the 23rd of the month. Thus reserve requirements were semi–lagged, so that the holding period started and ended later than the calculation period – so these periods overlapped.

If a bank failed to meet its reserve requirements, it had to pay a penal rate at 3% above the Lombard rate for its deficiencies. Excess reserves on average accounted for only 1% of reserves. Large excess reserves were only observed in cases of high inflow of foreign exchange. The reason for this is that reserve requirements in Germany exceeded what banks needed to hold as deposits for clearing purposes.

The once common practice of altering reserve requirements to adjust the monetary policy stance had largely been abandoned. Since the early 1970s, reserve requirements were steadily reduced (see Deutsche Bundesbank (1995, p. 131)). Nevertheless they remained above the level needed by commercial banks for clearing purposes. Yet it was seen as an important part of the implementation procedures by the Bundesbank. It argued that minimum reserve requirements served to stabilise short–term demand for reserves and were therefore helpful in exerting control over short–term rates. In order to

[7] It discounted their own bank promissory notes bearing no other signature.

implement an interest rate based operating procedure through periodic market operations, the Bundesbank had to predict the demand for bank reserves over some relevant horizon.

Whereas security and discount policies act on the supply side of money, reserve requirements operate on demand. By setting reserve ratios and interbank clearing rules, a central bank may determine reserves demand. In systems linking reserve holdings to banks' liabilities, reserve demand is sometimes very inelastic in the short–run. In the absence of accommodating operations by the central bank, banks can influence their demand for reserves only by changing the structure of liabilities and their pace of credit granting to some extent, borrow money abroad, sell securities and take advantage of averaging provisions. The smoothing of interest rates is especially easy to achieve under a reserve requirement system. As pointed out by Kasman (1992, pp. 21–23) in his comparison of monetary policy operating procedures in six industrial countries, there is a relationship between required reserves and overnight interest variability. In countries with low nonbinding reserve requirements, overnight rates are much more volatile than elsewhere. His findings support the view that central banks face greater difficulties in stabilising interest rates around desired levels when reserve requirements are eased. In the U.S. a decline in reserve requirements combined with the increased reluctance of banks to approach the discount window has been associated with a higher variability of the Federal Funds Rate. However, whether increased volatility reduces the ability of market participants to identify the monetary authority's intentions is an open issue, since longer–term interest rates might be more important in the transmission of monetary policy.

A further reason for a higher interest volatility in systems without binding reserve requirements is that money demand shocks have a stronger and more direct influence on interest rates. Reserve requirements on the other hand would automatically raise the banking sector's need for reserves and subsequently dampen the shock in credit demand (see Deutsche Bundesbank (1995, pp. 128–130)). Thus systems with no reserve requirements require a higher degree of day–to–day intervention, since there is greater need to smooth interest rate fluctuations. The Bundesbank was indeed rather inactive in its daily reserve management in comparison to the U.S. Federal Reserve Bank. The introduction of minimum reserve requirements in the European System of Central Banks in order to facilitate a policy of monetary targeting has been strongly favoured by the Bundesbank.

Reserve requirements sometimes raised concerns among private banks, since they reduce their profitability. Such regulations have led German banks to seek refinancing sources abroad. For this very reason, the Bundesbank drastically reduced reserve ratios and continued to provide discount loans at subsidised rates to a still significant extent.

Open issues. Considering the maturity of instruments employed it is quite surprising that they should have served to exert influence over the day–to–

day rate. The discount rate, the Lombard rate, the treasury bill selling rate and the repurchase agreement rate range from 1 day to 3 months. Thus, the Bundesbank engaged in a wide variety of money market instruments instead of using intervention strategies that span the money market term structure.

On the one hand, the Bundesbank's reserve management activities provided considerable control over short–term interbank rates. On the other hand, its influence must have extended to a maturity well beyond overnight rates to affect the money stock and economic activity. In the view of the Bundesbank, however, long–term rates were principally affected by market forces. There might have been an indirect influence on long–term rates if the central bank successfully affected the market's expectations on the future setting of short–term rates. The reason for this is that, through arbitrage, longer–term rates reflect market expectations of future short–term rates. This is suggested by the expectations model of the term structure of interest rates. Assuming risk neutrality, a linearised version might be used to link the short–term rate i_t to that of the long–term rate r_t (of T–period–maturity)

$$r_t = \frac{1}{T}\sum_{j=0}^{T-1} E(i_{t+j}|\Omega_t), \tag{2.1}$$

where Ω_t is the information set available to the public at time t. Drawing on Fisher (1930) the theory has been developed e.g. in Lutz (1940). Hence, transmission of interest rate policies throughout the money market term structure is possible only if the central bank credibly conveyed its intentions about the range in which the future day–to–day and other short–term interest rates were set. However, to serve this objective, money market instruments in Germany seemed neither that far developed nor officially used to meet this objective. So, despite its official statements, it seemed unclear what the intentions of the Bundesbank were in this respect. The statements even appeared somehow contradictory. As already mentioned, the Bundesbank stated that it pursued a policy of "indirect monetary targeting" - which is only possible if there is a stable relationship between the overnight rate and the intermediate and ultimate goals of stabilising money stock growth and the price level. This again seems only possible if it had a reasonable command over the yield curve spread. On the other hand, however, the Bundesbank stated that it did not intend to influence interest rates of a longer–term maturity, and that these interest rates were determined by market forces.

Questions are now arising considering the Bundesbank's statements about its policy of monetary targeting and the conduct of this policy in its day–to–day operations. What was termed a strategy of indirect monetary targeting was seen as the achievement of monetary goals by setting money market interest rates.

However, this is only feasible if there is a fairly stable relationship between the *Tagesgeldsatz* and the targeted aggregate M3. The validity of this presumption is not clear. From a theoretical point of view targeting of M3 would plausibly be possible if changes in the overnight money market rate influence the opportunity costs for holding M3. In this case monetary targeting is achieved by influencing at least one variable entering a demand equation for M3. Yet it might be argued that in the context of this equation the very short–term *Tagesgeldsatz* does not reliably reflect opportunity costs for holding M3. An influence on these opportunity costs is only conceivable if changes in the overnight rate have a predictable effect on the yield curve spread. This is altogether unclear.

In addition, it is only since 1985 that the Bundesbank explicitly stated that it pursued a call–rate regime. In the period from 1974 to 1984 it has not been that explicit. As mentioned above, the Bundesbank put special emphasis on the Lombard rate, but it is unclear how monetary targeting was conducted on a day–to–day basis. The question therefore arises – at least with respect to this subperiod – whether the Bundesbank conducted monetary targeting in terms of smoothing interest rates or bank reserves around a desired level. An interest rate regime throughout the post Bretton Woods era can be observed for Germany only if the instruments of Lombard and discount credit, swaps, reserve ratios and later on the *REPO*s were set to determine the *Tagesgeldsatz* and leave quantity decisions up to banks.

Beyond that, it remains open whether the evolution that took place in the Bundesbank's instruments throughout the decades had an effect on the conduct of the policy. Moreover, if monetary targeting was conducted in terms of smoothing interest rates, it would be interesting to know whether discretionary changes in interest rates might have been induced by deviations from the proposed target.

It is desirable to develop theoretically conclusive considerations in order to address these questions. Chapter 3 is mainly devoted to develop a framework linking money supply and demand, bank reserves and interest rates under specific monetary policy regimes. In Chapter 4 this model is empirically assessed.

2.2 Operating procedures and money supply

Due to the evolution in the Bundesbank's policy instruments during the past decades, it is difficult to make a clear cut distinction between different operating periods. In contrast to this, through subsequent explicit statements from the side of the Federal Reserve Bank, this has been a much easier task with respect to the United States, as it is documented, among others, in Bradley and Jansen (1986). Theoretically, there are several possible ways in which the Bundesbank could have conducted monetary targeting in terms of operating procedures.

1. Especially with respect to the period since 1985, when the *REPO*s became the main refinancing tool, one might surmise that the Bundesbank

through its choice of discount contingencies provided a limited amount of discount credit to achieve a certain target in its reversed security transactions. In this case, money demand shocks would have been directly be transmitted to the money market through the banks' demand for reserves. If the Bundesbank provided only a certain amount of *REPO*s and other open market transactions, the market would have cleared through adjustment in the overnight rate. In this case, reserves were exogenous to the money stock in the economy.

The scheme seems especially appropriate with respect to the use of the interest rate tender procedure to provide *REPO*s, when the amount and the rate applied were related more to market conditions. The procedure seemed to prove especially useful in tightening monetary policy.

However, considering the Bundesbank's statements that the overnight rate was the main tool to exert monetary policy, this seems improbable.

2. Given a stable demand equation with respect to the interest rate in the money market, monetary aggregates might have been changed by means of discretionary alterations in interest rates. This is what the Bundesbank might have had in mind when using the term "indirect monetary targeting" (see Deutsche Bundesbank (1994, p. 62)) with respect to its policy. One should be quite aware of the importance of a stable demand equation in this context. Here, money demand shocks are to be accommodated by an elastic supply of bank reserves both through discount and open market operations. The central bank chooses an interest rate consistent with the designated monetary target. Changes in interest rates will cause banks and the public to adjust their portfolio in the direction of the money target.
3. Following the concept of a standard money multiplier model in the spirit of Brunner (1961) or Brunner and Meltzer (1964), one might treat banks' reserves – as obtained from discount and open market operations – as exogenously determined by the central bank and independent of money demand disturbances. The approach served as standard paradigm in monetary macroeconomics textbooks and as a point of departure for empirical analyses (see, for example, Bomhoff (1977)) for money stock control. Originally, it was assumed that the money multiplier is independent of the policy actions of the central bank. Given a stable relationship between reserves and the money stock, the Bundesbank simply had to choose a certain level of reserves consistent with a given monetary aggregate. The market would have cleared through an adjustment in interest rates. Shifts in bank reserves should be identified with monetary policy actions. Thus, reserves should have been exogenous to the money stock. The usual keynesian liquidity effect is obtained by increases in money supply triggering decreases in interest rates.

Given these considerations, assuming an interest rate procedure for the period since 1985 seems most appropriate. In the case of the *REPO*s, the volume tender procedure was the most frequently used instrument to exert direct influence over short–term rates: the Bundesbank announced an interest rate consistent with its policy objectives and stood ready to grant loans on an elastic basis so that its interest rate target could be met. Therefore, below, the period since 1985 is referred to as an interest rate period. In the period from 1974 to 1985 this is not that clear–cut. During this period, interest rates have sometimes been excessively volatile – as for example in 1974 when the Bundesbank embarked on monetary targeting, and in the periods of monetary tightening in 1979 when the overnight rate was held consistently above the Special Lombard rate. This indicates that a money–multiplier approach could be adequate. Nevertheless, with respect to this time period, the Bundesbank stated that the Lombard rate was then its key policy instrument serving to stabilise money market rates (see Deutsche Bundesbank (1985, p. 51)). As an open–ended line of credit Lombard loans served to provide reserves on an elastic basis thereby stabilising money market rates. Hence, it might be concluded, that the Bundesbank had an operating procedure intact having similar implications for its policy of monetary targeting as in the case of the aforementioned "interest rate rule period". With reference to the "borrowed reserves procedure" adopted by the Federal Reserve Board in 1982, the period from 1974 to 1984 in Germany might be labelled "discount window borrowing procedure". The term used in the U.S. is not adequate when applied to Germany because *REPO*s that are to be excluded from discount loans were "borrowed reserves" in the sense that they are central bank loans to commercial banks.

2.3 A note on the identifiability of money demand

2.3.1 The identification problem

Money demand nowadays is analysed using equations in reduced form and by identifying estimated parameters with those of the structural form. This is appropriate if the central bank in the conduct of its monetary policy does not react to movements in money demand; otherwise, estimated parameters would constitute a mixture of demand and supply parameters.

At the individual level, explanatory variables in the demand equation might indeed be taken to be exogenous. Agents may be assumed to adjust their demand for nominal balances in response to changes in explanatory variables – it may indeed be assumed that money supply is completely passive at this level. The problem, therefore, arises from aggregation. At the macroeconomic level it might be doubted that money supply is equally elastic.

Hence, knowledge of the conduct of German monetary policy is crucial in order to assess whether empirical money demand equations are properly specified. Identification of the money stock with money demand is only possible if the central bank sets its monetary target independently from the variables in the money demand equation. Awareness of this is only scarcely reflected in the money demand literature. If there is feed back between money demand and supply in a multi–equation context, parameters in the demand function may be consistently estimated if there is an instrument variable at hand making movements in the supply independent of demand.

2.3.2 Money demand and monetary policy rules

These critical issues have only been scarcely appreciated throughout decades of empirical work on money demand. Problems with theoretical foundation of the choice of alternative dynamic specification and with parameter instability as arising from simultaneity were discussed in passing in the 1980s (see Gordon (1984), Cooley and LeRoy (1981)). Having largely overcome dynamic specification problems with the emergence of the cointegration literature, the issue meanwhile seems to have been jettisoned completely. The purpose of this study of the conduct of German monetary policy is to shed some light on whether this is justified. The discussion in this section attempts to clarify which conditions must hold for the conduct of monetary policy so as to ensure identifiability of money demand.

As already fiercely criticised in Cooley and LeRoy's (1981) scathing paper on this issue, the exclusion of simultaneity problems was based on a confounding of the term "exogeneity" as used in economics and in econometrics. It has often been argued that if the central bank stands ready to buy and sell securities at a given targeted interest rate, for a given period of time, then demand–for–money functions may be correctly identified (see Laidler (1980, p. 238)). It is readily shown, however, that this is neither a necessary nor sufficient condition to estimate money demand parameters consistently. Firstly, in a single equation context, the observed money stock can be identified with money demand if, and only if, the money supply is always completely elastic and, furthermore, if the central bank targets interest rates independently (in the probability sense) from present and past movements in the money stock. The latter condition is necessary for exogeneity of the interest rate to hold in an *econometric* sense. Hence, the observation that interest rates are not used to clear the money market but are instead set by the central bank on an autonomous basis for a given policy period, is not strong enough.

Next, consider the multi–equation approach as in the following simple theoretical framework treated in Gordon (1984):

$$M_t^d - P_t = \alpha_1 y_t + \alpha_2 i_t + u_t \qquad \text{with} \qquad \alpha_1 > 0, \alpha_2 < 0, \tag{2.2}$$

$$M_t^s = \beta_1 TR_t^s + \beta_2 i_t + v_t \qquad \text{with} \qquad \beta_1 > 0, \beta_2 > 0. \tag{2.3}$$

Here, equation (2.2) is a standard demand–for–money equation, where P_t, y_t, i_t denote logs of the price level, real income and the opportunity cost for holding real balances $M_t - P_t$. In equation (2.2) it is assumed that nominal money supply positively depends on the interest rate and total reserves supply; u_t and v_t are error terms.

Let us assume that the central bank indeed adopts an interest rate rule of the form $i_t = i_t^T + \eta_t$, where i_t^T is the central bank's interest target and η_t an error term. When estimating α_1 and α_2 difficulties may arise if η_t and u_t are correlated, and furthermore, if autocorrelation in u_t together with an effect of i_t^T on lagged money supply is observable. That is, it is to be excluded that M_t^s through choice of i_t^T is set to exert lasting influence on the money stock in response to present and past observations of M_t.

An estimated demand equation may thus tell nothing about parameters of money demand. Moreover, they will vary subject to changes in monetary policy regimes. In general, estimated parameters may be a mixture of money demand and supply parameters. Instability in money demand equations may reflect shifts in the central bank's operating regime rather than money demand. Concerning the specification of German money demand, it is therefore desirable to assess whether the behaviour of the Bundesbank and its policy rules have been subject to frequent changes.

It should be mentioned here that the debate about identification problems in the 1980s was largely motivated by issues concerning the theoretical foundations of the choice of alternative dynamic specifications. Error terms in empirical money demand equations have been found to exhibit high positive autocorrelation. This is, of course, an issue that has largely been settled by the cointegration literature. The salient features that scientists were concerned with at that time may well be viewed as being caused by the property of nonstationarity of the variables involved. Nevertheless, in the light of the above considerations, it might be viewed sceptically, whether it is sufficient to exclude a feedback between demand and supply in order to ensure identifiability of demand parameters. It appears unlikely that central banks conduct monetary policy independently from movements in variables entering the demand–for–money equation. In Germany, the Bundesbank explicitly stated that the targeted money stock also served as information variable and several empirical studies suggest that there is a feedback (see Clarida and Gertler (1996) and Bernanke and Mihov (1997)) from income and inflation to the money stock and interest rates.

2.3.3 Tracing the supply side using bank reserves?

In this study a further interesting issue concerning the simultaneity problem might be addressed: in his classic on the demand for money, Laidler (1977, p. 115–116) stated that identification is correct, if

> "...the supply function of money shifts independently of the demand–for–money function if the supply–of–money function contains at least one variable that does not appear in the demand function. It is not hard to establish that this is the case, for the level of

reserves made available by the central bank to the commercial banking system figures prominently in any theory of the supply of money and does not appear in any theory of the demand for money."

To put it more specifically, bank reserves as an explanatory variable must be excluded not only from the demand side, but also from the unobserved components of money demand. This view of the money supply process is directly opposed to the justification of identification on the ground that supply is completely elastic. In this case, money demand shocks should not even be partially accommodated by the central bank. This assumption seems even less likely to be valid. Nevertheless, from a theoretical point of view, it is therefore necessary to address this hypothesis empirically. In this case, reserves must be exogenous to the money stock and must be set independently in the probability sense from observed and unobserved components of money demand. The empirical study of the conduct of German monetary policy presented here is directly aimed at explicitly dealing with this controversial issue. At the same time it will be shown which interpretation of the money supply process is more appropriate, a "money market" approach, assuming that money supply is elastic, or the rival "credit market hypothesis" in the spirit of the Brunner–Meltzer money–multiplier approach.

2.4 A note on the identifiability of autonomous monetary policy actions

2.4.1 Common identification problems in *VARs*

There is a wide range of empirical studies on the identification and transmission of monetary policy. Identifying monetary policy is not only desirable in order to assess its stance compared to what it was under similar macroeconomic conditions, it is also necessary to evaluate alternative theories of monetary transmission and quantitative effects of policy changes on various macroeconomic variables. These judgements must be based on objective means of determining the direction and size of changes in the policy stance. The most important strand of literature is thereby based on multivariate time series models that identify statistical innovations in monetary aggregates or short–term interest rates with monetary policy actions. However, in this context, responses of macroeconomic variables due to monetary policy actions are often inconsistent with what might be presumed from traditional monetary theory. These phenomena termed "liquidity puzzle" or "price puzzle" are usually explained by the failure to identify autonomous actions of the central bank, so that the effects are contaminated by non–policy components as argued e.g. by Sims (1992, p. 997). The puzzles may as well be explained on methodological grounds. It has been common practice to use vector autoregressions (*VARs*) for multiple time series to identify innovations in the variables involved, as e.g. in Bernanke and Blinder (1992), Christiano and Eichenbaum (1992), Shapiro (1994), Sims(1980, 1992), and Bernanke and Mihov (1995, 1997). It might be conjectured that, even if "policy innovations" are correctly identified, these are not the object that need to be measured. This is discussed in greater detail in Chapter 4.

The problem has been triggered implicitly by Sims' (1980) prominent and often cited paper "Macroeconomics and reality". Employing German and U.S. macroeconomic data of money, real GNP, unemployment, wages, prices and import prices in a vector autoregression he illustrates that standard economic hypotheses which then lay at the core of macroeconomics are all too readily challenged on statistical grounds. The most challenging result to macroeconometrics arose from his testing of both standard monetarism and new–classical hypotheses. Adopting a monetarist view of the economy, cyclical variations in GNP should be "caused" by changes in money supply as usually assumed using money as an explanatory variable. In the context of a rational expectations view variables representing the real sector should have "causal" explanatory power with respect to wages and prices. However, Granger–causality tests reject exogeneity of the respective variables suggesting that the interaction among the variables and their joint evolution seem to have nothing to do with what was then believed in macroeconomic theory. Moreover, inclusion of the respective variables on the right–hand side of an econometric equation explaining business fluctuations or wage– and price setting seems inappropriate.

Standard assumptions concerning the identification and effects of monetary policy have been rejected even more explicitly in the subsequent studies of Litterman and Weiss (1985) and Gordon and Leeper (1992). Gordon and Leeper (1992) showed that the relationship between innovations in the monetary base (and especially broader monetary aggregates) and in interest rates is uncertain, varies over time and in most cases has the opposite sign than that predicted by the keynesian liquidity hypothesis. The phenomenon has henceforth been termed "liquidity puzzle". Litterman and Weiss (1985) showed that, once interest rates are included in a system containing money and output, money fails to Granger–cause economic activity. These results, reproduced in a wide range of empirical studies, have often been seen as supportive to the real business cycle theory developed in the 1980s (see e.g. Kydland and Prescott (1982) and King and Plosser (1984)). According to this view, the business cycle is caused by real factors such as unanticipated shocks in technology, tastes, and environmental impacts. The business cycle is considered to be a movement of a full employment equilibrium. Thus, monetary factors have no explanatory power, money is endogenous. The failure to detect a liquidity effect in the above mentioned empirical studies, however, does not necessarily support the real business cycle view. It might be argued that these empirical findings failed to appropriately identify monetary policy actions: employing a relatively broad monetary aggregate in the context of a system incorporating money, income and interest rates would lead to modelling a demand–for–money system rather than capturing the supply process of money, and, hence, its effect on economic activity.

2.4.2 Identifying monetary policy regimes

Empirical studies following the detection of the liquidity puzzle have been directed at capturing the conduct of monetary policy more appropriately. Searching for a variable containing valuable information of the monetary policy stance, in their study on U.S. monetary policy, Christiano and Eichenbaum (1992) draw a distinction between *"M–Rules"* and *"R–Rules"*. If the central bank conducts monetary policy in terms of targeting bank reserves – i.e. following an "M–Rule" – changes in a narrow aggregate such as nonborrowed reserves or M1 should trigger a decline in interest rates and increases in output and prices. In their study, a liquidity effect is detectable using nonborrowed reserves. If, on the other hand, the central bank aims at stabilising interest rates around desired levels ("R–Rule"), it is the Federal Funds Rate that should have predictive power with respect to the macroeconomic variables involved. With respect to both M–Rules and R–Rules for U.S. monetary policy, they find correlations between the Federal Funds Rate and nonborrowed reserves consistent with the liquidity–effect hypothesis. Nevertheless, the study is not directly aimed at modelling the conduct of monetary policy. It is a rather pragmatic approach: monetary policy is assumed to be conducted in terms of a variable having the best predictive power with respect to the evolution of the macroeconomic system and displaying correlations with the variables involved that are consistent with standard macroeconomic hypotheses.

In analogy to Christiano and Eichenbaum's (1992) "R–Rules", Bernanke and Blinder (1992) for the U.S. and Sims (1992) in a comparative study for Germany, France, UK, Japan and the U.S. investigate what effects unanticipated changes of overnight interest rates in the interbank money market might have on economic activity, prices and money in the context of a VAR (with the interest rate placed first in a Wold–ordering scheme to obtain impulse–responses[8]). Again, in Bernanke and Blinder (1992) it is assumed that movements in the Federal Funds Rate are genuine policy changes. In this case the Federal Funds Rate must be essentially unresponsive to changes in reserves demand within the policy period. The approach is justified on the ground that the Federal Funds Rate is a powerful predictor for macroeconomic variables rather than monetary aggregates. Using innovations in macroeconomic variables driving the demand for bank reserves as instruments for nonborrowed reserves, they show that the slope coefficient of nonborrowed reserves might be neglected statistically. When estimating a Federal Reserve

[8] Structural inference in multivariate time series is discussed in much greater detail below in Section 4.5.

reaction function they find that the Fed is pursuing a policy of "leaning against the wind" thereby lowering interest rates when unemployment rises and inflation decreases.

Sims' (1992) adoption of the interest rule hypothesis using a VAR comprising money, output, prices and the overnight interest rate, however, reveals patterns in the data that are in part inconsistent with standard assumptions on the effects of monetary policy. Across countries, the tendency of interest rate increases to predict high inflation is particularly striking. The phenomenon has been dubbed "prize puzzle" by Eichenbaum (1992). It might even be accompanied by an "output puzzle" eventually indicating zero responses in economic activity due to interest rate increases. Sims (1992) suggests that the phenomenon can be explained on the basis of *reverse causation* between interest rates and inflation: if the monetary authority bases its decision on more information than is contained in the VAR, what appears as unforecastable increases in prices is to some extent predictable to authorities. Monetary policy is tightened to counter a build–up of foreseen inflation so that actual prices rise less than they would have, had policy not contracted. In this case the interest rate is not exogenous to the system but rather *contaminated* by endogenous responses of policy to anticipated inflationary pressure generated by non–policy variables. For example in the case of a demand shock to the economy, an increase in the price level may thus mistakenly be attributed to monetary policy.

A slightly modified approach has been adopted by Strongin (1995) who studies the Federal Funds market as well. Assuming that the Fed largely accommodates reserve demand by providing total reserves on an elastic basis, it is assumed that political influence on the reserve market is exerted rather by altering the mix of borrowed and nonborrowed reserves supply. Interest rate innovations will then be determined both by suppply and demand innovations. To separate the contemporaneous components of reserve accommodation from interest rate effects resulting from controlling the composition of reserves, a reserve mix variable (nonborrowed reserves divided by the lag of total reserves) is constructed. Since total reserve demand is inelastic in the short–run, demand shocks would lead to large swings in the Federal Funds Rate if not met by the Fed. However, the Fed can tighten policy by reducing nonborrowed reserves and forcing banks to borrow more from the discount window. If, on the other hand, nonborrowed reserves were altered in exactly the same way as total reserves, demand shocks would leave the funds rate unaffected, permitting the Fed to target interest rates. The reserve mix variable constructed by Strongin (1995) reflects nonborrowed reserve growth orthogonal to total reserve growth. The method helps to overcome both the liquidity and the price puzzle, when implemented in a VAR.

A conclusive and yet broader study has been undertaken by Bernanke and Mihov (1995). With respect to different subperiods using a general model of the Federal Funds market in the context of a VAR for output and prices, they test the different identification schemes encountered in the literature: restrictions on a general reserves market model comprising the policy regimes discussed result in a specific "sub–model" reflecting a certain regime. The approach allows them to avoid the use of a single–policy indicator that might be affected by shocks to the demand for reserves and other factors, by directly separating demand and supply shocks. It turns out that among the four identification schemes (Federal Funds Rate targeting, nonborrowed reserves targeting, borrowed reserves targeting and targeting of nonborrowed reserves relative to total reserves) the Bernanke–Blinder (1992) Funds–Rate measure is appropriate for the periods prior to 1979 and after 1988 and the Strongin (1995) measure otherwise.

2.4.3 Narrative approaches

Largely inspired by the prominent historical analysis of Friedman and Schwartz (1971) of U.S. monetary policy from 1867 to 1960, a quite different attempt to identify monetary policy actions and to analyse its effects has been undertaken in Romer and Romer's (1989) "narrative approach". Based on their readings of documents of the Federal Open Market Committee (FOMC) meetings they created a dummy variable which is identified with a tightening of monetary policy. In particular, "they count as a shock only episodes in which the Federal Reserve attempted to exert contractionary influence on the economy in order to reduce inflation", they "look at times when concern about the current level of inflation led the Federal Reserve to attempt to induce a recession"(Romer and Romer (1989, p. 134)). That is, they take a more narrow approach towards identifying monetary policy than Friedman and Schwartz (1971) who looked for times when monetary policy was unusual as compared to the overall stance of the economy. Incorporating the dummy variable into a reduced form dynamic equation for U.S. industrial production they show that what is identified as contractionary policy has strong and persistent effects on output.

2.4.4 Unresolved issues

Although directed at the same set of problems, narrative approaches (as a further example, see Hamilton (1987)) and VAR approaches as discussed above have developed quite independently from each other.

A combination has been attempted by Leeper (1996). In a VAR implementation of the Romers' dummy he shows that the puzzling results known from the econometric literature are reproduced. Moreover – and more scathing – in an attempt to investigate the exogeneity of the dummies, he estimates a probit model describing the decision to contract monetary policy as a function of expected discounted variables such as output and prices. Even though only lagged macroeconomic variables are included in the system, 5 out of the

7 Romer dummies are predicted from past observations of the data! Thus their measure contains substantial endogenous components and – besides its inherent subjectivity – fails to overcome the short–comings of the time series models.

Thus, considering either VAR or the narrative approaches as reviewed in this section, it seems difficult to reconcile the endogeneity issue endemic to studies of monetary policy.

2.5 Evidence from recent empirical analyses of German monetary policy

2.5.1 Was there no role for monetary aggregates in Germany?

In recent years there have been several empirical investigations of the conduct of monetary policy in Germany. The studies seem to have been partly inspired by the political debate concerning the construction of the European Central Bank and the shape of its policy. The Bundesbank strongly favoured the implementation of a policy of monetary targeting. However, the empirical studies cast doubt on the assumption that the Bundesbank indeed followed a policy of monetary targeting. With the exception of the central banks in Germany and Switzerland, monetary targeting as practised by several central banks in industrialised countries has largely been abandoned. Due to uncertainties in the relationship between monetary targets and the inflation rate as arising from financial innovations and currency substitution, several industrialised countries (New Zealand, Canada, the United Kingdom, Sweden, Finland, Italy and Israel) are now relying on direct inflation targeting (for a documentation see Leidermann and Svensson (1995)). In the western industrialised countries, apart from (until very recently) the Swiss National Bank the Bundesbank was the sole remaining monetary targeter – and from its record and its reputation as a tough inflation fighter it had become the monetary targeter *par excellence.* However, it might be conjectured that even in Germany there has been only a weak role for monetary targeting throughout the past decades for at least two reasons. First, the Bundesbank's record in meeting its monetary target had been poor, as already pointed out in Section 2.1.1. Second, from the empirical point of view it might be doubted that there was a reliable relationship between the aggregate targeted and inflation and output (see, for example, Estrella and Mishkin (1996)). It might therefore be doubted that the Bundesbank might be described as a monetary targeter, and, moreover, one might wonder why the Bundesbank intended to enforce monetary targeting as a rule for European monetary policy.

This is the issue from which Clarida and Gertler's (1996) and Bernanke and Mihov's (1997) empirical analyses of German monetary policy take their point of depature. The common aim of their studies is to analyse to what extent the Bundesbank targeted inflation rather than monetary aggregates. In order to model the conduct of day–to–day policy, they develop quite different models of the German money market that might be considered more or less appropriate.

In order to identify monetary policy actions Clarida and Gertler (1996) employ a structural *VAR* containing the day–to–day rate, real M3 and the DM/US \$ exchange rate as policy variables influenced by the central bank and as non–policy variables international commodity prices, industrial production, retail sales, the price level and the Federal Funds Rate (see Clarida and Gertler (1996, p. 26)). To incorporate hypotheses on money demand and supply, in the structural part of the system, it is assumed that, as usual, money demand for $M3$ contemporaneously depends on the day–to–day rate and retail sails. In an interest rate equation termed money supply equation, the day–to–day rate is contemporaneously made dependent on the price level, real money balances and the exchange rate. Hence, it is assumed that the Bundesbank uses the overnight rate as the main tool. Their empirical results suggest that the Bundesbank aggressively raises interest rates in response to inflationary pressure and that shocks to money demand have no significant effect on interest rates or on any other variables except the money stock itself. Moreover, the Bundesbank seems to ease interest rates – followed by an eventual economic expansion – if the DM is appreciating against the dollar. Thus, there seems to be little evidence that the Bundesbank pursues a strategy of monetary targeting. Instead it pursues a strategy of leaning against the wind in the sense that it tightens monetary policy if output and inflation are rising (see Clarida and Gertler (1996, p. 36)). The evidence is stressed by a further analysis of how the Bundesbank sets interest rates in response to expected deviations of output and inflation from their steady–state values (see Clarida and Gertler (1996, pp. 34–46)). They conclude that – besides some influence from the real economy – the "goal of a low long–term inflation rate is paramount" (Clarida and Gertler (1996, pp. 46–47)).

It might be objected that the interpretation of the interest rule equation as a money supply relationship seems dissatisfying since an aggregate for money supply is not involved: it remains open whether the Bundesbank provided liquidity on an elastic basis. Moreover, there is no statistical investigation whether the daily management of monetary policy is indeed conducted in terms of interest rates or in terms of a narrow monetary aggregate having a stable relationship with M3. It might be conjectured that supply and demand components are not properly separated and, hence, their conclusions are vague.

2.5.2 Did the Bundesbank pursue a Lombard rate regime?

A more explicit approach towards both the analysis of the money market and the Bundesbank's final objective has been undertaken by Bernanke and Mihov (1997). This study is largely a copy of their analysis of the conduct of U.S. monetary policy (Bernanke and Mihov (1995)) concerning the German case. They use a structural *VAR* containing a model of the German reserve market and nonpolicy variables (German industrial production, CPI, Dow–Jones index of commodity prices) to test for different identification schemes in the reserve market model. However, a broad monetary aggregate such as M3 is *not* included in the system in order to capture demand–for–money shocks (see Bernanke and Mihov (1997, pp. 1031–1043)). Employing the measure of monetary policy as derived from this model, they aim at studying to what extent monetary policy responds to money demand shocks and inflation. Modelling the reserve market, they assume that total reserves demand depends negatively on the interest rate and that the demand for Lombard loans depends on the spread between the Lombard and the call rate. In the context of the *VAR* employing monthly data they investigate the interaction among the Lombard– and call rate, total reserves and Lombard loans demand and nonborrowed reserves supply innovations to test for a call rate regime, a nonborrowed reserves targeting and a Lombard rate targeting regime (see Bernanke and Mihov (1997, pp. 1031–1043)).

Throughout the period 1975.01 to 1990.06 they find evidence that monetary policy in Germany can best be described as a Lombard rate regime. Clearly, it might be objected that this conclusion inappropriately reflects the evolution that took place in the Bundesbank's policy instruments since the 1980s. With respect to different subperiods they conclude that a call rate regime might plausibly be assumed for the time since *REPO*s have been used more extensively in 1985. A nonborrowed reserves regime is strongly rejected throughout the whole period. However, there might be some objections as to how the respective components in the reserve market are measured. Total reserves are measured as required reserves as of January 1974 (that is the Bundesbank's use of "Central Bank Money" less currency in circulation) and nonborrowed reserves are total reserves less Lombard loans, thereby implying that discount loans are included as part of nonborrowed reserves.

This approach seems to be inspired by the motivation to construct a model for the German market that mimicks their 1995–model of the Federal Funds market. This is especially reflected in their measurement of nonborrowed reserves since, in the U.S., nonborrowed reserves are the main source of central bank credit and the use of discount loans, or "borrowed reserves", is reserved for emergency needs. Consequently, Lombard loans are seen as the sole source of borrowed reserves in Germany. Hence, their measurement of the reserve component may not properly reflect the salient features in the evolution of money market instruments in Germany. Firstly, it does not directly account for the extensive supply of *REPO*s since 1985. Secondly, the construction of both total reserves and nonborrowed reserves does not account for the Bundesbank's practice most frequently used in the 1970s to change discount contingencies especially as a means to neutralise foreign exchange market interventions. And thirdly, the construction of reserve demand implies no link to the money stock in the economy. It is thus not quite clear how money market instruments are related to the Bundesbank's intermediate strategy.

Assuming that the Lombard rate is the Bundesbank's main policy tool, they address this very question by investigating whether – given forecasts of inflation and the Lombard rate as obtained from a *VAR* – money growth forecasts will have additional predictive information for the Lombard rate. Their answer is that in a Granger–causality sense, this is the case. However, forecast error variance decompositions suggest that, in the short–term, the Lombard rate is dominated by its own shocks, and in the long–term by shocks to the inflation forecast. Like Clarida and Gertler (1996), they conclude "that the Bundesbank is better characterised as an inflation targeter than as a money targeter" (Bernanke and Mihov (1997, p. 1049)).

The literature reviewed in this section delivers the picture that the Bundesbank seems to have made its monetary targets subservient to a policy of inflation targeting. One might wonder then, what the Bundesbank's fuss concerning the conduct of future monetary policy in Europe was all about.

However, considering the empirical implementation of the Bundesbank's policy adopted in the studies, the result seems not surprising. The Bundesbank has never claimed to be a pure monetary targeter. As outlined in Section 2.1.1 the monetary target is derived from some implicit assumptions about the trend in output and an inflation objective. Moreover, observations of the *present* money stock are seen as informative about the *future* course of inflation given some specific degree of capacity utilisation. Clearly, it would be more adequate to empirically implement this specific attitude more appropriately when inferring about the central bank's reaction function.

Moreover, the question remains open, whether the results found in these studies may be reproduced when trying to develop a model for the German money market reflecting the evolution in the Bundesbank's policy tools more appropriately and where a direct link between the money stock and reserves is established. It is the purpose of the following section to develop a model reflecting both of these salient features.

3. Theoretical framework

> *"The quantity theorist also holds that there are important factors affecting the supply of money that do not affect the demand for money.[...] A stable demand function is useful precisely in order to trace out the effects of changes in supply, which means that it is useful only if supply is affected by at least some factors other than those regarded as affecting demand."*
>
> MILTON FRIEDMAN (1956, PP. 16–17)

3.1 Basic considerations

A simple theoretical model is presented below that is used to identify money demand and monetary policy actions. A similar model has been used by Nichols , Small and Webster, Jr. (1983) , Pecchi (1993), Roley (1987), and Roley and Walsh (1985) to theoretically assess the Fed's monetary policy. Albeit less explicit several empirical studies rest on the ideas behind this set–up. The analyses of Bernanke and Mihov (1995, 1997) discussed above might be seen as an adoption of this model. With this framework at hand, it will be possible to model the Bundesbank's operating procedures as discussed in Section 2.2. The theoretical implications derived here are then used in the context of the empirical model presented in Chapter 4 to assess whether it is an appropriate description of German monetary policy.

The first element is a standard money demand equation relating the demand for nominal balances negatively to the overnight in the money market:

$$M_t^d = \alpha_0 - \alpha_1 i_t + u_t \tag{3.1}$$

with

$$u_t = \rho u_{t-1} + \varepsilon_t^d, \qquad 0 < \rho < 1. \tag{3.2}$$

Thereby ε_t^d is a white noise process (w.n.), that is, a mean–zero, serially uncorrelated process.

With $\alpha_1 > 0$ money demand depends negatively on the overnight interest rate i_t, the opportunity cost for holding money, and in addition, money demand shocks are given a certain degree of persistence, assuming positive autocorrelation for the mean zero process u_t. One might object that the inclusion of an interest rate for assets with a longer–term maturity in equation (3.1) would be more appropriate. A reduction in demand for nominal balances through a rise in the overnight rate is probably possible only if there is a stable relationship between short–term and long–term interest rates as stated above in equation (2.1). Indeed, several empirical studies of Germany suggest that the central bank controls the yield curve spread through its short–term instruments (see, for example, Estrella and Mishkin (1997)). The constant term α_0 represents effects from the price level and nominal GNP, which are excluded from this model.

Total supply of reserves TR_t^s is being composed of reserves as borrowings from the discount window DL_t (the sum of Lombard and discount loans) and credits from open market operations OMP_t of the central bank (*REPO*s, government securities and other short–term open market instruments as discussed in Section 2.1.2).

The demand for discount loans DL_t is assumed to be positively dependent on the spread between the discount rate d and the call rate:

$$DL_t = \beta_0 + \beta_1(i_t - d). \tag{3.3}$$

If the spread is rising it becomes more profitable to borrow from the discount window: $\beta_1 > 0$. With total reserves supply $TR_t^s = DL_t + OMP_t$,

$$TR_t^s = OMP_t + \beta_0 + \beta_1(i_t - d) + v_t, \qquad v_t \sim \text{w.n.}, \tag{3.4}$$

if the supply of discount loans is assumed to be elastic. From now on, the discount rate d might be set constant and dropped from the equation. The error term v_t might be seen either as policy errors or as the Bundesbank's discretionary use of the total reserves supply to influence the future money supply. According to this v_t and OMP_t should suffice certain properties reflecting the means by which monetary policy is conducted and which are therefore to be modified.

Total reserves demand in the banking sector depends on reserve requirements [(reserve requirement ratio k)$\times$(money stock M_t)] plus a white noise error term:

$$TR_t^d = kM_t^d + w_t, \qquad w_t \sim \text{w.n.}. \tag{3.5}$$

If either the money stock or reserve ratios are rising, demand for total reserves will rise. Equation (3.5) reflects the Bundesbank's use of a combination of contemporaneous and lagged reserve requirements in a simplified way. The equilibrium condition is thus given by:

$$TR_t^d = TR_t^s. \tag{3.6}$$

Besides, it is assumed that the central bank pursues the following policy rule:

$$M_t^T = M_t^* + \lambda(E(M_{t-1}|\Omega_t) - M_{t-1}^*), \tag{3.7}$$

where Ω_t is the information set available to the public at time t. Note that due to publication lags money demand shocks are realised only with a lag of one month, i.e.[1] $DE(M_{t-1}|\Omega_t) = \epsilon_{t-1}$. Equation (3.7) states that the monthly monetary target M_t^T depends on the previously announced long–term monetary target M_t^* and the degree λ (with $0 \leq \lambda \leq 1$) to which the central bank accommodates money demand shocks in the previous period. The long–term monetary target M_t^* is chosen following the Bundesbank's quantity theoretic approach, depending on its forecast of potential output growth, velocity and a specific inflation "target" as outlined in Section 2.1.1.

Assuming that the long–term monetary target is equal to a (base) level of the money stock, set at some previous time n periods ago (M_{t-n}^B) that is targeted to grow at rate g, the equation might be used to derive the reaction of some future monthly money target $M_{t+j|t}^T \equiv E(M_{t+j}^T|\Omega_t)$ subject to the central bank's information on deviations of the previous period's money stock from its long–term path:

$$\begin{aligned} M_{t+j|t}^T &= (1+g)^{n+j} M_{t-n}^B \\ &+ \lambda^{1+j}[E(M_{t-1}|\Omega_t) - (1+g)^{n-1} M_{t-n}^B] \qquad \text{with} \quad j = 0, 1, 2, \ldots \end{aligned} \tag{3.8}$$

Note that, like impulse–response or multiplier analysis in time series econometrics, innovations as observed only at a given point in time t are considered.

3.2 Interest rate operating procedure (from 1985 on)

If the central bank pursues a policy of monetary targeting in terms of interest rate targeting as discussed in Section 2.2, it might be assumed that within the policy period the central bank sets a monthly interest target i_t^T consistent with its monetary target. Shifts in i_t^T are then discretionary policy changes aimed at definitely altering the level of money market rates. They are thus given a certain degree of persistence.

$$i_t = i_t^T + e_t, \tag{3.9}$$

[1] In the following $DE_t(x_t)$ denotes the revision of the public's expectation of a certain variable due to its realisation of specific shocks. It might be written as $DE_t(x_t) \equiv E(x_t|\Omega_{t-1}) - E(x_t|\Omega_t)$ whereby Ω_t represents the public's information set before and Ω_{t-1} after the realisation of the shock at time t. $DE_t(x_{t+j}) = E(x_{t+j}|\Omega_{t-1}) - E(x_{t+j}|\Omega_t)$ is the revision of expectations on the future value of some variable due to innovations observed at time t.

where

$$e_t = he_{t-1} + \varepsilon_t^i \qquad \text{with} \quad 0 < h < 1, \qquad \varepsilon_t^i \sim \text{w.n.} \tag{3.10}$$

is a shock to the policy rule.

Given a level of i_t^T, the central bank has to accommodate money demand shocks by an elastic supply of bank reserves to maintain the interest target. The supply of total reserves is therefore completely passive. In this case, equation (3.6) might be rewritten using (3.4) and (3.5) and solving for OMP_t.

$$OMP_t = -\beta_0 - \beta_1(i_t^T + e_t) + kM_t + u_t^s. \tag{3.11}$$

Shocks to the supply of OMP_t^s $u_t^s = w_t - v_t$ are assumed to be non–discretionary policy errors. That is, in this case the central bank does not use reserves supply to target the money stock. Hence, they are given no persistence.

Interaction among the variables

The assumption of this policy practice implies specific patterns of interaction among the variables involved in the above model. Solving equation (3.1) for i_t and taking expectations yields interest rate responses to shocks in money demand.

$$DE_t(i_{t+j}) = -\frac{1}{\alpha_1}DE_t(M_{t+j}) + \frac{1}{\alpha_1}E(u_{t+j}|\Omega_t). \tag{3.12}$$

The second term in this equation represents the persistence of money demand shocks ε_{t-1}^d at time $t+j$, $j+1$ periods ago. It can be derived from the demand equation (3.1) in combination with iterations[2] on (3.2), where $E(u_{t+j}|\Omega_t) = \rho^{j+1}\varepsilon_{t-1}^d$. The first term in (3.12) represents the effects of money *stock* responses to shocks to money demand. From policy rule (3.8) and by iteration[3] it follows how this shock is accommodated: $DE_t(M_{t+j}) = \lambda^{j+1}\rho\varepsilon_{t-1}^d$. Thus, the interest rate response to a money demand shock is given by:

$$DE_t(i_{t+j}) = \frac{1}{\alpha_1}(\rho^{j+1} - \lambda^{j+1}\rho)\varepsilon_{t-1}^d. \tag{3.13}$$

That is, i_t *may rise or fall* – depending on the central bank's desire to control money demand shocks as expressed through control parameter λ.

Further inspection of the policy rule (3.9) and (3.10) reveals that responses to innovations in i_t itself are positive and petering out depending on parameter h:

[2] Note that, if $\varepsilon_{t-1}^d \neq 0$ and $\varepsilon_{t-1-i}^d = 0 \quad \forall \quad i \neq 0$, $u_{t-1} = \varepsilon_{t-1}^d$, so that $u_{t+1} = \rho u_t = \rho^2\varepsilon_{t-1}^d; \ldots; u_{t+j} = \rho^{j+1}\varepsilon_{t-1}^d$.

[3] The shock to demand observed at time t is $\rho\varepsilon_{t-1}^d$. It is accommodated according to parameter λ: $DE_t(M_t) = \lambda\rho\varepsilon_{t-1}^d; DE_{t+1}(M_t) = \lambda^2\rho\varepsilon_{t-1}^d; \ldots; DE_{t+j}(M_t) = \lambda^{j+1}\rho\varepsilon_{t-1}^d$.

$$DE_t(i_{t+j}) = h^j \varepsilon_t^i. \tag{3.14}$$

The higher h, i.e. the more lasting the effect will be, the more the central bank would be able to exert influence on long–term interest rates as argued above in Section 2.1.2. Given the linearised version of the expectations model of the term structure of interest rates as stated in (2.1), it might be argued that the central bank may affect longer term interest rates by successfully influencing expectations of future short–term rates using its policy instruments.

Responses to the *supply of reserves* are not present in future values of i_t since they are assumed to be policy errors and thus do not represent discretionary shifts in monetary policy. Responses in the money stock may be derived from equation (3.1) together with (3.9) and (3.10):

$$DE_t(M_{t+j}) = -\alpha_1 h^j \varepsilon_t^i + \rho^{j+1} \varepsilon_{t-1}^d, \tag{3.15}$$

that is money demand will decrease when i_t is rising through a tightening of monetary policy and, furthermore, money demand shocks ε_{t-1}^d persist. Again, there is no persistent reaction to the supply of reserves through OMP_t. Proceeding analogously with equation (3.11) and using (3.13), it might be shown that

$$DE_t(OMP_{t+j}) = -\beta_1(h^j \varepsilon_t^i) + (k - \beta_1)(\frac{1}{\alpha_1}(\rho^{j+1} - \lambda_j \rho)\varepsilon_{t-1}^d). \tag{3.16}$$

If there is a positive innovation in money demand leading to higher interest rates, then on the one hand OMP_t should decrease, whilst on the other hand it should increase because of a higher demand for refinancing resources through minimum reserve requirements. In addition, OMP_t will decrease if monetary policy is tightened. Table 3.1 summarises the interaction among the variables under this interest rate rule.

	Positive innovation to		
Response in	OMP_t	i_t	M_t
$E_t(OMP_{t+j})$	0/+	−	+/−
$E_t(i_{t+j})$	0	+	+/−
$E_t(M_{t+j})$	0	−	+

Table 3.1. Interaction among the variables under an interest rate rule

3.3 An alternative approach: reserves targeting

Following the concept of a money multiplier model (as frequently used in the literature), reserves might be assumed to be exogenous to the money market. Given a stable relationship between reserves and the money stock as in Brunner (1961) or Brunner and Meltzer (1964), the Bundesbank simply had to choose a certain level of reserves consistent with a desired amount of money. The reserves market would then clear through an adjustment in the interest rate i_t. Hence, to achieve the monetary target, it provides a certain target in its open market operations. (3.4) might thus be rewritten

$$TR_t^s = OMP_t^T + \beta_0 + \beta_1(i_t - d) + v_t \tag{3.17}$$

with

$$v_t = \sigma v_{t-1} + \varepsilon_t^s, \qquad |\sigma| < 1, \varepsilon_t^s, v_t \sim w.n.. \tag{3.18}$$

Furthermore, it might be assumed that, consequently, parameter h in (3.10) is now equal to zero – assuming that the reserve market is completely cleared by an adjustment in interest rates. Nevertheless, this might be the case only at times of a severe tightening of monetary policy. Apart from targeting bank reserves, it might be plausible to assume that the central bank smoothes interest rates to a certain extent. Therefore, to keep the exposition general, a pure regime of reserves targeting is not assumed and, hence, parameter h in (3.10) is not set equal to zero. Interest rate responses may be derived using the equilibrium condition for supply and demand (3.6) in combination with (3.18) and (3.19):

$$kM_t + w_t = OMP_t^T + \beta_1(i_t - d) + v_t.$$

Solving for i_t and taking expectations gives

$$DE_t(i_{t+j}) = \frac{k}{\beta_1} DE_t(M_{t+j}) - \frac{1}{\beta_1}(OMP_{t+j}^T) + h^j \varepsilon_t^i,$$

revealing that expected interest rates depend on the central bank's use of reserves supply (as well as on accommodation and persistence of money demand shocks):

$$DE_t(i_{t+j}) = \frac{k}{\beta_1}[(\rho^{j+1} - \lambda^j \rho)\varepsilon_{t-1}^d] - \frac{1}{\beta_1}\sigma^j \varepsilon_t^s + h^j \varepsilon_t^i.$$

Note that the usual keynesian *liquidity effect* is reflected in the second term of this equation.

Money stock responses are derived from the demand–for–money equation (3.1) where responses to i_t are now augmented by effects of, say, the supply of reserves on interest rates:

$$DE_t(M_{t+j}) = -\alpha_1(h^j \varepsilon_t^i + \frac{1}{\beta_1}\sigma^j \varepsilon_t^s) + \rho^{j+1}\varepsilon_t^d,$$

where the first term represents money stock responses through changes in interest rates induced by the supply of open market papers and by changes in the interest target. The second term reflects persistence of money demand innovations.

There is a multiplier effect from reserves to the money stock: if the supply of reserves rises, the money stock should increase. Responses to the overnight rate may be observable but should not be persistent if changes in i_t are not induced by policy discretion of the central bank.

Finally, responses of OMP_ts are the same as in the case of the interest rule policy discussed above with the exception that a higher persistence in the supply of reserves should now be observable. Table 3.2 summarises these considerations. Note that the higher the willingness of the monetary authority to let the reserves market clear through interest rate changes, and the stronger the central bank targets bank reserves the weaker should be responses in M_t and OMP_t to interest rate movements.

	Positive innovation to		
Response in	OMP_t	i_t	M_t
$E_t(OMP_{t+j})$	+	−	+/−
$E_t(i_{t+j})$	−	+	+/−
$E_t(M_{t+j})$	+	−	+

Table 3.2. Interaction among the variables under a reserves targeting procedure

3.4 Discount window borrowing procedure (1975–1984)

As described in Section 2.2 it might be assumed that, in the periods from 1975 through 1984 as well, the Bundesbank used its policy tools to stabilise interest rates. Nevertheless, given the higher interest volatility throughout this period, a different approach treating banks' reserves as exogenous policy variable might be appropriate, too. However, both alternatives are not analysed again. The results are straightforward.

First, let us assume that – as in the case of the interest rule period – discount and Lombard loans are set so as to meet the appropriate interest target consistent with the desired amount of money:

$$i_t = \gamma_0 + \gamma_1 DL_t^T + v_t + \eta_t \qquad \text{with} \tag{3.19}$$

$$\eta_t = h\eta_{t-1} + \varepsilon_t^i \quad v_t, \varepsilon_t^i \sim \text{w.n.}, |h| < 1. \tag{3.20}$$

Reserves are defensively used – so as to offset shocks in money demand; they are not used to induce policy discretionary changes, so that v_t is given no persistence. Again, M_t and i_t are exogenous to the amount of reserves made available by the Bundesbank. Impulse–response functions must equal those of the interest rule period: proceeding analogously as before, responses in the interest rate are given as in (3.13) and (3.14). Interest rates might rise or fall due to money demand shocks depending on the control parameter λ.

M_t decreases in response to a positive innovation in i_t. Solving (3.6) for discount loans and taking expectations gives:

$$DE_t(DL_{t+j}) = \beta_1 h^j \varepsilon_t^j + (k + \beta_1)(\frac{1}{\alpha_1}(\rho^{j+1} - \lambda^{j+1}\rho)\varepsilon_{t-1}^d).$$

Responses in DL_t are therefore unique. If a shock in money demand leads to higher interest rates, this – together with the need for higher reserves because of reserve requirements – will drive up the demand for discount loans and, hence, the stock of it.

There are no responses to innovations in DL since they are only used to induce changes in the interest target. Table 3.3 summarises the interaction among the variables under this policy rule. They are only slightly different from the interest rule period as discussed before.

	Positive innovation to		
Response in	DL_t	i_t	M_t
$E_t(DL_{t+j})$	0/+	+	+
$E_t(i_{t+j})$	0	+	+/−
$E_t(M_{t+j})$	0	−	+

Table 3.3. Interaction among the variables under the discount borrowing rule

3.5 Concluding remarks

It should have become clear from this section that the money stock, interest rates and bank reserves must interact in a specific manner reflecting the central bank's policy regime. The empirical analysis for Germany presented in Chapter 5 is aimed at revealing theses specific patterns with respect to different subperiods in order to draw conclusions about the Bundesbank's operating procedure.

4. Analysis of time series using linear state space models

4.1 Basic concepts

"The reports of the death of large–scale macroeconomic forecasting models are not *exaggerated."*
FRANCIS X. DIEBOLD (1998, P. 175)

4.1.1 Common approaches to multivariate time series analysis

The econometric analysis of time series has undergone quite dramatic changes since the beginning of the 1980s. Sims' (1980) paper discussed in Section 2.4, raised a serious challenge to the credibility of identifying assumptions used thus far in structural time series analysis, especially in the context of simultaneous equation systems. The criticism led to a growing acceptance of the use of economically largely unrestricted multiple time series models to assess the interaction among the variables involved for policy and forecasting purposes. The use of vector autoregressions has in effect now become an econometric standard method, as extensively reflected in time series analysis textbooks (see Hamilton (1994)). A second major blow to the use of large–scale macroeconometric models in the 1980s originated from Engle and Granger's (1987) seminal paper on cointegration in economic time series. The concept that most economic time series contain nonstationary components in the form of unit roots made traditional structural approaches suspicious to "spurious regression" problems and, at the same time, seemed to solve the dynamic specification problems econometric analysis had to deal with thus far. It has now become common practice to use vector error correction models (*VECM*s) where the time difference of the variables is related to the variables in the level – thereby incorporating contemporaneous relationships between the levels interpreted as long–term equilibrium.

This approach now comes along with an extensive apparatus for model specification and testing for structural economic restrictions. Despite the fact that it is amenable only to a very limited set of questions, it seems to have virtually erased the use of large–scale econometric models in the academics profession.

A related and yet somehow different approach is used in this study. Despite its usefulness in structural analysis, practitioners are quite aware of the sensitivity of results from *VARs* or *VECMs* to the final model choice. Due to multicollinearity inherent in the approach, the sampling error of parameter estimates tends to be large so that it is difficult to find the proper model order.

4.1.2 The system theoretic approach

Using a state space representation for vector–valued time series as suggested by Aoki (1990) derived from linear systems theory to capture the underlying process, the variance of parameter estimates can be reduced considerably. Hence, it is claimed that, by adopting this approach, structural inference should be more robust towards model selection. In addition to this – as will be shown in Section 4.7 – the approach offers a more direct and intuitively appealing representation of nonstationary time series. A common trend representation related to Stock and Watson (1988) is used that turns out to be a dual representation of error correction models used in econometrics.

In the case of *VARs*, lagged endogenous variables enter the right hand side of the system in order to model the dynamics. Using a state space modelling approach in the way suggested by Aoki (1990) time series are viewed as being generated by systems transforming information in past and present *exogenous signals* into future observations. The signals are used as *state variables* incorporated in a state space model. The state vector is thereby interpreted as minimal sufficient statistics of the process uniquely determining the future evolution of the dynamic system – given the future time path of further exogenous variables that may additionally be incorporated. Inference on the evolution of the unobservable state variables is drawn by *filtering* and *smoothing* using observed variables given a known state space model that satisfies certain regularity conditions. This system theoretic approach has been developed in the engineering literature and, together with mathematical control theory, gained the status of an independent discipline in the field of electrical engineering and applied mathematics.

Naturally, in the context of this study, the representation is focused exclusively on the properties of state space models that arise from their application for specific econometric purposes. It is therefore often established on a heuristic basis.

Since time series are viewed to be generated by unobserved exogenous signals, state space models are used to construct filters with which to detect the unobservable signal, given the observed series from a system where both signals and noise are entering. This is crucial in order to obtain in–sample and out–of–sample forecasts. Roughly, the filter that has its output closest to the correct or useful signal and, therefore, forecasts of the observed series closest to the true value will be considered as resulting from the best filter.

However, the methodology applied here is retained only to a certain class of models allowing the construction of filters which suffice specific basic conditions. First, the modelling technique involves operation in discrete time. Discrete–time statistical theory is simpler than continuous–time statistical theory, since the theory of random sequences is simpler than that of continuous–time processes. Moreover, this is analogous to the common approach in time series econometrics. It arises naturally in the field of econometrics where certain statistics or economic indices are available periodically and not on a continuous basis. Second, it is desirable to find an optimal filter, at least in the sense that it is free from stability problems. Finally, the model used for the analysis is linear in a minimum mean–square–error sense, as it is the case with most econometric techniques.

4.1.3 Filtering and smoothing

Using a dynamic system to forecast time series involves both *filtering* and *smoothing* in order to recover the signal contaminated by noise from the observed series. It is necessary that the system is *causal* in the sense that its output at time $t = t_0$ is in no way dependent on inputs applied subsequent to $t = t_0$. If the system in question is a discrete time system, the signal at time t to be measured might be denoted z_t. The signal z_t is not directly observable – or is measured with an error – so that it differs from the measurement y_t which is actually available. Generally, filtering of y_t involves recovery of z_t from y_t. So, some noisy measurement of the system is used to obtain information about some quantity that is internal to the evolution of the system. Filtering in a more specific sense, however, means the extraction of information at time t about z_t using measurement only *up until* time t. Consequently, information after time t is not used. Smoothing differs from filtering in the sense that information available *after* time t can be used. That is, information necessary to obtain smoothed estimates of z_t is available only with a delay.

The difference can be illustrated if we take the example of reading hastily written handwriting (the example is from Anderson and Moore (1976), p. 11). Each word is tackled sequentially and when a word is reached that is particularly difficult to interpret, words preceding and following the difficult word might be used to obtain information about it. Now let us assume that the handwriting corresponds to y_t and the meaning of the words to z_t. If only words before the difficult word are used to trace z_t, this might be called filtering, and if information after it is used, this corresponds to smoothing. Finally, when the aim is to obtain at time t information on future values of the system z_{t+k} and y_{t+k} $(k = 1, 2, 3, \ldots)$ this might be called *prediction*.

4.2 The linear state space model

The class of discrete–time systems used in this study is the following general finite–dimensional state space model:

$$z_{t+1} = A_t z_t + v_t \tag{4.1}$$
$$y_t = C_t z_t + D_t x_t + e_t, \qquad t = 1, 2, \ldots \tag{4.2}$$

Since system matrices are dependent on time, the system is referred to as a time variant (see Harvey (1993), pp. 81–105) state space model. It is therefore particularly useful with respect to modelling nonstationary time series in a specific way (see Kitagawa (1981)).

The system involves observable variables y_t and x_t which are endogenous and exogenous variables respectively. The variable z_t corresponds to the unobservable state variable that, together with the noise sequences e_t and v_t and the exogenous variables x_t, determine the evolution of y_t. The term 'state' refers to the condition – state of nature – in which a dynamic system happens to be at a point in time. Equations (4.1) and (4.2) may correspond to a scalar as well as a vector valued system (with matrix dimensions defined accordingly). Since observable variables appear only in (4.2) it is called observation or measurement equation, whereas (4.1) is referred to as state or transition equation. Equation (4.2) specifies the relation between the observable data and the state vector. Consequently, matrix C_t is called observation matrix and e_t is called measurement noise. Note that exogenous variables x_t might be included in equation (4.1) as well.

Assuming time independent matrices, the following time invariant state space model is derived:

$$z_{t+1} = A z_t + v_t \tag{4.3}$$
$$y_t = C z_t + D x_t + e_t, \qquad t = 1, 2, \ldots \tag{4.4}$$

Let y_t be a $(k \times 1)$ vector of – for the moment – weakly stationary time series to be analysed, e_t and v_t serially uncorrelated noise sequences of dimension $(k \times 1)$ and $(r \times 1)$ respectively, z_t the unobservable state vector and x_t a $(m \times 1)$ vector of exogenous variables. Parameter matrices A, C, D are $(n \times n)$, $(k \times n)$, and $(k \times r)$ respectively.

The system's dynamic evolves according to the eigenvalues in transition matrix A. The system is asymptotically stable if, and only if, all the eigenvalues of A are less than one in magnitude – see Section 4.3.2 below. Furthermore, assume for the moment that

$$E(e_t e'_\tau) = \begin{cases} \Delta & \text{for } \ t = \tau \\ 0 & \text{otherwise,} \end{cases}$$

and

$$E(v_t v'_\tau) = \begin{cases} K & \text{for } \ t = \tau \\ 0 & \text{otherwise,} \end{cases}$$

where Δ is of dimension $(k \times k)$ and K $(n \times n)$, that is $\{e_t\}$ and $\{v_t\}$ are individually white processes in a general sense. Additionally let $E(z_t z_t') = \Pi$. That is, v_t and e_t are usually orthogonal, so that

$$E(v_t e_\tau') = 0 \quad \forall \quad t, \tau = 1, 2, 3, \ldots$$

and

$$\begin{aligned} E(z_t e_\tau') &= 0 \quad \forall \quad t, \tau = 1, 2, 3, \ldots, \\ E(v_t e_\tau') &= 0 \quad \forall \quad t, \tau = 1, 2, 3, \ldots. \end{aligned}$$

Finally, it is claimed that the sequence $\{z_t\}$ is a *Markov process*, that is, if $t_1 < t_2 < \cdots < t_m < t$ the probability density of z_t conditioned on $z_{t_1}, z_{t_2}, \ldots, z_{t_m}$ is simply the probability density of z_t conditioned on z_{t_m}. This is due, first, to the causality of the system (as mentioned above in Section 4.1.2), and second, to the whiteness of v_t: using the lag operator defined as $Lz_{t+1} \equiv z_t$ (4.3) may be rewritten

$$\begin{aligned} z_{t+1} &= (1 - AL)^{-1} v_t \\ &= A^{t+1} z_0 + \sum_{i=0}^{t} A^i v_{t-i} \end{aligned}$$

or

$$z_{t+1} = A^{t_m+1} z_{t_m} + \sum_{i=t_m}^{t} A^i v_{t-i}.$$

The summation in this equation involves v_{t-i} for $i \geq t_m$ with $t_m > t_l$ for all $m > l$. Thus all v_is are independent of $z_{t_1}, z_{t_2}, \ldots, z_{t_{m-1}}$, so that knowledge of these values contains no information about v_i. Of the sequence $z_{t_1}, z_{t_2}, \ldots, z_{t_m}$ only z_{t_m} is relevant for conditioning z_{t+1}, which is the essential property of the Markov process (see Anderson and Moore (1976), p. 18). Figure 4.1 depicts the system represented by (4.3) and (4.4).

It displays the feature that the time series contained in y_t are viewed to be generated by a system transforming past and present exogenous signals and noise variables into future observations. Given the future time path of the exogenous variables x_t the state vector contains a minimal set of information uniquely determining the evolution of the system (4.3) and (4.4).

In the more commonly known application of state space models in econometrics, model regression coefficients are treated as states, so as to allow for time varying coefficients (see Hamilton (1994, pp. 399–403)). Constructing the transition equation, it is then either assumed that coefficients follow a random walk or that they fluctuate stochastically around a constant value. In contrast to this, the approach in this study adopts a linear scheme to the data generating process.

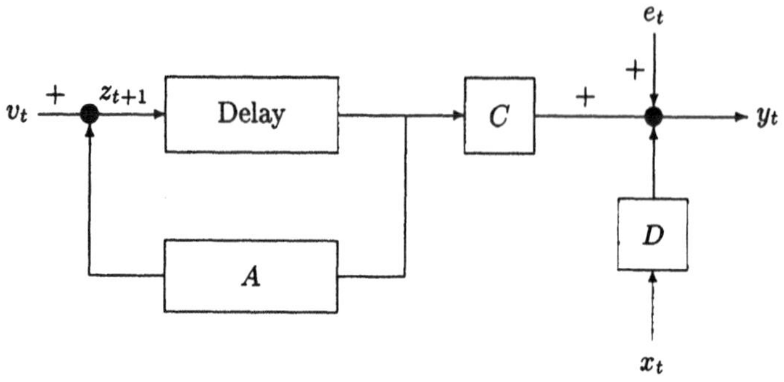

Fig. 4.1. Graphical representation of model (4.3)–(4.4)

4.3 Specific properties of the linear model

4.3.1 Innovation state space representation

By setting matrix D in (4.4) equal to zero and thereby eliminating the set of exogenous variables x_t the following system is derived:

$$z_{t+1} = Az_t + v_t, \tag{4.5}$$
$$y_t = Cz_t + e_t. \tag{4.6}$$

From 4.6 it follows[1]

$$y_{t|t-1} = Cz_{t|t-1} \qquad \text{and} \qquad z_{t+1|t-1} = Az_{t|t-1}.$$

The terms $v_{t|t-1}$ and $e_{t|t-1}$ drop out because they are assumed to be uncorrelated.

As information on y_t becomes available at time t, the forecast of z_t and y_t conditioned on this information can be updated using the formula of updating a linear projection (see Anderson and Moore (1979, p. 39) and for the proof: Harvey (1989, pp. 165–166)) : If z and y are jointly Gaussian, i.e.

$$\begin{pmatrix} z \\ y \end{pmatrix} \sim N\left(\begin{pmatrix} \mu_z \\ \mu_y \end{pmatrix}, \begin{pmatrix} \Sigma_{zz} & \Sigma_{zy} \\ \Sigma_{yz} & \Sigma_{yy} \end{pmatrix}\right), \tag{4.7}$$

where μ_z and μ_y correspond to the processes' unconditional means and Σ_{ii}, $i = y, z$, denotes respective variance–covariance matrices, then

$$(z|y) \sim N[\mu_z + \Sigma_{zy}\Sigma_y^{-1}(y - \mu_y), \quad \Sigma_z - \Sigma_{zy}\Sigma_y^{-1}\Sigma_{yz}]. \tag{4.8}$$

[1] Note that e.g. $y_{t|t-1} \equiv E(y_t|\Omega_{t-1})$ where Ω_{t-1} denotes information available at time $t-1$.

That is, $z_{t+1|t-1}$ can be updated as more information becomes available using the following projection:

$$z_{t+1|t} = Az_{t|t-1} + E[(z_t - z_{t|t-1})(y_t - y_{t|t-1})'] \\ \times E[(y_t - y_{t|t-1})(y_t - y_{t|t-1})']^{-1} \times (y_t - y_{t|t-1}). \tag{4.9}$$

Observing that e_t denotes the innovation component to y_t: $e_t = y_t - y_{t|t-1}$, (4.9) can equivalently be stated:

$$z_{t+1|t} = Az_{t|t-1} + Be_t,$$

where $B = E[(z_t - z_{t|t-1})e_t'][e_te_t']^{-1}$ is of dimension $(n \times k)$.

Thus, a system is derived called the ***innovation form*** (see Aoki (1991, pp. 5–6)) of the linear state space model (4.5) and (4.6):

$$z_{t+1} = Az_t + Be_t, \tag{4.10}$$

$$y_t = Cz_t + e_t. \tag{4.11}$$

The term "innovation form" corresponds to the feature that e_t has been shown to be the innovation component of y_t. The system is graphically depicted in Figure 4.2.

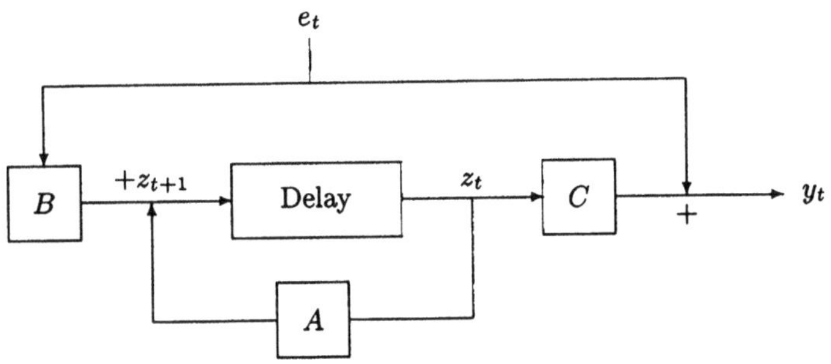

Fig. 4.2. Graphical representation of system (4.10), (4.11) in innovation form.

4.3.2 Linear state space models and time series models

There is a systematic relationship between linear state space models and time series models in vector–AR–, MA– or $ARMA$–form. State space models can be converted into time series models in a specific way and vice versa.

Theoretically they are thus equivalent in the input–output sense. Different methods exist to carry one representation over into the other. Aoki (1990, pp. 23–31) and Hamilton (1994, pp. 374–376) propose different methods for univariate processes.

A generic approach is represented in this section in order to demonstrate the algebraic equivalence between specific state space models and *ARMA* models.

When transforming time series models into state space representations it is desirable to produce state space models of *minimal dimension*, a concept that is referred to in the following section in more detail. For the moment note that a state space model is called minimal if its state dimension n cannot be reduced further. The property is not only desirable because nonminimal representations might contain redundant and useless information producing inefficiencies. It is a technical precondition for the model estimation algorithm which will be presented in Section 4.6. Moreover, procedures for filtering and smoothing will break down if applied to a nonminimal model.

Passage from ARMA to state space representations. A general method of transforming time series models into a state space representation has become known as *Gilbert's method* (see Aoki (1991, pp. 4–5)). Consider the vector–valued $ARMA(p,q)$ model for a k–variate series y_t

$$A(L)y_t = B(L)u_t, \tag{4.12}$$

with

$$A(L) = I_k - A_1L - \cdots - A_pL^p,$$
$$B(L) = I_k + B_1L + \cdots + B_qL^q,$$

and where the polynomials in L, $A(L)$ and $B(L)$, suffice the usual invertibility and stability conditions. Hereby u_t is assumed to be a mean–zero and serially uncorrelated process. Hence, the determinant of the autoregressive part is nonzero $|A(L) \neq 0|$, so that it might be inverted to rewrite (4.12) in a *transfer–function representation*:

$$y_t = [A^{-1}(L)]B(L)u_t = G(L)u_t, \tag{4.13}$$

where elements in $G(L)$ are rational functions in L. Using $A^{-1}(L) = \frac{1}{|A(L)|}(\text{adjoint}(A(L)))$, the transfer function is now put into a *matrix fraction representation* (see Aoki (1976, p. 54)):

$$G(L) = \frac{1}{d(L)}N(L),$$

where

$$d(L) = |A(L)|,$$

and $N(L)$ is the product of the adjoint matrix of $A(L)$, adjoint$(A(L))$, and $B(L)$. For cases in which the roots of this polynomial are distinct, stable and known, the construction of a state space model according Gilbert's method applies. Assume that the degree of $d(L)$ – the number of characteristic roots in A – is equal to n. The determinant of A might be factored as[2]

$$|A| = \prod_{i=1}^{n}(\lambda - \lambda_i).$$

Then $G(L)$ might be expanded into partial fractions:

$$G(L) = \sum_{i=1}^{n} \frac{N_i}{(\lambda - \lambda_i)}$$

where N_i is the residue matrix of $G(L)$ evaluated at a specific $\lambda = \lambda_i$:

$$N_i = \lim_{\lambda \to \lambda_i} G(L)$$

(see Aoki (1976, p. 54)). That is, the infinite sum $G(L) = [A^{-1}B(L)]$ is transformed into the sum $\sum_{i=1}^{n} \frac{N_i}{(\lambda-\lambda_i)}$, where each term $\frac{N_i}{(\lambda-\lambda_i)}$ again constitutes an infinite sum. Assume that rank$(N_i) = r_i$, N_i might then be expressed as the product of two rank r_i matrices C_iE_i.

Clearly, this maximal rank factorisation is arbitrary, and hence, the state space model derived from it is not unique: $N_i = C_iE_i$ with $C_i \ldots (k \times r_i)$, $E_i \ldots (r_i \times k)$. For different roots λ_i matrix N_i will be of different rank. The state vector derived from this factorisation is defined as

$$z_{i,t+1} \equiv \lambda_i I_{r_i} z_{i,t} + E_i u_t \qquad i = 1, \ldots, n,$$

where $z_{i,t+1}$ and $z_{i,t}$ is of dimension, $(r_i \times 1)$, $\lambda_i \quad (1 \times 1)$, $I_{r_i} \quad (r_i \times r_i)$, and $E_i \quad (r_i \times k)$, $u_t \quad (k \times 1)$. More compactly, constructing the state vector

$$z_{t+1} = \begin{pmatrix} z_{1,t+1} \\ z_{2,t+1} \\ \vdots \\ z_{n,t+1} \end{pmatrix}$$

this may be written

$$z_{t+1} = Az_t + Eu_t \tag{4.14}$$

with

[2] In $d(L)$ and the other polynomials L is replaced by λ in order to solve it for λ_i since L denotes only a particular operator, see Hamilton (1994, pp. 30–31).

$$\underset{(n\times n)}{A} = \operatorname{diag}(\lambda_1 I_{r_1}, \ldots, \lambda_n I_{r_n}),$$

$$= \begin{pmatrix} \lambda_1 I_{r_1} & & & 0 \\ & \lambda_2 I_{r_2} & & \\ & & \ddots & \\ 0 & & & \lambda_n I_{r_n} \end{pmatrix} \quad \text{and}$$

$$E = \begin{pmatrix} E_1 \\ \vdots \\ E_n \end{pmatrix}.$$

The observation equation is

$$y_t = Cz_t,$$

where $C = (C_1, \ldots, C_n)$.

Because C_i and E_i are not unique, this representation is not unique. However, the choice of A determining the dynamic behaviour of the system is unique. As indicated below it depends exclusively on the eigenvalues in transition matrix A which are not affected by the choice of C_i and E_i.

As demonstrated by Aoki (1990, p. 37) the model derived by Gilbert's method is of minimal dimension. Quite interestingly this is not so much a direct transformation of an *ARMA* model into state space form but rather a conversion of a transfer function into state space form using its partial fraction expansion.

Passage from state space into *MA(∞)*–representation. Conversely, the transfer function representation in (4.13) is easily derived from state space model (4.10) and (4.11).

Using $Lz_{t+1} \equiv z_t$, (4.10) may be rewritten $z_{t+1} = (I - AL)^{-1}Be_t$. With $G(L) \equiv CL[(I - AL)^{-1}B] + I$, the transfer function from the exogenous noise process e_t to the data vector y_t is

$$y_t = G(L)e_t.$$

Expansion of $G(L)$ using

$$\Gamma_i \equiv CA^{i-1}B \tag{4.15}$$

with $i = 1, 2, \ldots$ yields the *MA(∞)* representation of the process

$$y_t = (I + \Gamma_1 L + \Gamma_2 L^2 + \cdots)e_t. \tag{4.16}$$

Passage from state space to *ARMA(p,q)*–representation. A straightforward method of transforming the state space represenation of a vector valued series into *ARMA* form can now be adopted using the following useful theorem (see Aoki (1976, pp. 385–388)).

Theorem 4.3.1 (Cayley–Hamilton Theorem). *Every matrix satisfies its own characteristic equation considered as the matrix polynomial: If the characteristic equation of the $(n \times n)$ matrix A is defined*

$$\varrho(\lambda) = |\lambda I_n - A| = \lambda^n - A_1\lambda^{n-1} - \cdots - A_n = 0$$

the corresponding matrix polynomial in A is

$$\varrho(A) = A^n - A_1 A^{n-1} - \cdots - A_n I_n = 0.$$

Hence,

$$\varrho(A) = 0.$$

In order to convert the state space model contained in (4.10) and (4.11), first solve the state equation (4.10) for period $t+n$, where n is the number of states equivalent to the number of distinct characteristic roots in matrix A. Then

$$\begin{aligned} z_{t+n|t+n-1} &= A^n z_{t|t-1} \\ &\quad + \begin{pmatrix} B & AB & A^2B & \cdots & A^{n-1}B \end{pmatrix} \begin{pmatrix} e_{t+n-1} \\ e_{t+n-2} \\ \vdots \\ e_t \end{pmatrix}. \end{aligned}$$

Using this equation the following system of equations is derived by solving the observation equation for $i = 1, 2, \ldots, n$.

$$\begin{aligned} y_t &= C z_{t|t-1} + e_t, \\ y_{t+1} &= CA z_{t|t-1} + \begin{pmatrix} I & CB \end{pmatrix} \begin{pmatrix} e_{t+1} \\ e_t \end{pmatrix}, \\ y_{t+2} &= CA^2 z_{t|t-1} + \begin{pmatrix} I & CB & CAB \end{pmatrix} \begin{pmatrix} e_{t+2} \\ e_{t+1} \\ e_t \end{pmatrix}, \\ \vdots &= \vdots \\ y_{t+n} &= CA^n z_{t|t-1} \\ &\quad + \begin{pmatrix} I & CB & CAB & CA^2B & \cdots & CA^{n-1}B \end{pmatrix} \begin{pmatrix} e_{t+n} \\ e_{t+n-1} \\ e_{t+n-2} \\ \vdots \\ e_t \end{pmatrix}. \end{aligned} \tag{4.17}$$

Let Φ_i denote the coefficients of the characteristic polynomial of A:

$$|\lambda I_n - A| = \lambda^n - \Phi_1 \lambda^{n-1} - \cdots - \Phi_n I_n.$$

Starting with the last equation in the set of equations (4.17) multiply the preceding one by $-\Phi_1$, the equation before that by $-\Phi_2$ and so on, finally arriving at the first equation to be multiplied with $-\Phi_n$. Summing over the whole set of equations resulting from (4.17) yields

$$\begin{aligned} & y_{t+n} - \Phi_1 y_{t+n-1} - \cdots - \Phi_n y_t = \\ & C[A^n - \Phi_1 A^{n-1} - \cdots - \Phi_n] z_{t|t-1} \\ & + e_{t+n} + \Theta_1 e_{t+n-1} + \cdots + \Theta_n e_t, \end{aligned} \tag{4.18}$$

where Θ_i's are implicitly defined by calculation of the respective coefficients for e_{t+i}. From the Cayley–Hamilton Theorem above

$$A^n - \sum_{i=1}^{n} \Phi_i A^{n-i} = 0,$$

and thus cancelling out the states, the *ARMA*-representation

$$\begin{aligned} & y_t - \Phi_1 y_{t-1} - \cdots - \Phi_n y_{t-n} = \\ & e_t + \Theta_1 e_{t-1} + \cdots + \Theta_n e_{t-n} \end{aligned} \tag{4.19}$$

is derived, where the *AR* and *MA* polynomials are of the same specific degree $n = q = p$.

4.3.3 Minimality

As mentioned in the previous section, it is desirable to derive a model of *minimal* dimension. Minimality directly corresponds to the concept of parsimony in econometrics. The property results from specific regularity conditions for system matrices A, B, and C in (4.10) and (4.11). It is essential both in the model building procedure and for making forecasts on the output vector y_t.

Nonminimal models produce technical difficulties so that estimation of the system matrices will be impossible, and filtering algorithms to extract the unobserved state vector z_t will break down.

The concept of minimality is related to the *observability* and *controllability* property of the system discussed in this study. Both these properties are of specific importance in the engineering literature where a given relationship between the input process e_t and the output y_t is desired. There is an important and interesting difference as to how e_t is treated in econometrics and in control theory: Whereas in econometrics e_t would be viewed as a *stochastic* "innovation" process as stated in the context of (4.10) and (4.11), a typical control theoretic perspective would be to treat e_t as a *deterministic* process, and more specifically, as an instrument used to steer the variables z_t and/or y_t in a desired way. With this deterministic concept in mind it should be easier to understand the controllability and observablitity property.

First, *controllability* refers to whether it is possible to find an input e_t causing the state z_t or the output y_t to behave in a certain way. Finding an input e_t to steer z_t or y_t is equivalent to a "servomechanism problem": it is concerned with making certain variables associated with a dynamic system, for example, a telescope or a rocket, follow a particular path or take on particular values at one point in time. Controllability of a model has to do with the effectiveness of control instruments in influencing the dynamic behaviour of y_t. In the case of a dynamic macroeconomic model used for a policy implication study, for example, it is necessary that the desired time path of y_t be associated with some specific existing set of policy instruments e_t. It is the existence condition of e_t for some targeted value of y_t or z_t. The dynamic system (4.10) and (4.11) is called completely controllable at time t_0 if an instrument vector e_t exists on some finite time interval $t_0 \leq t \leq t_1$ such that the initial state z_{t_0} moves to the targeted state z_{t_1}.

The property of *observability* refers to the reconstructability of the system's data from the observed data y_t. It is the existence condition for the value z_t which is not directly observable. The dynamic system (4.10) and (4.11) is called observable if over some time interval $t_0 \leq t \leq t_1$ the observations of y_t over the same time interval uniquely determine z_{t_0}. If a system fails to fulfil this property it will be impossible to uncover the unobservable state from a set of observable data. Any filtering scheme to recover z_t from y_t will then break down. Intuitively it should be clear that observability is especially important for forecasting purposes. The following theorems state which regularity conditions should hold for the nonsingular system matrices A, B, and C so that the system is controllable and observable.

Theorem 4.3.2 (Controllability). *The n–dimensional linear system*

$$z_{t+1} = Az_t + Be_t$$

is controllable if and only if the rank of

$$\mathcal{C} = (B \quad AB \quad A^2B \quad \cdots A^{n-1}B)$$

is equal to n.

Proof: Aoki (1976, p.80) or along the lines of Brockett (1970, pp. 74–80).

Theorem 4.3.3 (Observability). *The n–dimensional linear system*

$$z_{t+1} = Az_t + Be_t, \quad y_t = Cz_t$$

is completely reconstructible or observable if and only if the rank of

$$\mathcal{O} = \begin{pmatrix} C \\ CA \\ CA^2 \\ \vdots \\ CA^{n-1} \end{pmatrix}$$

is equal to n.

Proof: Aoki (1976, pp. 109–111) or along the lines of Brocket (1970, pp. 88-90).

If both of these properties are fulfilled the system is called minimal:

Definition 4.3.1 (Minimality). *The state space model (4.10) and (4.11) is called* minimal *if matrices A and B constitute a* controllable *pair and matrices A and C an* observable *pair.*

Roughly speaking a state space model is called minimal if its state dimension n cannot further be reduced. The property corresponds to the concept of parsimony in econometrics.

What is more, as indicated earlier, it should be observed that the dynamic behaviour of the system (4.10) and (4.11) is entirely determined by the evolution of the system's state z_t according to the dynamic modes contained in transition matrix A. The following proposition applies:

Proposition 4.3.1 (Stability). *The time–invariant linear system (4.10) and (4.11) is asymptotically stable if the eigenvalues λ_i in A are distinct and if $|\lambda_i| < 1 \quad \forall \quad i = 1, 2, \ldots, n$.*

Proof: Aoki (1976, pp. 119–121). This is, of course, a precondition for observability and controllability.

The rank condition for the observability and controllability matrix can equally be stated as the positive definiteness condition for the product of the transpose of the respective matrices with itself. Aoki (1990, pp.41–42) states that $\text{rank}(\mathcal{O}) = n$ if and only if $G_{\mathcal{O}} = \mathcal{O}'\mathcal{O} > 0$ and $\text{rank}(\mathcal{C}) = n$ if and only if $G_{\mathcal{C}} = \mathcal{C}'\mathcal{C} > 0$ where $G_{\mathcal{O}}$ and $G_{\mathcal{C}}$ are called observability and controllability gramian respectively . This leads to another useful definition:

Definition 4.3.2. *A linear state space model $z_{t+1} = Az_t + Be_t$ and $y_t = Cz_t + e_t$ is called a* balanced representation *if its controllability gramian and its observability gramian are positive definite and equal to the same diagonal matrix:*

$$\mathcal{O}'\mathcal{O} = G_{\mathcal{O}} = G_{\mathcal{C}} = \mathcal{C}'\mathcal{C} > 0$$

This particular property touches on the issue of identifiability of parameter estimates: principally, the unobservable state variable z_t could be scaled in any desired way, thereby producing arbitrary choices of parameter matrices. However, it is necessary to find state variables with minimal variance. Finding a *balanced representation* is concerned with the problem of choosing system matrices for state space representations in order to properly scale input and output variables e_t and y_t so as to avoid inappropriate choices for state variables (see Aoki (1990, p. 60)). The model estimation procedure outlined in Section 4.6 is especially aimed at constructing balanced state space representations of time series.

4.4 Signal extraction using the Kalman filter

4.4.1 Filtered forecasts

In order to use the system (4.10) and (4.11) for forecasting purposes, it is necessary to obtain information about the unobservable signal vector z_t uniquely determining the evolution of the vector of the set of observable variables contained in y_t. As indicated in the introductory Section 4.1 recovering the signal contaminated by noise from the observed series involves filtering and smoothing.

The following subsection introduces the Kalman filter that serves this very purpose. It is a function of the system matrices and represents a recursive algorithm for optimally updating a linear projection for the system as more information sequentially becomes available with time.

Let $z_{t|t-1} \equiv E(z_{t+1}|y_{t-1}^-)$ denote the linear projection of z_{t+1} on y_t^-, where y_t^- is defined

$$y_t^- = \begin{pmatrix} y_t \\ y_{t-1}^- \end{pmatrix}.$$

In order to initialise the filter, the unconditional moments of the state vector z_t may be used:

$$z_{0|-1} = E(z_1)$$

which is equal to zero in the context of (4.10) and (4.11) and

$$\Pi_{0|-1} = E(\Pi_1) = \Pi.$$

Given these starting values $z_{0|-1}$ and $\Pi_{0|-1}$, the goal is to calculate $z_{t|t-1}$ and $\Pi_{t|t-1}$ as more information becomes available through time. From the observation equation (4.11) it follows,

$$y_{t|t-1} = Cz_{t|t-1} \tag{4.20}$$

which is associated with the forecast error:

$$\begin{aligned} &E[(y_t - y_{t|t-1})(y_t - y_{t|t-1})'] \\ &= E[C'(z_t - z_{t|t-1})(z_t - z_{t|t-1})'C] + E[e_t e_t'] \qquad (4.21) \\ &= C'\Pi_{t|t-1}C + \Delta, \qquad (4.22) \end{aligned}$$

since e_t and z_t are orthogonal. As information on y_t becomes available at time t, the forecast of z_t and y_t is updated using the formula of updating a linear projection (4.7),(4.8), where projections of z_t conditioned on y_t are derived. Analogous to (4.9) $z_{t|t-1}$ can be updated using

$$z_{t|t} = z_{t|t-1} + E[(z_t - z_{t|t-1})(y_t - y_{t|t-1})'] \times E[(y_t - y_{t|t-1})(y_t - y_{t|t-1})']^{-1} \times (y_t - y_{t|t-1}), \tag{4.23}$$

where

$$E[(z_t - z_{t|t-1})(y_t - y_{t|t-1})'] = E[(z_t - z_{t|t-1})(C(z_t - z_{t|t-1}) + e_t)'] = \Pi_{t|t-1}C'.$$

This result together with (4.22) may be used to rewrite (4.23)[3]:

$$z_{t|t} = z_{t|t-1} + \Pi_{t|t-1}C'(C\Pi_{t|t}C' + \Delta)^{-1}(y_t - Cz_{t|t-1}). \tag{4.24}$$

The updating equation (4.23) can now be used to forecast $z_{t+1|t} = Az_{t|t}$. Substituting accordingly gives the Kalman updating equation:

$$z_{t+1|t} = Az_{t|t-1} + A\Pi_{t|t-1}C'(C\Pi_{t|t-1}C' + \Delta)^{-1}(y_t - Cz_{t|t-1}), \tag{4.25}$$

which is analogous to (4.9). Equation (4.25) or (4.9) respectively can equivalently be stated as

$$z_{t+1|t} = Az_{t|t-1} + K_t(y_t - Cz_{t|t-1}), \tag{4.26}$$

where

$$K_t \equiv A\Pi_{t|t-1}C'(C\Pi_{t|t-1}C' + \Delta)^{-1} \tag{4.27}$$

is called the *Kalman filter gain* and, hence, where the unconditional moment matrix $B = A\Pi C'(C\Pi C'+\Delta)^{-1}$ resulting from (4.9) is referred to as Kalman filter matrix.

The mean square error of the forecast associated with (4.26) can now be shown to be given by the so-called *Ricatti-equation*:

$$\begin{aligned}\Pi_{t+1|t} &= E[(z_{t+1} - z_{t+1|t})(z_{t+1} - z_{t+1|t})'] \\ &= E[(Az_t + Be_t - Az_{t|t})(Az_t + Be_t - Az_{t|t})'] \\ &= A\Pi_{t|t}A' + B\Delta B',\end{aligned} \tag{4.28}$$

since cross-products are cancelled out. Forecasts on $z_{t+1|t}$ and $y_{t+1|t}$ derived in this way may be called *filtered forecasts* since only information up until time t is used. Figure 4.3 graphically depicts this recursive algorithm.

[3] This might be shown to be associated with the mean square error

$$\Pi_{t|t} = \Pi_{t|t-1} - \Pi_{t|t-1}C'(C\Pi_{t|t-1}C' + \Delta)^{-1}C\Pi_{t|t-1}.$$

The error is implied by the formula of updating a linear projection (4.8):

$$\begin{aligned}\Pi_{t|t} &= E[(z_t - z_{t|t})(z_t - z_{t|t})'] \\ &= E[(z_t - z_{t|t-1})(z_t - z_{t|t-1})'] - E[(z_t - z_{t|t-1})(y_t - y_{t|t-1})'] \\ &\quad \times E[(z_t - z_{t|t-1})(z_t - z_{t|t-1})']^{-1}E[(y_t - y_{t|t-1})(z_t - z_{t|t-1})'].\end{aligned}$$

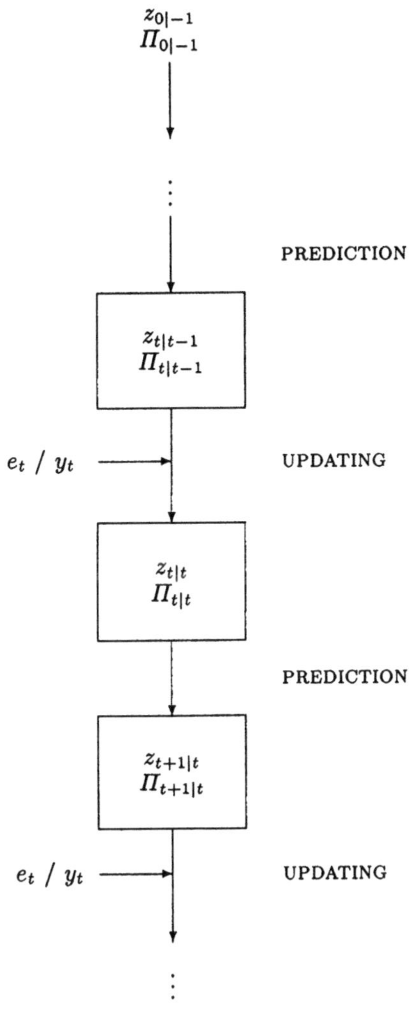

Fig. 4.3. The Kalman filter

4.4.2 Smoothed forecasts

Clearly, these forecasts can be further improved if information after time t is used. Thus *smoothed* forecasts on the state and the output vector may be produced using the full set of data $y_1, y_2, \ldots, y_t, \ldots, y_T$.

Given some "true" value for z_{t+1} the estimate of $z_{t|t+1}$ can be improved using the formula for updating a linear projection as above:

$$\begin{aligned} E(z_t|z_{t+1}) &= z_{t|t} + E[(z_t - z_{t|t})(z_{t+1} - z_{t+1|t})'] \\ &\times E[(z_{t+1} - z_{t+1|t})(z_{t+1} - z_{t+1|t})']^{-1}(z_{t+1} - z_{t+1|t}), \end{aligned}$$

where

$$\begin{aligned} &E[(z_t - z_{t|t})(z_{t+1} - z_{t+1|t})'] \\ &= E[(z_t - z_{t|t})(Az_t + Be_t - Az_{t|t})'] \\ &= E[(z_t - z_{t|t})(z_t - z_{t|t})'A'] \\ &= \Pi_{t|t}A'. \end{aligned}$$

Note that the term $E[(z_{t+1} - z_{t+1|t})(z_{t+1} - z_{t+1|t})']$ is given by (4.28). Hence,

$$\begin{aligned} E(z_t|z_{t+1}) &= z_{t|t} + \Pi_{t|t}A'\Pi_{t+1|t}^{-1}(z_{t+1} - z_{t+1|t}) \\ &= z_{t|t} + S_t(z_{t+1} - z_{t+1|t}) \end{aligned} \tag{4.29}$$

with

$$S_t \equiv \Pi_{t|t}A'\Pi_{t+1|t}^{-1}.$$

Thus, the sequence of smoothed forecasts is obtained proceeding backwards through the sample $y_1, y_2, \ldots, y_T$ given the Kalman filter estimates $\{z_{t|t}\}_{t=1}^T$, $\{z_{t+1|t}\}_{t=1}^T$, $\{\Pi_{t|t}\}_{t=1}^T$, and $\{\Pi_{t+1|t}\}_{t=1}^T$. The algorithm is initialised using $z_T = z_{T|T}$ and proceeding backwards through time using the smoothed estimates as "true values".

4.4.3 The use of the Kalman filter in econometrics

The Kalman filter has proved to be an extremely useful tool in econometrics. Sometimes the state vector z_t is given a structural interpretation, representing unobserved variables such as expectations. This is especially applicable to models of learning behaviour (for an overview see Cuthbertson, Hall and Taylor (1992, pp. 191–223)). Moreover, the Kalman filter is sometimes used to calculate the likelihood function for some specified time series model. This is so because time series models can easily be converted into state space models as illustrated in Section 4.3.2. The most prominent application, however, is the use of the filter to model time varying parameters in econometrics. Parameters might simply be assumed to evolve according to the Markov process specified in the transition equation of the state space model. This is achieved by assuming, for example, that parameters follow a random walk or some mean reverting stochastic process. For an overview of these various applications see Hamilton (1994, pp. 372–408) and Harvey (1993, pp. 100–103).

A computer algorithm for the Kalman–filter is presented in Appendix A.2. It is based on the notation in Lütkepohl (1993, pp. 428–434) because it is more compact than that in the above section where a more heuristic derivation has been used.

4.5 Structural analysis

4.5.1 Impulse–responses to orthogonal innovations

As in the case of vector autoregressions, state space models summarise the joint empirical distribution of economic variables without imposing structural restrictions. A prominent method of using such theoretically neutral time series models to assess structural relationships among the variables is given by the *impulse–response function*: Given the $MA(\infty)$–representation of a multivariate process it is possible to trace what effect – loosely speaking – an unanticipated change in a specific variable will have on the time path of each variable in the system. More specifically, as pointed out by Sims (1980, p. 21) this change is unanticipated in the sense of not being predicted from past values of variables in the system. (For an exposition with respect to vector autoregressions, see Hamilton (1994, pp. 318–323)). The method is as well referred to as multiplier analysis or innovation accounting. The dynamic multipliers of the state space model (4.10) and (4.11) are given by

$$\Gamma_i = CA^{i-1}B \qquad i = 1, 2, \ldots \tag{4.30}$$

which can be easily demonstrated using the *transfer function representation* of (4.10) and (4.11) (see Anderson and Moore (1976, pp. 340–346)) as demonstrated above: (4.10) may be rewritten $z_{t+1} = (I - AL)^{-1}Be_t$. With $G(L) = CL[(I - AL)^{-1}B] + I$ the transfer function from the exogenous noise process e_t to the data vector y_t is

$$y_t = G(L)e_t.$$

Expansion of $G(L)$ using Γ_i as defined above yields the $MA(\infty)$–representation of the process:

$$y_t = (I + \Gamma_1 L + \Gamma_2 L^2 + \cdots)e_t.$$

As extensively discussed in the VAR literature, impulse–response functions are appropriate for structural inference only if e_t is a process of orthogonal innovations to different components of y_t. Ideally, Δ should therefore be of diagonal structure. If there are contemporaneous relationships among the variables in the system, shocks to different variables might not independently occur in one variable at a time, so that innovations in these variables are correlated. Thus it is likely that an innovation in one variable is accompanied by a shock in another variable. Impulse–responses will then represent a mixture of shocks to different variables. Hence, dynamic multipliers will be contaminated by cross correlation and will not accurately reflect the true pattern of interaction.

4.5.2 Impulse–responses to non–orthogonal innovations using a Wold–ordering scheme

Using a minimum set of structural assumptions that are used to explain these cross correlations in e_t, it is possible to derive responses to orthogonal innovations v_t. Cross correlations among shocks will be reflected in the off–diagonal elements of $E(e_t e_t') = \Delta$ in the state space model (4.10), (4.11). If Δ is not a diagonal matrix, it might be decomposed so that

$$\Delta = TDT', \tag{4.31}$$

where $E(v_t v_t') = D$ is diagonal and T of full rank.

As an example for the problem of how to decompose Δ as in (4.31), let us consider an empirical implementation of the money market model as presented in Section 3.2. If a multivariate time series model is chosen so as to model the series $y_t = (OMP_t \quad i_t \quad M_t)'$, where OMP_t, denotes the supply of reserves via open market operations, i_t the day–to–day rate and M_t the money stock in the economy, the problem is to specify how innovations in these variables are contemporaneously correlated given an estimate of Δ. Generally, in the following system, these relationships are *not* identified:

$$\begin{aligned} OMP_t &= t_{12} i_t + t_{13} M_t + v_{OMP,t} \\ i_t &= t_{21} OMP_t + t_{23} M_t + v_{i,t} \\ M_t &= t_{31} OMP_t + t_{32} i_t + v_{M,t} \end{aligned}$$

or

$$\begin{aligned} OMP_t - t_{12} i_t - t_{13} M_t &= v_{OMP,t} \\ i_t - t_{21} OMP_t - t_{23} M_t &= v_{i,t} \\ M_t - t_{31} OMP_t - t_{32} i_t &= v_{M,t}. \end{aligned}$$

These equations can equivalently be written as:

$$y_t = T v_t \qquad \text{or} \qquad T^{-1} y_t = v_t,$$

where

$$T = \begin{pmatrix} 1 & -t_{12} & -t_{13} \\ -t_{21} & 1 & -t_{23} \\ -t_{31} & -t_{32} & 1 \end{pmatrix} \qquad \text{and where} \qquad v_t = \begin{pmatrix} v_{OMP,t} \\ v_{i,t} \\ v_{M,t} \end{pmatrix}$$

is a process of orthogonal innovations. In order to solve this identification problem, T is usually assumed to be of triangular shape, e.g.

$$T = \begin{pmatrix} 1 & -t_{12} & -t_{13} \\ 0 & 1 & -t_{23} \\ 0 & 0 & 1 \end{pmatrix}.$$

This results in the following recursive system:

$$\begin{aligned} OMP_t &= t_{12} i_t + t_{13} M_t + v_{OMP,t} \\ i_t &= t_{23} M_t + v_{i,t} \\ M_t &= v_{M,t}. \end{aligned}$$

In this example, M_t is affected only by own innovations $v_{M,t}$, whereas the remaining variables are not. Apart from own innovations they are influenced by those in M_t and/or i_t. Under the assumptions the process of non–orthogonal innovations

$$e_t = T v_t$$

imposes a recursive structure on the innovation process, where M_t is not affected by innovations in any of the other variables, and i_t not by those in OMP_t, whereas OMP_t may be influenced by any variable in the system Thus $E(e_t e_t') = \Delta$ is decomposed so that $\Delta = TDT'$, where $E(v_t v_t') = D$ is a diagonal matrix. Assuming a triangular shape of T results in a specific contemporaneous causality structure which has been dubbed "Wold–ordering" (see Hamilton (1994, p. 323)). In our example, contemporaneous innovations "first" feed exclusively into M_t, "then" – together with the innovation $v_{i,t}$ – into i_t, and "finally" into into OMP_t. In order to obtain dynamic multipliers, (4.30) is corrected as

$$\Gamma_i = CA^{i-1}BT \qquad i = 1, 2, \ldots. \tag{4.32}$$

A procedure for calculating impulse–response functions subject to different identification schemes is presented in Appendix A.3. Note that, if diagonal elements in T are equal to one, Γ_i will represent responses to one–standard–error innovations in each variable.

There is yet the problem of *calculating* the elements in T and D given an estimate of Δ. Principally, this problem amounts to solving the system of nonlinear equations implied by (4.31): In our example, it is given by[4]

[4] Thereby t_{ij}, δ_{ij} and d_{ij} correspond to the $i-j$–th elements in T, Δ and D respectively with $i, j = 1, 2, 3$.

$$\begin{aligned}
\delta_{11} &= d_{11} t_{12}^2 d_{22} + t_{13} t_{23} d_{33} \\
\delta_{21} &= d_{12} = -t_{12} d_{22} + t_{13} t_{23} d_{33} \\
\delta_{31} &= d_{13} = -t_{13} d_{33} \\
\delta_{22} &= d_{22} - t_{23} d_{33} \\
\delta_{32} &= d_{23} = -t_{23} d_{33} \\
\delta_{33} &= d_{33} .
\end{aligned}$$

The unknown elements in D and T are derived by solving this set of equations. The conventional approach in time series econometrics is to circumvent this problem by using a Cholesky decomposition of Δ (see Hamilton (1994, p. 82)), where matrix T can directly be derived in the desired triangular shape. Computer software packages providing tools for analysing multivariate time series routinely resort to this algorithm. However, a serious drawback of this is, of course, that the practitioner is always forced to implement a specific Wold–ordering in the system, even though a different identification scheme might be more appropriate.

4.5.3 Impulse–responses to non–orthogonal innovations: Beyond the Wold–ordering scheme

In the context of this study it has been desirable to follow a more generic approach to structural analysis. In the light of the discussion of the money market model presented in Chapter 3, for example, it is readily seen that a Wold–order would be inappropriate for structural analysis, whatever operating regime is considered. Assuming an interest rate operating procedure, it has been shown that there should be no contemporaneous effects from the supply of reserves through open market operations on the money stock and interest rates. If, in addition, money demand shocks have no contemporaneous effect on interest rates, T might be specified as

$$T = \begin{pmatrix} 1 & t_{12} & t_{13} \\ 0 & 1 & 0 \\ 0 & t_{32} & 1 \end{pmatrix} . \tag{4.33}$$

In this case, the set of nonlinear equations resulting from (4.31) is given by

$$\begin{aligned}
\delta_{11} &= d_{11} + d_{22} t_{12}^2 + d_{33} t_{13} \\
\delta_{21} &= d_{12} = t_{12} d_{22} \\
\delta_{31} &= d_{13} = d_{22} t_{12} t_{32} + d_{33} t_{13} \\
\delta_{22} &= d_{22} \\
\delta_{32} &= d_{23} = d_{22} t_{32} \\
\delta_{33} &= d_{33} .
\end{aligned}$$

Solution for T and D using a Newton–type iterative algorithm. The solution of this set of equation can be done by using a conventional Newton–type iterative algorithm. Let

$$f(x) = f\begin{pmatrix} d_{11} \\ d_{22} \\ d_{33} \\ d_{12} \\ d_{13} \\ d_{32} \end{pmatrix} = \begin{pmatrix} d_{11} + d_{22}t_{12}^2 + d_{33}t_{13} - \delta_{11} \\ t_{12}d_{22} - \delta_{21} \\ d_{22}t_{12}t_{32} + d_{33}t_{13} - \delta_{31} \\ d_{22} - \delta_{22} \\ d_{22}t_{32} - \delta_{32} \\ d_{33} - \delta_{33} \end{pmatrix}.$$

Given sensible starting values x_0, the solution $\bar{x}$ can be found using

$$\begin{aligned} x_{j+1} &= x_j - \frac{f(x_j)}{J(x_j)}, \\ \bar{x} &= \lim_{j\to\infty} x_{j+1} \qquad \text{for} \qquad j \geq 0. \end{aligned}$$

Thereby $J(x)$ denotes the Jacobi–matrix containing the analytical derivatives of $f(x)$ evaluated at x.

This scheme has several disadvantages. The algorithm will converge to the solution $\bar{x}$ only if the initial values x_0 are chosen appropriately. Besides, the algorithm bears the risk of "overshooting" the true solution. And, in addition to this, each time the identification scheme is changed, both the equations and the analytical derivatives are to be calculated again. This is, of course, a tedious task.

A direct solution for T and D. A different algorithm has been developed for the purposes in this study serving to avoid this task. From (4.31):

$$\begin{aligned} D &= T^{-1}\Delta(T^{-1})' \qquad \text{and} \\ T &= (D^{-1}T^{-1}\Delta)'. \end{aligned}$$

From these equations the solution $\bar{T}$ and $\bar{D}$ can be found using the following iterative algorithm:

$$\begin{aligned} D_{j+1} &= (T_j^*)^{-1}\Delta((T_j^*)^{-1})' \\ T_{j+1} &= ((D_j^*)^{-1}(T_j^*)^{-1}\Delta)' \\ \bar{D} &= \lim_{j\to\infty} D_{j+1} \\ \bar{T} &= \lim_{j\to\infty} T_{j+1} \qquad \text{for} j \geq 0. \end{aligned}$$

Thereby, D_j^* and T_j^* represent iterative solutions for T and D with the *known* elements – the zeros and ones! – set equal to their theoretical values. It turned out to be sufficient to initialise T_0^* using a $(k \times k)$ (in the example a (3×3))

identity matrix. The code for this algorithm can be found in Appendix A.5. It is more efficient than the Newton-type algorithm.

Convergence of the algorithm is due to Banach's fix point theorem[5] (see Heuser (1986, p. 35)), stating that if a function $\phi : R^N \to R^N$ is contracting, that is $||\phi(x) - \phi(y)|| \leq L||x - y||$ with fixed positive $L < 1$, then ϕ will have a fix point $\hat{x}$ in x so that $\phi(\hat{x}) = \hat{x}$. The speed of convergence in the algorithm is approximated by the norms of the matrix function $||T||$ and $||D||$ respectively.

Some critical remarks on the use of dynamic multipliers. One should be aware of the fact that impulse–responses might, of course, vary substantially depending on the structural assumptions imposed. This will be more dramatic the more off–diagonal elements in Δ approach the diagonal elements in absolute size. If on the other hand Δ is nearly diagonal each component in e_t can be treated as the original source of disturbances. Equation (4.30) can then be interpreted as reflecting effects of one variable on another excluding effects arising from contemporaneous relationships among the variables in the system.

Moreover, one should be quite aware of the limits of multiplier analysis with respect to policy analysis: only *innovations* in variables are used that could not have been anticipated on the basis of earlier information. So reactions of endogenous variables to systematic changes in policy variables cannot be considered in this context. In the case of a variable considered as policy variable it remains therefore unclear whether a *policy innovation* is indeed the object one wants to measure. More specifically, if the change in policy is due to the fact that the authority received information on other variables in the system, then the effect of the policy on the other variables will mix together the effect of the policy with the effect of the forecast on policy from the system.

4.5.4 The forecast error variance decomposition

Given the sequences of impulse–responses, it is possible to calculate the forecast error variance decomposition for the state space model

$$\Psi_h = \sum_{s=1}^{h} \psi_s \qquad \begin{array}{l} s = 1, \ldots, h. \\ h = 1, 2, \ldots \\ i, j = 1, 2, \ldots, k, \end{array} \tag{4.34}$$

where the i–j–th element in ψ_s is equivalent to the portion of the i–th variable's forecast error as accounted for by errors in the j–th variable in the system at forecasting horizon s. A procedure for calculating the sequences is given in Appendix A.4.

Thereby Ψ_h reflects the forecast error variance in the variables as contributed by each variable in the system *up until* forecasting horizon h. The

[5] I am grateful to Burkhard Peter for suggesting to take advantage of the theorem.

variance decomposition is simply calculated from the sequence of impulse–responses (see Hamilton (1994, p. 324)). Therefore, the critical remarks made above also apply in this context. The forecast error variance decomposition is a further conventional tool for structural analysis in muliple time series analysis. Using the sequence contained in (4.34), it is possible to assess which variables are more endogenous or more exogenous to the system under investigation: if a specific variable accounts for virtually no variance in the forecast error in the other variables, they are exogenous to that respective variable. For an outline of the concept of exogeneity in time series econometrics, see Ericsson (1992).

4.5.5 Distribution of impulse–response functions

Methods of calculating error bounds for dynamic multipliers. In a strict statistical sense, neither the sequence of impulse–responses nor that of variance decompositions give evidence in how far one variable is influenced by innovations in another variable of the system. This will only be the case if the sequences are significantly different from zero at some time horizon, as pointed out in Runkle's (1987) criticism of Sims (1980).

It has therefore sometimes become common practice to compute confidence intervals for impulse–responses, in order to assess whether economic results are statistically significant that are derived from theoretically neutral time–series models for vector–valued processes. Runkle (1987) proposed two different methods of obtaining error bounds for dynamic multipliers.

First, they might be derived analytically given the distribution of parameter estimates of the model. Since impulse–responses Γ_i are a function of parameter matrices, they have a distribution with the same mean and variance $G_s \Omega G_s'$ where Ω is the variance of parameter estimates and G_s the analytical derivative of Γ_i evaluated at the given value of parameter estimates (see Hamilton (1994, p. 336)). It is a quite tricky task to derive these analytical derivatives, especially in the case of orthogonalised multipliers (see Hamilton (1994, pp. 336–340)). Expressions for the distribution of parameter estimates as obtained from the model building algorithm to estimate state space models presented in section 4.6 below are given in Aoki (1990, pp. 177–183).

As a possible alternative Runkle (1987) suggested to use Monte Carlo or resampling methods. For an exposition, see Hamilton (1994, pp. 337–338). Since theoretical results on the asymptotic distribution of impulse–responses from linear state space models as applied in this study are not available, this approach seems to be especially applicable. The resampling methods suggested by Efron and Tibshirani (1986, 1993) conveniently substitute computer based simulation techniques in place of the complicated theoretical analysis. It avoids assumptions on the asymptotic distribution of parameter estimates and all analytical difficulties of any kind. The analyst is free to obtain statistics for whatever complicated estimators constrained only by the burden of computer time.

Confidence bounds from bootstrap replications. The aim is to simulate the distribution of estimators and impulse–response sequences resulting from it by generating large numbers of artificial observations from the actual data and the estimated residuals. Similar to the case of the $AR(1)$–model treated in Efron and Tibshirani (1993, pp. 92–99), in the context of a vector valued state space model the algorithm proceeds as follows:

1. Given an estimated time series model for a $(k \times 1)$ data series y_t $(t = 1, \dots, T)$, calculate the residuals $\tilde{e}_t$.
2. Using a random number generator independently draw $\mathcal{B}$ bootstrap samples of size T: $\{\tilde{e}_t^{*1}, \tilde{e}_t^{*2}, \dots, \tilde{e}_t^{*b}, \dots, \tilde{e}_t^{*\mathcal{B}}\}$ $\forall$ $t = 1, \dots T$. Thus, a bootstrap sample $\hat{y}_t^{*b}$ $(t = 1, \dots, T)$ is obtained by sampling $\tilde{e}_t$ with replacement and calculating y_t^{*b} given $\tilde{e}_t^{*b}$ and estimated coefficients of the time series model.
   For most situations $\mathcal{B}$ in the range 50 to 200 is quite adequate. In the simulations for the empirical part of the study 1000 replications have been used to construct the relevant statistics.
3. For each bootstrap sample evaluate the test statistic of interest, say the impulse–response sequences $\hat{\Gamma}_i^{*b}$, $b = 1, \dots, \mathcal{B}$ as from (4.32).
   The bootstrap generates many replications of the impulse response estimate conditional on the estimated coefficients $\tilde{A}$, $\tilde{B}$, $\tilde{C}$, $\tilde{\Delta}$ and $\tilde{e}_t$, as though they where the population values.
4. A confidence interval can be constructed for $\hat{\Gamma}_i$ of the form $[\hat{\Gamma}_i^{*(\alpha)}, \hat{\Gamma}_i^{*(1-\alpha)}]$ based on the α and $1 - \alpha$ percentiles of the empirical distribution of the bootstrap estimate $\hat{\Gamma}_i^{*b}$.

In the implementation of the algorithm, bootstrap samples producing non–stationary and non–minimal models have been dropped out. The purpose of this is to prevent pushing stationary and minimal models into non–stationary or non–minimal regions. This might be justified on the ground that it has asymptotically no effect: it does not restrict the parameter space of the stochastic realisation estimator.

The algorithm has the advantage of avoiding all parametric assumptions. Using draws from the *actual* data set results in carrying out the bootstrap nonparametrically. Of course, as in a usual Monte Carlo experiment y_t^{*b} may as well be randomly drawn from a distribution of $\tilde{e}_t$ assuming an estimate for this distribution.

However, apart from parametric assumptions, a further problem with conventional Monte Carlo studies in this context is that disturbances are to be generated given estimates of how orthogonal innovations feed into the system generating contemporaneously correlated disturbances. Hence, implementing a common Monte Carlo study requires assumptions on the distribution of orthogonal innovations and on how they interact contemporaneously thereby generating nonorthogonal innovations e_t subject to estimates of matrices T and D as in (4.31). All this is not required using the bootstrap algorithm. Moreover, the measured distribution of estimates reflects the small sample distribution. It is therefore not necessary to rely on asymptotic theory.

The presentation of confidence bounds for dynamic multipliers should be especially useful in the context of this study: firstly, up until now, error bounds have never been calculated in the context of state space models. Secondly, comparing the intervals from a *VAR* and a state space model should indicate which implementation produces more efficient estimates. This task is retained to Chapter 5.

4.6 Model selection and estimation

4.6.1 The model building algorithm

As mentioned in Section 4.1 modelling of multiple time series using *VAR*s or *VECM*s has some drawbacks. It is commonly known that parameter estimates may vary considerably with changes in the model choice. Due to multicollinearity inherent in the approach the sampling error of parameter estimates is large. Model selection criteria tend to be flat and practitioners are quite unaware of how adding or deleting specific lags in the model specification might contribute to explain the dynamics of the underlying process. More specifically, the "importance" to be assigned to adding or deleting some specific lag is unclear even though this might change economic results in terms of dramatic changes in the shape of impulse–responses.

Both these drawbacks – the problems with inefficiency and model selection – are claimed to be overcome in the estimation and model selection procedure for the state space model (4.10), (4.11) as developed in Aoki (1990, pp. 105–112). First, the approach of using the states as minimal sufficient statistics to explain the dynamic behaviour in the observed data offers a more parsimonious representation of time series. Second, the modelling procedure inherently ranks the states according to their importance for the dynamics of the process, thus facilitating model selection.

Aoki (1990) suggests a procedure using estimated autocovariances that are implied by the underlying process to derive parameter estimates of state space model (4.10), (4.11). Note that this state space model has been assumed to be weakly stationary. Given T observations of the mean–zero $(k \times 1)$ data vector y_t, $t = 1, \ldots, T$, compute the maximum likelihood autocovariances by $\hat{\Lambda}_i = T^{-1} \sum_{t=i}^{T-i} y_{t+i} y_t'$, $i = 0, 1, \ldots, 2p$, where p is chosen so as to capture the structure of the underlying process and y_t is a mean–zero process. Using these autocovariances, the following $(kp \times kp)$ block band counterdiagonal matrix might be constructed:

$$\hat{H}_p = \begin{pmatrix} \hat{\Lambda}_1 & \hat{\Lambda}_2 & \dots & \hat{\Lambda}_p \\ \hat{\Lambda}_2 & \hat{\Lambda}_3 & \dots & \hat{\Lambda}_{p+1} \\ \dots & \dots & \dots & \dots \\ \hat{\Lambda}_p & \hat{\Lambda}_{p+1} & \dots & \hat{\Lambda}_{2p-1} \end{pmatrix}. \tag{4.35}$$

A matrix of this specific shape is called Hankel matrix. Using the notation

$$y_{t-1}^- = \begin{pmatrix} y_{t-1} \\ y_{t-2}^- \end{pmatrix} \quad \text{and} \quad y_t^+ = \begin{pmatrix} y_t \\ y_{t+1}^+ \end{pmatrix} \tag{4.36}$$

y_{t-1}^- recursively stacks y_{t-1} over $y_{t-2} \dots$ and analogously y_t^+ stacks y_t over $y_{t+1} \dots$. Hence the Hankel matrix (4.35) relates future with past observations of y_t: $H_\infty = E(y_t^+ y_{t-1}^{-\prime})$.

For sufficiently large values of p the *rank* of the Hankel matrix is *equal to the number of states* required to summarise the information contained in the data series: this rank result is known as the *Kronecker theorem* in the engineering literature (see Aoki and Havenner (1991, pp. 16–18)). It is therefore desirable to determine the rank of $\hat{H}_p$. In order to obtain a system of *minimal dimension* by determining the rank of $\hat{H}_p$, a singular value decomposition is used to approximate

$$\hat{H}_p = U \Sigma V',$$

where U and V' are orthonormal (i.e. $U'U = V'V = I_{kp}$) and Σ is a diagonal matrix containing the singular values of $\hat{H}_p$ arranged in decreasing order $s_1 \geq s_2 \geq \dots \geq s_{kp} \geq 0$. Matrix $\hat{H}_p$ is approximated by deleting singular values in Σ "close" to zero, and retaining only n remaining singular values thereby determining the state dimension in the system. Let $\tilde{\Sigma}_n$ denote the matrix used to approximate Σ. Since formal statistical testing of singular values is difficult, the number of states n is determined by choosing a break point, i.e. a large jump, in the singular values. Singular values close to zero can be regarded as corresponding to a weak subsystem of the system which contributes little to its input–output behaviour and may be due to the presence of noise. Justification for eliminating relatively small singular values is given by the fact that the rank of the Hankel matrix H_∞ should be finite if the underlying process is indeed a finite ARMA(p,q) with $p, q < \infty$. Asymptotically, $n = rank(H_\infty) \leq kr$, where $r = \max(p, q)$ (as illustrated in Section 4.3).

Model specification by condition number: A large jump in Σ is not necessarily observed. As an alternative, let n be such that it equals a pre–set value: Aoki and Havenner (1991, pp. 16–18) suggest computing ratios of subsequent singular values s_i $i = 1, \dots, kp$ to the first singular value s_1 and to choose n so that $s_{n+1}/s_1 \leq (1/\sqrt{T})$.

80% inclusion rule: Alternatively, Mittnik (1987, pp. 91) suggests determining the state dimension n, such that the portion of the sum of the largest singular value equals approximately 80%: $\sum_{i=1}^{n} s_i / \sum_{i=1}^{kp} s_i \simeq 0.80$. From an econometric perspective, model order selection seems to lack statistical foundation. It is therefore desirable to specify the model more on the basis of formal statistical testing. Model specification tests aimed at determining the state dimension are therefore presented at the end of this section.

Given an estimate of n, the "Kronecker index" of the system, the Hankel matrix may now be approximated using the non–zero singular values retained in Σ. The approximation is thus given by

$$\tilde{H}_n = \tilde{U}_n \tilde{\Sigma}_n \tilde{V}_n'.$$

Thereby matrices $\tilde{U}_n$ and $\tilde{V}_n$ are defined in accordance with the approximating matrix $\tilde{\Sigma}_n$. It is extremely important not to choose too large a value of n. This might produce a nonminimal model, so that the estimation algorithm will break down.

Now let $E(z_{t+1}y_t') = \Omega$. Theoretically, this cross covariance matrix can be derived from the system in (4.10) and (4.11) and it can be shown to suffice $\Omega = A\Pi C' + B\Delta$. By recursive substitution, Λ_i might be calculated as

$$\Lambda_i = E(y_{t+i}y_t') = CA^{i-1}\Omega \qquad i = 1, 2, \ldots .$$

So H_∞ might be factorised into

$$H_\infty = \mathcal{O}\mathcal{K} = \begin{pmatrix} C \\ CA \\ CA^2 \\ \vdots \end{pmatrix} \begin{pmatrix} \Omega & A\Omega & A^2\Omega & \cdots \end{pmatrix}, \tag{4.37}$$

where the observability matrix $\mathcal{O}$ and the controllability matrix $\mathcal{K}$ are implicitly defined[6] by (4.37). Shifting the given Hankel matrix $\hat{H}_p$ up one submatrix row and filling the bottom row with $\hat{\Lambda}_{p+1} \ldots \hat{\Lambda}_{2p}$, the following "shifted" Hankel matrix

$$\hat{H}\uparrow = \begin{pmatrix} \hat{\Lambda}_2 & \hat{\Lambda}_3 & \ldots & \hat{\Lambda}_{p+1} \\ \hat{\Lambda}_3 & \hat{\Lambda}_4 & \ldots & \hat{\Lambda}_{p+2} \\ \ldots & \ldots & \ldots & \ldots \\ \hat{\Lambda}_{p+1} & \hat{\Lambda}_{p+2} & \ldots & \hat{\Lambda}_{2p} \end{pmatrix} \tag{4.38}$$

is obtained. Denote the first row of submatrices in (4.35) $\hat{H}^C = (\hat{\Lambda}_1, \ldots, \hat{\Lambda}_p)$ and the first column submatrices $\hat{H}^\Omega$. Then it can be observed that system matrices are theoretically related to H_p in the following way:

---

[6] Note that controllability in terms of matrix $\mathcal{K} = \begin{pmatrix} \Omega & A\Omega & A^2\Omega & \cdots \end{pmatrix}$ is defined as the existence condition of z_t for some targeted value y_t. This is in contrast to the concept of controllability in terms of the controllability matrix $\mathcal{C}$ in Theorem 4.1.

$$H \uparrow = \mathcal{O}A\mathcal{K}, \tag{4.39}$$
$$H^{\Omega} = \mathcal{O}\Omega, \tag{4.40}$$
$$H^{C} = C\mathcal{K}. \tag{4.41}$$

These relationships can be solved for A, Ω, and C. Let $\tilde{\Sigma}_n^{1/2}$ denote the matrix containing the square roots of singular values in $\tilde{\Sigma}_n$ on the main diagonal line. Since $V'V = U'U = I$ and observing that $\tilde{H}_n = \tilde{U}_n \tilde{\Sigma}_n^{1/2} \tilde{\Sigma}_n^{1/2} \tilde{V}_n' = \tilde{\mathcal{O}}\tilde{\mathcal{K}}$, estimates of matrices A, Ω, C are given by

$$\tilde{A} = \tilde{\Sigma}_n^{-1/2} \tilde{U}'_n \hat{H} \uparrow \tilde{V}_n \tilde{\Sigma}_n^{-1/2} \tag{4.42}$$
$$\tilde{\Omega} = \tilde{\Sigma}_n^{-1/2} \tilde{U}_n' \hat{H}^{\Omega} \tag{4.43}$$
$$\tilde{C} = \hat{H}^{C} \tilde{V}_n \tilde{\Sigma}_n^{-1/2}. \tag{4.44}$$

Note that $\Lambda_0 = E(y_t y_t') = C\Pi C' + \Delta$, so that $\Delta = \hat{\Lambda}_0 - C\Pi C'$. To estimate Π, the following equation

$$\begin{aligned} \tilde{\Pi} &= \tilde{A}\tilde{\Pi}\tilde{A}' + \tilde{B}\tilde{\Delta}\tilde{B}' \\ &= \tilde{A}\tilde{\Pi}\tilde{A}' + (\tilde{\Omega} - \tilde{A}\tilde{\Pi}\tilde{C}')(\hat{\Lambda}_0 - \tilde{C}\tilde{\Pi}'\tilde{C}')^{-1}(\tilde{\Omega} - \tilde{A}\tilde{\Pi}\tilde{C}')', \end{aligned} \tag{4.45}$$

which is equivalent to the matrix *Ricatti equation*[7], is to be solved for $\tilde{\Pi}$. The solution of this equation is tricky and usually proves to be the bottleneck in the estimation procedure.

Solutions of Ricatti equations are not unique. A whole class of symmetric positive definite matrices $\tilde{\Pi}_i$ solves for (4.45). When ordered by using partial ordering of symmetric positive semidefinite matrices, $\tilde{\Pi}_{\text{Min}} \leq \cdots \leq \tilde{\Pi}_{\text{Max}}$ the smallest matrix $\tilde{\Pi}_{\text{Min}}$ is to be used since, of course, the state vector with the smallest covariance matrix is needed.

Matrix $\tilde{\Pi}_{\text{Min}}$ may be found either by a Newton–type iterative scheme or non–iteratively by using symplectic matrices. For a detailed exposition of these techniques see Aoki (1990, pp. 78–83), Dorfman and Havenner (1992, pp. 322–323) and the references made therein. Both methods are implemented in the source code for model estimation presented in Appendix A.1. Using the iterative scheme matrix $\tilde{\Pi}_{\text{Min}}$ should be calculated using a zero matrix as starting value:

$$\begin{aligned} \tilde{\Pi}_j &= 0 \qquad \text{for} \qquad j = 0 \\ \tilde{\Pi}_{j+1} &= \tilde{\Pi}_j + \epsilon[f(\tilde{\Pi}_j) - \tilde{\Pi}_j] \\ \tilde{\Pi}_{\text{Min}} &= \lim_{j\to\infty} \tilde{\Pi}_{j+1} \qquad \text{for} \qquad j \geq 1 \end{aligned} \tag{4.46}$$

[7] To derive (4.45), note that theoretically $B = (\Omega - A\Pi C')\Delta^{-1}$ and $\Delta = \Lambda_0 - C\Pi C'$. That is, $B\Delta B = (\Omega - A\Pi C')\Delta^{-1}\Delta(\Delta^{-1})'(\Omega - A\Pi C')'$, where Δ is symmetric positive definite.

where

$$f(\tilde{\Pi}_j) = \tilde{A}\tilde{\Pi}\tilde{A}' + \tilde{B}\tilde{\Delta}\tilde{B}'$$
$$= \tilde{A}\tilde{\Pi}\tilde{A}' + (\tilde{\Omega} - \tilde{A}\tilde{\Pi}\tilde{C}')(\hat{\Lambda}_0 - \tilde{C}\tilde{\Pi}'\tilde{C}')^{-1}(\tilde{\Omega} - \tilde{A}\tilde{\Pi}\tilde{C}')' \tag{4.47}$$

and where the step length ϵ corresponds to some small positive value. In order to prevent the algorithm from overshooting the solution, it is convenient to use a variable step length for ϵ.

The solution technique inevitably leads to an early elimination of unsuitable models: if the selection of the state dimension n above fails to produce a model of minimal dimension, the algorithm in (4.46), (4.47) will break down. Estimation should then be restarted with a different (in most cases lower) order approximation of the Hankel matrix.

Finally, Δ and B are given by

$$\tilde{\Delta} = \hat{\Lambda}_0 - \tilde{C}\tilde{\Pi}\tilde{C}', \tag{4.48}$$
$$\tilde{B} = (\tilde{\Omega} - \tilde{A}\tilde{\Pi}\tilde{C}')\tilde{\Delta}^{-1}. \tag{4.49}$$

$\tilde{\Delta}$ must be positive definite and $\hat{\Lambda}_0$ of full rank since it is assumed that none of the components of the data vector y_t are collinear at any time.

4.6.2 Salient features of the algorithm as compared with *VAR*s

The feature of the singular value decomposition used to derive estimates for the state space model imply some specific advantages.

Nestedness under misspecification:. First, the leading principal coefficient submatrices are unchanged by the addition of states. This property is referred to as "*strict nestedness*" (Aoki and Havenner (1991, p. 27)). Reduced rank approximations are obtained by simply eliminating the corresponding rows and columns in matrices A and C. The model includes not only smaller models as subcases but also produces exactly the same finite sample estimates for certain parameter matrices. Aoki and Havenner (1991, p. 27) argue that, for example, if a model with state dimension $n = 2$ resulting in matrices $\tilde{A}$, and $\tilde{C}$ of dimension (2×2) and $(k \times 2)$ respectively is augmented by additional states, then the first (2×2) submatrix in $\tilde{A}$ and the first two columns of $\tilde{C}$ will be unchanged. Thus parameters from a lower order model should be known from a model of higher dimension. This feature contrasts neatly with the fact that model coefficients in *VAR*s might change dramatically with the model choice. Note, however, that the procedure advocated by the authors results only in a partially nested state space model. Estimates of matrices $\tilde{A}$ and $\tilde{C}$ have the nestedness property, whereas $\tilde{B}$ has not. For each specific number of states n, $\tilde{B}$ is calculated by solving the Ricatti equation. This solution will vary given different specifications of the state dimension n resulting in different estimates of matrix $\tilde{B}$.

Second, even in the case of misspecification, the leading principal submatrices should not only be identical to those that would be obtained in the "true" model but are also *consistent*.

These specific properties result from the balanced representation of the model derived from the singular value decomposition as used in the estimation algorithm. An estimate of the observability matrix is given by $\tilde{\mathcal{O}} = \tilde{U}_n \tilde{\Sigma}_n^{1/2}$ and of the controllability matrix by $\tilde{\mathcal{K}} = \tilde{\Sigma}_n^{1/2} \tilde{V}_n$ (see Aoki (1990, p. 113)).

And finally, the singular value decomposition brings states into the model in order of decreasing singular values, the *most important* effects modelled *first*! In the case of misspecification one can be sure at least not to have excluded the most important states and conversely, if the model is artificially augmented by additional "unimportant" states this will have virtually no effect on the dynamic behaviour of the system.

These properties contrast neatly with the difficulties of finding the final model order for vector-autoregressive representations of time series; in model order selection for *VAR*s, it often proves to be difficult to assign "importance" to specific additional lags and, furthermore, adding or deleting lags might considerably change the system's dynamic behaviour.

It can be shown that the solution for model parameters given by the method introduced in this section is equivalent to an instrumental variable technique (see Aoki (1990, p. 109–112)). For example, it can be shown that the instrumental variable estimator of matrix C using the state vector as instrument results in the same relation as implied by (4.44) in the above procedure (Aoki (1990, p. 110)).

Given this instrumental variable interpretation of matrix estimates it is possible to derive the asymptotic distribution of parameter estimates. The results are presented in Aoki (1990, pp. 177–183).

States as sufficient statistics:. In the above approach the model order to capture the dynamics in y_t is considerably reduced and, hence, offers a more parsimonious representation using the state variable z_t as statistic for the observed series. The dimension of the state space model should be considerably smaller than that of a *VAR*. How can this be justified on theoretical grounds? The reason is that sufficient information contained in z_t^- is minimal, whereas that in y_t^- is not.

Let $R \equiv E(y_t^- y_t^{-\prime}))$. Then the orthogonal projection of y_t^+ on y_t^- is given by the least squares formula

$$E(y_t^+ | y_{t-1}^{-\prime}) = H_\infty R^{-1} y_{t-1}^- \tag{4.50}$$

using $H_\infty = E(y_t^+ y_{t-1}^{-\prime})$. Therefore, y_{t-1}^- is a sufficient statistic to uniquely determine the time path of y_t.

However, according to Aoki and Havenner (1991) a *minimal* sufficient statistic can be used by introducing the state vector z_t: The orthogonal projection of y_t^+ on the linear manifold spanned by y_t^- can be written

$$E(y_t^+ | y_{t-1}^-) = \mathcal{O} z_{t|t-1}, \tag{4.51}$$

where $\mathcal{O}$ is the observability matrix as defined in (4.37). The relation is obtained by solving the state difference equation recursively for y_t^+. Equating (4.50) and (4.51) gives

$$H_\infty R^{-1} y_{t-1}^- = \mathcal{O} z_{t|t-1}. \tag{4.52}$$

Given some finite approximation for H_∞, and hence of $\mathcal{O}$ which will then be of full column rank, this implies

$$z_{t|t-1} = S y_{t-1}^- \tag{4.53}$$

with $S \equiv \mathcal{O}^{-1} H R^{-1}$. The aggregating matrix S reduces the dimension of y_{t-1}^- to just n states, where y_{t-1}^- contains lags long enough to encompass the actual model order. Given a model specification where S is of full rank, the information in y_{t-1}^- is preserved so that the states are minimal sufficient statistics for information contained in y_t.

Approximation of autocovariance sequences:. Time series models basically attempt to approximate autocovariance sequences of data. It is well known that the reduced–rank approximation of the Hankel matrix containing the sample autocovariance sequences is optimal in the sense of a Hankel norm[8], which does, of course, not necessarily mean that it is the best approximation. In theory, the approximation error of a matrix using the singular value decomposition is measured as

$$||H - \tilde{H}_n||_H = s_{n+1}$$

(see Aoki and Havenner (1991, p. 28)). However, as pointed out and illustrated by Mittnik (1991, p. 81–85), the approximation of sequences of autocovariances as arising from estimated model parameters is not as close as this measure would suggest: The approximation of the Hankel matrix using the singular value decomposition generally destroys the Hankel property of $\hat{H}_p$ or $\tilde{H}_n$, respectively. Hence, the entries of $\tilde{H}_n$ do not represent an autocovariance sequence. For that reason, the autocovariance sequences resulting from the estimated state space model derived from $\tilde{H}_n$ do not necessarily approximate the original (sample) autocovariances as closely as the reduced–rank Hankel approximation ($\tilde{H}_n$) of $\hat{H}_p$ itself would do.

4.6.3 Model specification tests

Aoki–C Test Aoki (1990, pp. 157–159) develops a test to choose the model dimension n in the estimation procedure presented in this subsection. The

[8] The Hankel norm of a matrix Ξ (denoted $||\Xi||_H$) is given by the square root of the sum of all squared elements in Ξ.

idea behind it is to test whether excluded canonical correlations related with some specified model order are jointly significant. For an illustration of how the state vector is related to the canonical variables of the data vector, see Aoki (1988b, pp. 605–606). Aoki (1988b) shows that the test is equivalent to a test on the ratio of determinants of the error covariance matrix Δ_i from different model orders $n = i$.

Let λ_n denote the ratio of determinants of the error covariance matrix Δ_{kp} – associated with the largest possible order – by Δ_n raised to the power p:

$$\lambda_n = \left(\frac{|\Delta_{kp}|}{|\Delta_n|}\right)^p. \tag{4.54}$$

It can be shown that the ratio defined in (4.54) is equal to $(I - P^2)$ where P^2 is a diagonal matrix containing the canonical correlations left out by the specification with n states, and I is an $(kp - n)$–order identity matrix. From Bartlett (1939), it is known that a constant multiplied by the log of the determinant of the excluded canonical correlations is an asymptotically Chi–squared distributed random variable. In order to achieve a better approximation to the Chi–squared distribution it is convenient to multiply this log determinant by a different constant.

Thus the test statistic for the $(kp-n)$ smallest canonical correlations may be written:

$$\begin{aligned} C(n) &= -[T - n - \frac{1}{2}(kp+1)]\ln(\lambda_i) \\ &= -[T - n - \frac{1}{2}(kp+1)]\ln\left(\frac{|\Delta_{kp}|}{|\Delta_n|}\right)^p, \end{aligned} \tag{4.55}$$

where $C(n)$ is asymptotically Chi–squared distributed with $(kp-n)^2$ degrees of freedom. Specification of the state dimension n may thus be found by starting with the largest possible specification and subsequently reducing n thereby computing $C(j)$ until it is large enough to reject the H_0 of no significant excluded canonical correlations. It may be shown that the test statistic can be calculated without actually estimating state space models of different order:

The following equivalence holds (see Dorfman and Havenner (1995, p. 108)):

$$|\Delta_j|^p = |I_p \otimes \Delta_j| = |R - H_j R^{-1} H_j'|, \tag{4.56}$$

where R is defined as in (4.50) and H_j is the Hankel matrix approximated by retaining j singular values from the decomposition of the original. Then λ_n can be expressed as

$$\hat{\lambda}_j = \frac{|\hat{R} - (U\Sigma V')\hat{R}^{-1}(V\Sigma U')|}{|\hat{R} - (\tilde{U}_j\tilde{\Sigma}_j\tilde{V}_j')\hat{R}^{-1}(\tilde{V}_j\tilde{\Sigma}_j\tilde{U}_j')|}, \tag{4.57}$$

where U, Σ, V correspond to the singular value decomposition of the original Hankel matrix and $\tilde{U}_j$, $\tilde{\Sigma}_j$, $\tilde{V}_j'$ are defined as in the context of (4.35)-(4.45). Substituting (4.57) into (4.55) shows that model specification testing can be conducted without estimation of model parameters.

As noted by Dorfman and Havenner (1995, p. 109) the test cannot suffer from gaps or inconsistencies in the model order because canonical correlations are ordered in the same manner as singular values. Proceeding from a general model of order kp downwards to a specific one of order n will not result in changing significance levels. Given a specific significance level, the test should automatically and uniquely determine n.

Dorfman–M Test A different test based on model coefficients has been suggested by Dorfman (1991, pp. 67–73). To develop the test statistic, write the model in stacked form:

$$y_t^+ = \mathcal{O} z_t + \mathcal{T} e_t^+, \tag{4.58}$$

where $\mathcal{O}$ is the observability matrix and $\mathcal{T}$ a lower block triangular Toeplitz matrix[9] resulting from solving (4.11) recursively for elements in y_t^+ so that, for example,

$$\mathcal{T} = \begin{pmatrix} I & 0 & 0 & 0 \\ CB & I & 0 & 0 \\ CAB & CB & I & 0 \\ CA^2B & CAB & CB & I \end{pmatrix} \tag{4.59}$$

if the dimension of y_t^+ is four. From (4.37), the estimator for $\mathcal{O}$ can be expressed as

$$\tilde{\mathcal{O}} = \tilde{H}\tilde{\mathcal{K}}^{-1} \tag{4.60}$$

where, as above, the inverse of the controllability matrix $\mathcal{K}$ is given by

$$\tilde{\mathcal{K}}^{-1} = \tilde{V}_n \tilde{\Sigma}_n^{-1/2}.$$

Given a specific approximation of the Hankel matrix as in (4.37) the dimension of $\mathcal{O}$ will be $(kp \times n)$. In the case of inclusion of unnecessary states in the model the coefficients in $\mathcal{O}$ which multiply that state have a probability limit equal to zero. Hence, testing the joint significance of a particular column in $\mathcal{O}$ provides a statistical test of the significance of the state associated with that particular column.

Let $\tilde{\mathcal{O}}_{kp}$ denote the observability matrix of the largest possible model. It can be shown (see Dorfman (1991, p. 71)) that $\tilde{\mathcal{O}}_{kp}$ is asymptotically normally distributed as follows: let

$$\tilde{o}_{kp} = \text{vec}(\tilde{\mathcal{O}}_{kp}),$$

then

[9] A matrix of block–band lower triangular shape is called Toeplitz matrix.

$$\sqrt{T}(\tilde{o}_{kp} - o_{kp}) \xrightarrow{L} N[0, (\mathcal{K}R^{-1}\mathcal{K}')^{-1} \otimes (\mathcal{T}\Delta^{+}\mathcal{T}'),] \tag{4.61}$$

where $\Delta^{+} = (I_p \otimes \Delta)$, the covariance matrix of e_t^{+}, and $R = E(y_{t-1}^{-}, y_{t-1}^{-'})$. The controllability matrix $\mathcal{K}$ is estimated by

$$\mathcal{K} = \mathcal{O}\mathcal{K} = \tilde{\Sigma}^{-1/2}\tilde{U}'\tilde{H}.$$

The test statistic can be simplified in the following way: let $\Psi = \mathcal{K}R^{-1}\mathcal{K}'$ and ψ_{ij} the i–j–the element in Ψ. Let $\tilde{o}_j$ be the j–th element of $\tilde{o}_{kp}$. The test statistic for the null that all coefficients in the j–th column of $\tilde{\mathcal{O}}_{kp}$ are equal to zero can be written

$$M(j) = \tilde{o}_j'[T\psi_{jj}(\mathcal{T}\Delta^{+}\mathcal{T})^{-1}]\tilde{o}_j \tag{4.62}$$

which is asymptotically distributed as Chi–squared variable.

Again, due to the strict nesting property, coefficient values are numerically unchanged by addition or deletion of columns in $\tilde{\mathcal{O}}_{kp}$. Since columns in $\tilde{\mathcal{O}}_{kp}$ are orthogonal to each other the test may thus be conducted sequentially as in the case of Aoki's test. It is therefore not necessary to re–estimate the model under different specifications. And again, since singular values are ordered largest to smallest, significance levels will change consistently by moving from a given approximation to a lower order approximation. First, the test statistic is calculated for a state space model with a maximum set of states, $M(j)$ with $j = kp$ and, next, this calculation is repeated subsequently for $j = j - 1$ as long as the hypothesis that all coefficients in that column of $\tilde{\mathcal{O}}_{kp}$ equal zero is not rejected. Choose the state dimension $n = j$ for which $M(j)$ rejects the null hypothesis.

4.7 Modelling nonstationary time series and common stochastic trends

4.7.1 Detrending and common trend representation in econometrics

From a perspective of empirical economics, it is essential to identify different components in data series that drive fluctuations in the respective series: in macroeconomics, output series are decomposed into long–run and short–run components. Thereby the long–run component is driven by real factors such as capital accumulation, population growth and technical change, and short–run transitory components are assumed to be driven by nominal or monetary factors. Examination of both components is usually subject to different economic disciplines: the first one is explained by growth theory the second by business cycle theory. For examples, see Lucas (1973) and Barro (1978).

In order to detrend economic time series, it has become common practice in econometrics to assume that variables follow a random trend, apart from some deterministic trend component, and to hypothesise that the random trend has a unit root. It is thereby assumed that the first difference of the series is stationary. The approach has been developed in Beveridge and Nelson (1981) and Nelson and Plosser (1982). A recent application to German post–war GDP data, together with an empirical assessment of the power of unit root tests involved, may be found in Assenmacher (1998).

Detrending is not only desirable from an economic perspective: in the detrending procedure, time series are transformed in order to render them weakly stationary, since time series models are usually applicable only to nonstationary processes.

Given a vector–valued time series the adoption of this approach implicitly assumes that the number of unit roots is equal to the number of components in the data series. However, if different components of the data vector share the same random walk components, this information contained in the level of the series will be lost in the detrending procedure.

For that reason, in the cointegration literature following Engle and Granger (1987), the trend component of multiple time series is modelled by seeking a small number of common factors that may cause a large number of economic variables to change. In Engle and Granger's (1987) approach the vector of the time difference of some variables $(1 - L)x_t$ is related to a combination of level variables z_{t-1}. The combination $z_t = x_t - \alpha y_t$ is interpreted to implicitly express a long–run relationship $x = \alpha y$ so that z_t measures deviations from the equilibrium. Using an error correction model it is assumed that these deviations affect the short–run behaviour in x_t. Hence, time series are decomposed by associating the short–run or fast–acting behaviour with the stationary components of the series and the long–run or slow–acting and persistent behaviour with some nonstationary components of the series. If variables share nonstationary components, i.e. they are cointegrated, then slower dynamic modes can be aggregated out from their dynamic behaviour by a suitable linear combination of the variables.

To test and estimate models for cointegrated variables, Engle and Granger (1987) and Johansen and Juselius (1990) use an error correction representation, and Stock and Watson (1988) implicitly a common trends representation. Meanwhile the approaches are extensively documented in the textbook literature (see Hamilton (1994, pp. 570–656)). As it is known, some specific assumptions are made in this approach that might be considered to be too restrictive. Despite the drawback that common random walk components cannot be modelled explicitly, it is assumed that only contemporaneous components of the data vector might form a stationary linear combination. This is not sufficiently general because there are $ARMA$–models whose first differences are *not* weakly stationary, as will be illustrated. Moreover, in order to establish cointegrating relationships among economic variables, it is necessary to impose unit roots. The common trend component *must* evolve according to a random walk. A vast set of tests is now available (see e.g. Hamilton (1994, pp. 435–570)) to test for the existence of unit roots in time series.

Practitioners are quite aware of the poor power of these tests as well as their sensitivity towards assumptions concerning the underlying data generating process that are to be made when implementing the tests. A further drawback of Stock and Watson's (1988) common trend representation is that the trend cannot be modelled explicitly. They provide only a tool to test for the number of common trends based on traditional $ARMA$–modelling of time series.

The linear state space modelling approach to nonstationary time series offers a more general and direct representation: in analogy to the common trends representation of Stock and Watson (1988), it is assumed that components of multivariate time series share the same stochastic trend, exhibiting a high degree of persistence. This common trend is explicitly modelled using the state vector in the state space model as in (4.10) and (4.11).

4.7.2 Modelling trend and cycle

The dichotomy of the approach. As in Engle and Granger (1987), Aoki (1991) uses a two step modelling procedure, whereas in the first step a trend model is fitted to the data and residuals are used to build a model for the cyclical behaviour of the data. This procedure takes advantage of the well–known fact that in the first step, the limiting distribution of the estimates is invariant to autocorrelation in the residuals. Through explicitly modelling the trend component in the series, the imposition of unit roots in the procedure is avoided. In the modelling procedure eigenvalues in transition matrix A are implicitly separated into those near (or on) the unit circle, determining the long–term behaviour, and into remainders representing transitory components. A recursive structure is implemented so that short–term components feed into longer–trend dynamics of the data vector y_t.

Following Aoki (1988a, p. 90), it can be shown that, if in the transition equation

$$x_{t+1} = Ax_t + Be_t \tag{4.63}$$

the $(n \times n)$ matrix A is of rank k and has the structure $A = DEC$, where D, E, and C are $(n \times k)$, $(k \times k)$, $(k \times n)$ respectively, then (4.63) can be aggregated using a new state vector

$$z_t = Cx_t :$$

$$C(x_{t+1}) = (CDE)Cx_t + CBe_t,$$

or

$$z_{t+1} = Fz_t + CBe_t,$$

where $F = CDE$. Therefore, because $CA = CDEC$, the condition for aggregation of dynamic matrices is $CA = FC$. This specific property is used when aggregating out trend and cyclical components from the system (4.10), (4.11).

Assume that the $(n \times n)$ matrix A has k eigenvalues near (or on) the unit circle assigned to class c_1 and remaining $(n-k)$ eigenvalues assigned to class c_2.

Let P be an $(n \times k)$ matrix which is an orthogonal matrix containing columns which are normalised characteristic vectors associated with the eigenvalues in c_1, where $P'P = I_k$. Furthermore, let us assume that S is an orthogonal $n \times (n-k)$ matrix with columns that are normalised characteristic vectors associated with the eigenvalues in class c_2, so that $S'S = I_{(n-k)}$. They satisfy

$$\begin{aligned} AP &= P'\Lambda, \qquad \text{and} \\ S'A &= \Phi S' \end{aligned} \tag{4.64}$$

where Λ and Φ are diagonal matrices containing eigenvalues on the main diagonal line. Matrices Λ and Φ can be shown to be orthogonal:

Multiplication of the first relation in (4.64) from the left with S' and the second one from the right with P and subtracting the latter from the former gives

$$0 = S'P\Lambda - \Phi S'P.$$

Because Λ and Φ have no eigenvalues in common by construction, it follows that

$$S'P = 0 \tag{4.65}$$

(see Householder (1964, p. 30 and p. 169)). The state vector z_t in (4.10) can be decomposed following

$$z_t = S\tau_t + P\xi_t, \tag{4.66}$$

where $S'z_t = \xi_t$ and $P'z_t = \tau_t$ from the above orthogonality conditions. Thus the system (4.10) can be represented as

$$\begin{aligned} S\tau_{t+1} + P\xi_{t+1} &= A[S\tau_{t+1} + P\xi_{t+1}] + Be_t \\ &= AS\tau_{t+1} + AP\xi_{t+1} + Be_t. \end{aligned} \tag{4.67}$$

In order to extract two subsystems having eigenvalues in both classes c_1 and c_2 respectively, first multiply (4.67) from the left by S' using (4.64) and (4.65) to derive a dynamic equation for τ_t:

$$\tau_{t+1} = \Phi\tau_t + S'Be_t, \tag{4.68}$$

where $\tau_t = S'z_t$ is the aggregated state vector.

Second, to derive a dynamic equation for ξ_t multiply (4.67) from the right by P', using again (4.64) and (4.65):

$$\xi_{t+1} = \Lambda\xi_t + P'AS\tau_t + P'Be_t \tag{4.69}$$

with the vector $\xi_t = P'z_t$ aggregating out long–run dynamics. (4.68) and (4.69) may be displayed in the following recursive representation:

$$\begin{bmatrix} \xi_{t+1} \\ \tau_{t+1} \end{bmatrix} = \begin{bmatrix} \Lambda & P'AS \\ 0 & \Phi \end{bmatrix} \begin{bmatrix} \xi_t \\ \tau_t \end{bmatrix} + \begin{bmatrix} P' \\ S' \end{bmatrix} Be_t. \tag{4.70}$$

The observation equation (4.11) may be written

$$y_t = CP\xi_t + CS\tau_t + e_t. \tag{4.71}$$

In (4.70) eigenvalues belonging to classes c_1 and c_2 are separately displayed as block diagonal matrices, and short–term dynamics contained in τ_t recursively affect the longer–term stochastic trend ξ_t through term $P'AS$. This is similar to the recursive structure developed in Engle and Granger's (1987) error correction model, where deviations from the long–term equilibrium are assumed to act on short–term dynamics of the system. A structure where roles of eigenvalues retained in classes c_1 and c_2 are reversed might be established as well (see Aoki (1988a, p. 92–94)): the same procedure may be used to produce a dynamic representation focusing on the effects that long–run equilibrium relations will have on shorter–run dynamcis. In this case, the state space model turns out to be a dual representation of the error correction model introduced by Engle and Granger (1987) .

If Λ contains only eigenvalues with unit magnitudes, then ξ_t is a nonstationary process representing random walk components whereas τ_t corresponds to the stationary dynamics in the process driving y_t.

The two step modelling procedure. In order to build a recursive model for y_t as in (4.70) and (4.71), Aoki (1991, pp. 8–11) suggests a two step modelling procedure as in Engle and Granger (1987), where in the first step a trend model is estimated whose residuals are used in the second step to build a model for the short–run behaviour of the data. To establish the validity of the two–step modelling procedure, properties of parameter estimates are given in Aoki (1991, pp. 19–24, 1990, pp. 206–217).

First stage Without imposing unit roots, detrending of y_t is achieved by estimating the trend model

$$\begin{aligned} \xi_{t+1} &= \Lambda\xi_t + Gy_t^* \\ y_t &= D\xi_t + y_t^*. \end{aligned} \tag{4.72}$$

In (4.72) $\xi_{t+1|t}$ is the vector of conditional means of the unobservable trend components after the removal of nonstationary or near–nonstationary trends. If Λ contains only unit roots, then ξ_t represents random walk components and, moreover, if in this case Λ is of rank k (the dimension of the data vector y_t) and the system matrices are identity matrices, the detrended series y_t^* is identical to the time difference of the original series. In this case, (4.72) includes simple differencing of the series as subcase. More generally, if the dimension of ξ_t is less than that of y_t, then the components of the data vector are cointegrated. The stationary component y_t^* will usually be highly autocorrelated – with estimation results still holding. Note that (4.72) displays a scheme where the stationary component y_t^* serves as input that together with ξ_t drives the output process y_t.

In the context of (4.72), the dynamics of the common stochastic trend assumed in Stock and Watson (1988) is explicitly modelled and ξ_t need not evolve according to a random walk because it is not necessary to impose unit roots on the transition matrix Λ in order to detrend y_t. Furthermore, if the dimension of the state vector is smaller than k, ξ_t might be called common factor of the data series so that components of y_t are cointegrated. Note that in the case of cointegration, matrix D serves to distribute the common trends among the data series. Any vector μ' orthogonal to D might be called *cointegrating vector* in the sense of Engle and Granger (1987) since it cancels out the stochastic trend component $\mu' D \xi_t = 0$ so that $\mu' y_t = \mu' y_t^*$ contains only transitory and innovation components.

In order to assess long–run and possibly cointegrating relationships, it is crucial to determine the dimension of the vector ξ_t. In the algorithm presented in Section 4.6, the ratio of singular values of the Hankel matrix (4.35) provides an important indication of the size of the state dimension. As will be shown in the empirical implementation of the model in Chapter 5, determination of the state dimension using the singular value decomposition is especially easy in this first step of the model building procedure because of huge jumps in the singular values of the Hankel matrix $\hat{H}_p$.

Of course, the tests developed by Aoki (1990, pp. 157-159) and Dorfman (1991) as presented in Section 4.6 may as well be used to determine the dimension of ξ_t. Vinod and Basu (1995) use cointegration tests as developed by Johansen and Juselius (1990) to determine the number of common factors contained in ξ_t.

Note that there is an analogy in the approach adopted by Johansen and Juselius (1990) and the state space modelling approach: whereas in the traditional cointegration literature the trace statistic is used to rank cointegrating relationships due to their relative importance this is done implicitly using the singular value decomposition to estimate the trend model, where states (and, hence, resulting cointegration relationships) are ordered in accordance to their relative importance[10]

Since only long–run relationships are captured by (4.72) the order of autocovariances used to construct the Hankel matrix $\hat{H}_p$ in (4.35) should be chosen to be low. Usually $p = 1$ is chosen in practice (see e.g. Aoki (1991, p. 13) or Aoki (1988a, p. 603)). It will be shown below in this section that

[10] For a discussion of the consequences of misspecification of the state dimension n in this modelling step for the asymptotic distribution of parameter estimates see Aoki (1991, pp. 9-11).

the construction of the state vector implies cointegration relationships among lagged or non-contemporaneous variables, which is certainly a useful generalisation as compared to the original concept. Hence, note that the more lags are included to construct H_p, the more likely (4.72) will also contain cointegrating relationships among lagged variables.

Second stage In the second step, a state space model is built to capture the dynamics in the detrended weakly-stationary part of the data vector y_t, y_t^* which is obtained from the residuals for the first stage.

$$\begin{aligned} \tau_{t+1} &= J\tau_t + Ke_t \\ y_t^* &= M\tau_t + e_t. \end{aligned} \tag{4.73}$$

In order to construct model (4.73), the order p (the order of autocovariances to construct H_p) and n, the state dimension, is to be chosen so that e_t is a white noise sequence. In this step it is essential to choose p sufficiently large so as to capture all remaining dynamics in y_t.

A possible strategy for model order selection could be to use the model selection criteria known from traditional time series modelling: the final prediction error criterion (FPE), Akaike's information criterion (AIC), the Hannan–Quinn–criterion or the Schwarz–criterion (for an exposition see, for example, Lütkepohl (1993, pp. 128–132)). In order to determine n, again the tests presented above or the use of a preset value for the ratios of singular values might be used. In practice, however, the model selection order as derived from formal statistical testing or any of the above criteria might prove unsatisfactory because this might still produce noncontrollable and/or unobservable representations. The state dimension n is then to be changed slightly in order to obtain a model of minimal dimension. Thus, model order selection remains to rest somehow on an ad–hoc–basis. Sometimes a considerable degree of experience and acquaintance with the technique is required for the practitioner to successfully implement the model. The strategy used in the implementation of the model in this study was first to choose both p and n as large as possible and then to reduce p successively as long as the representation still produces white noise residuals e_t. In order to test for whiteness in e_t, the usual single equation tests known from time series econometrics have been used: the Durbin–Watson test statistic, the Box–Pierce and Ljung–Box test statistic (for an exposition see Kmenta (1990, p. 332)).

The two components of the model obtained from the two stages can now be put into the following joint model

$$\begin{bmatrix} \xi_{t+1} \\ \tau_{t+1} \end{bmatrix} = \begin{bmatrix} \Lambda & GM \\ 0 & J \end{bmatrix} \begin{bmatrix} \xi_t \\ \tau_t \end{bmatrix} + \begin{bmatrix} G \\ K \end{bmatrix} e_t, \tag{4.74}$$

and the observation equation (4.11) may be written

$$y_t = D\xi_t + M\tau_t + e_t, \tag{4.75}$$

with $E(e_t e_t') = \Delta$.

As hypothesised in the theoretical exposition introducing this section, in this specification short–run dynamics affect trend components through term GM.

Matrix D serves to distribute the common trends among the data series. Any cointegrating vector μ' orthogonal to D will cancel out the trend component $\mu' D\xi_t = 0$ so that $\mu' y_t = \mu'(M\tau_t + e_t)$ contains only cyclical and innovation components.

An intuition is yet to be given why the complete model (4.74) and (4.75) cannot be obtained in a single step using the algorithm presented in section 4.6. It has already been pointed out that the modelling procedure takes advantage of the invariance of the estimation process at the first stage to particular properties of the residual process. Moreover, if data series contain random trend components, then covariance matrices used to construct the Hankel matrix (4.35) contain large disparate magnitudes dominated by large variances arising from trend movements. As already mentioned, ratios of the largest to the next largest singular values of the Hankel matrix are huge when there are significant random components. Trend components will then dominate cyclical components, so that there are jumps in singular values so huge that it is impossible not to ignore components of the data vector with small variances arising from cyclical components (see Aoki (1991, pp. 16-17)).

4.7.3 A useful generalisation for cointegrated time series

The model contained in (4.74) and (4.75) provides an important and useful generalisation to the dynamic context of Engle and Granger's (1987) original concept of cointegration. Since state vectors are often formed by stacking lagged variables – as e.g. in equation (4.53) above – it may be shown that cointegration for state vectors may imply cointegration among lagged variables as well (see Aoki (1990a, pp. 210–211)).

Engle and Granger (1987) treat only a limited class of *VAR*–models. Hence, the approach of taking the time difference of the data will not always render them stationary. This will be the case if there are stationary combinations not only among contemporaneous components of the data vector (see Aoki (1990a, p. 211)). As an example, consider the following *VAR* representation which lies outside the class of models treated in the cointegration literature.

$$y_t = \Phi_1 y_{t-1} + \Phi_2 y_{t-2} + u_t$$

with

$$y_t = \begin{bmatrix} y_{1,t} \\ y_{2,t} \end{bmatrix} \qquad \Phi_1 = \begin{bmatrix} 1 & 0 \\ 1 & 1 \end{bmatrix}, \qquad \Phi_2 = \begin{bmatrix} 0 & 0 \\ -\alpha & 0 \end{bmatrix}, \qquad \text{and}$$

$$E(u_t u_\tau') = \begin{cases} \Delta & \text{for} \quad t = \tau \\ 0 & \text{otherwise.} \end{cases}$$

Taking time differences of the two components in the data vector y_t gives

$$\begin{aligned} (1-L)y_{1,t} &= u_1 \\ (1-L)y_{2,t} &= y_{1,t-1} - \alpha u_2. \end{aligned}$$

Clearly, the time difference of $y_{2,t}$ is related to $y_{1,t-1}$, which is a random walk. There is no stationary linear combination of the two components of y_t so that the detrending procedure adopted in the cointegration literature will not result in a stationary specification for y_t.

However, a common trend specification producing stationarity in the detrending procedure may be found using a state space model for y_t. Stacking y_t over the first component of y_{t-1} produces a state vector

$$z_t \equiv \begin{bmatrix} y_{1,t} \\ y_{2,t} \\ y_{1,t-t} \end{bmatrix}.$$

The construction of the respective model is straightforward. The resulting state space model is of minimal dimension. It allows for linear combinations not only of contemporaneous components of data but data vectors at different time instants. Note that this more general notion of cointegration possibly implies a dimension of the state vector equal or even larger than that of the data vector. This should not be the case if the state space model is used in analogy to the original concept.

4.7.4 Properties of the decomposition into permanent and transitory components

The approach of decomposing macroeconomic time series into permanent and transitory components presented in this section has the further advantage of relating the algorithm closer to what might reasonably be assumed for the data generating process. In a sense, the practice of taking time differences of macroeconomic variables does in fact render the series stationary, but by no means does it *remove* the random trend from the series. Explicit modelling of the long–run stochastic trend using (4.74) and (4.75), however, will in effect *detrend* the observed series y_t.

The problem was originally discussed in Nelson and Plosser's (1982) paper on the introduction of trend– and difference–stationary processes (see Nelson and Plosser (1982, p. 141-142)): when testing for unit roots in economic time series, a decision is to be made whether to include a deterministic time trend into the series or not, thereby assigning possible permanence in the series to both the trend and the cyclical component or to the cyclical component alone.

Nelson and Plosser (1982) argue that persistence (i.e. the detection of a unit root) is due to nonstationarity in the trend component whereas the cycle might be assumed to be stationary. In their study on fluctuations in U.S. GNP series they cannot reject the hypothesis that the series are a nonstationary stochastic process with no tendency to return to a trend line. Hence, the model hypothesised to capture the specific properties of the data generating process is assumed to be:

$$y_t = \bar{y}_t + c_t,$$

where y_t is the log of an output series and $\bar{y}_t$ and c_t refer to the trend and cyclical component respectively with

$$\begin{aligned} \bar{y}_t &= (1 - L)^{-1}\theta(L)v_t \\ c_t &= \psi(L)u_t, \end{aligned} \tag{4.76}$$

where y_t is a univariate series, v_t and u_t are mean–zero, serially uncorrelated processes. The finite lag polynomials $\theta(L)$ and $\psi(L)$ satisfy the usual stationarity and invertibility conditions. Note that no drift is included in (4.76) and that nonstationarity is assigned only to $\bar{y}_t$.

As pointed out by Nelson and Plosser (1982), the problem of separating out the permanent component $\bar{y}_t$ from the observed data y_t may be thought of as a *signal extraction problem* from a model with *unobserved* components. The problem has been addressed in Hodrick and Prescott (1997) where it is assumed that the trend component evolves smoothly over time, i.e. it is assumed to be stationary, whereas nonstationarity is assigned to the cyclical component. However, adopting this approach when (4.76) is true the magnitude and duration of the cyclical component will be overstated – and possibly monetary or nominal factors relative to real factors in explaining business cycle fluctuations.

As practised in time series econometrics, first differencing of the series will not remove the stochastic growth component. If in (4.75) it is simply assumed that $\theta(L) = \psi(L) = 1$ so that

$$y_t = \bar{y}_t + u_t \qquad \text{with} \quad \bar{y}_t = \bar{y}_{t-1} + v_t.$$

Taking differences results in

$$(1 - L)y_t = v_t + u_t - u_{t-1},$$

which is indeed stationary, but the trend component is *not* removed because the innovation in the *permanent component is part of the first difference.*

The issue can be stated in broader terms referring to the decomposition proposed by Beverdige and Nelson (1982) implicitly adopted in the common trends representation of Stock and Watson (1988):

The decomposition suggested by Beveridge and Nelson (1982) for the univariate case can be stated:

$$y_t = y_{t-1} + \Psi(L)u_t,$$

where $\Psi(L)$ and u_t are defined as in (4.76). The features of this decomposition can be illustrated for a multivariate series y_t, where y_t is of dimension $(k \times 1)$.

Adopting the common trends representation implied by Stock and Watson (1988), the trend component in (4.76) might be rewritten

$$\bar{y}_t = D\xi_t \tag{4.77}$$

where ξ_t and D are of dimension $(n \times 1)$ and $(k \times n)$, and

$$\xi_t = \xi_{t-1} + (I_n \quad 0_{n,k-n})\varepsilon_t.$$

I_n denotes a $(n \times n)$ identity matrix and $0_{n,k-n}$ a $(n \times (k-n))$ matrix of zeros. The innovation process ε_t simply contains white noise innovations to the trend part ξ_t and the cyclical part c_t:

$$\varepsilon_t = \begin{pmatrix} v_t \\ u_t \end{pmatrix}; \qquad v_t, u_t \sim \text{w.n.}.$$

The cyclical part evolves as stated in (4.76) with the parameter matrix defined accordingly. Therefore e_t, v_t and u_t are of dimension $((n+k) \times 1)$, $(n \times 1)$ and $(k \times 1)$. As long as $n < k$, the k series contained in y_t share n common trends contained in ξ_t: if the number of unit roots is smaller than k, the data series y_t are cointegrated. The transfer function from the noise process ε_t to the observed data y_t can now be shown to be

$$y_t = \left[D(I_n - L)^{-1}(I_n \quad 0_{n,k-n}) + \Psi(L)\right]\varepsilon_t, \tag{4.78}$$

where it can readily be seen that innovations ε_t *contemporaneously* affect both the cyclical component $\Psi(L)u_t$ and the random trend component $D(I_n - L)^{-1}(I_n \quad 0_{k-n})v_t$.

The state space decomposition introduced with (4.72)–(4.75) is different in this respect. For model equations (4.74) and (4.75) it can be shown that the transfer function from the exogenous noise process e_t to the data vector y_t is given by:

$$y_t = \left[(I_n - \Lambda L)^{-1}(DGL) + I_k\right]\left[(I_k - JL)^{-1}(MKL) + I_k\right]e_t. \tag{4.79}$$

If $\Lambda = I_n$ is assumed as in Stock and Watson (1998) with $n < k$ the transfer function for the permanent component may be written

$$\bar{y}_t \equiv (I_n - L)^{-1}(DGL)\left[(I_k - JL)^{-1}(MKL) + I_k\right]e_t \tag{4.80}$$

and for the cyclical component

$$c_t \equiv \left[(I_k - JL)^{-1}(MKL) + I_k\right] e_t. \tag{4.81}$$

In (4.80) the permanent component is *not* contemporaneously affected by e_t but rather by past values of e_t whereas in (4.81) e_t contemporaneously affects c_t. The property is not fulfilled by the decomposition implied by (4.77) which is in the spirit of Beveridge and Nelson (1981). These considerations reflect the very fact that e_t is the input–process of the model specified in (4.74) and (4.75). As illustrated above it drives the stationary part y_t^* of the series that again serves as input process in the observed series y_t.

5. Empirical implementation and results

5.1 Is a multiplier approach adequate to model German money supply?

In order to identify the Bundesbank's operating procedure serving its intermediate strategy a state space model is estimated to assess the interaction among interest rates, bank reserves and the money stock. As argued in Chapter 3 specific patterns of interaction will give evidence on monetary policy regimes.

5.1.1 Data

The total sampling period under investigation ranges from January 1975 to April 1997. Throughout the analysis monthly data are used. This period is divided into three different subperiods. Separation of the first subperiod (Period I) is motivated by the fact that a change in the Bundesbank's operating procedure took place in February 1985. As argued in Section 2.1 in the 1970s and the beginning of the 1980s the banks' main source of central bank credit was discount window borrowing, i.e. the use of Lombard and Special Lombard lending facilities, and discount credits. This changed, when in February 1985 the Bundesbank raised the Lombard rate to a level above that used in its *REPO* operations so as to discourage banks from the use of Lombard lending and to re–establish its function as a last resort–assistance at times of financial stress. It was then that *REPO*s became the banks' main refinancing instrument. Furthermore, the Bundesbank argues that the more and more extensive use of open market operations served to exert more influence on the overnight interest rate in the interbank money market. Hence, it is possible, that from 1985 on the Bundesbank placed more importance on smoothing interest rates relative to previous years.

The second subperiod (Period II) from February 1985 onwards ends with May 1990, the month before German unification. The rest of the year 1990 is excluded from the analysis for several reasons. First, structural breaks may arise from the horizontal shift in the money stock and bank reserves in June 1990. Second, measurement of bank liquidity is difficult, since east German banks initially were excluded from open market operations because they had no access to high quality trade bills and securities. Instead, they were allowed to discount bills of lower quality through traditional discount operations. (For a documentation, see the respective monthly reports of the Bundesbank). The final subperiod is January 1991 to April 1997 (Period III)[1].

5.1.2 Results

In order to assess the model presented in Chapter 3 the vector of endogenous variables y_t is defined $y_t = (DL_t \quad i_t \quad M_t)'$ for Period I and $y_t = (OMP_t \quad i_t \quad M_t)'$ for Period II and III. In order to meet zero initial conditions for the state vector ($\xi_{-1|0}$ in (4.74) and (4.75)), i_t is mean–adjusted and M_t and DL_t or OMP_t respectively are divided by their initial values. Logarithms are then extracted.

The scaling of the variables not only facilitates visual inspection of the interaction among them. It also stabilises the estimation algorithm by facilitating the choice of the state variable and, hence, specification of the state covariance matrix Π solving the Ricatti equation (4.45).

Model specification is defined m(p,n) and m*(p,n) where p indicates the number of lags used to construct the Hankel matrix and n refers to the number of states included. m(p,n) indicates the model order of the stochastic trend model (4.72) and m*(p,n) that of the detrended series y_t^* as in (4.73). A top–down strategy was used to find p so that the noise process e_t might be considered as white–noise–sequence. Given some specific lag length p the number of states was selected using the singular value decomposition of the Hankel matrix. Using a preset value as suggested by Aoki and Havenner (1991, pp. 16–18) (see Section 4.6) proved to be especially useful to construct the trend–model. However, in the second step of the estimation

[1] In correspondence with the money market model presented in Chapter 3 the amount of discount credits, DL_t, is measured as the sum of Lombard and discount credits. Note that Lombard loans include the Special Lombard lending facilities as well. A plot of the data series could be found in Chapter 2, Figure 2.6. The data are taken from the statistical part of the monthly reports of the Bundesbank. Lombard and Special Lombard lending facilities can be found under position II.3.IV, the amount of bills bought by the central bank to provide credit to the domestic banking sector is taken from the Bundesbank balance sheet (Position III.1). The sum of credit available through open market operations, OMP_t, is measured as the sum of *REPO*s and what is termed "very short term equalisation operations" by the Bundesbank. Both can be found under Position II, 3, IV: "II Bankstatistische Gesamtrechnung: 3 Zentralbankgeldbedarf der Banken und liquiditätspolitische Maßnahmen der Bundesbank – IV Stand im Monatsdurchschnitt". Note that these short–term equalisation operations constitute the sum of short–term reversed transactions (Schnelltender), foreign exchange swaps and reversed exchange transactions (Devisenswap– und pensionsgeschäfte), short–term treasury bills (kurzfristige Schatzwechselabgaben) and credit from the Bundesbank's deposit policy (§17–Verlagerungen) as explained in section 2.1.2 above.

algorithm, the application of this method sometimes led to an unobservable and/or noncontrollable, i.e. nonminimal, specification, so that it was impossible to solve the matrix Ricatti equation (4.45). In this case the state dimension n has been varied slightly – in most cases it had been reduced. The impulse–response functions resulting from the specification have indeed been very robust towards the choice of the state dimension. This is a highly desired property especially from the viewpoint of a *VAR*–practitioner. As argued in Section 4.6 this is due to the nestedness–property of the estimation algorithm. The most important states are always included in the model and even if "important" states are excluded, this will have only minor effects because of their unimportance relative to those already included.

In practice model selection turns out to require substantial proficiency with state space modelling of time series. The promise is not redeemed that model specification is easier than in the case of *VAR*s and more specifically that it might be conducted on an automatic basis using the tests discussed in 4.6 given a preset "significance"–level. The problem with these criteria is that they might either produce models that are nonminimal or nonstable or turn out to fit the data very poorly. Beyond these problems the dichotomy of system dynamics in the two step modelling procedure is often not reflected in the empirical application. Detrending of the series in the first step is often not achieved, since eigenvalues of the transition matrix J in (4.73) resulting from modelling residuals of the trend model may indicate substantial remaining persistence.

Hence, a more pragmatic approach had to be adopted in this application. The predominant aim was to build joint models that produce white–noise–residuals. Values of Aoki's C–Test and Dorfman's M–Test where used only in the sense whether they indicated that any substantial dynamics have been neglected by the some specific model. They could not be used so as to automatically find a model order. Finally attention has been paid to whether the two parts of the model reflect the salient features of the detrending method applied in this context.

Results for 1991.01–1997.04 Let us start the presentation of empirical results begining with an illustration of the implementation of a state space model for $y_t = (OMP_t \quad i_t \quad M_t)$ (Period III). In the first step, the sequence of singular values from the decomposition of a Hankel matrix H_p with $p = 1$ is given in Table 5.1. Note that a jump in the ratios of singular values

s_1	s_2	s_3
0.0820	0.0433	0.0049

Table 5.1. Singular values of trend part for small model (1991.01–1997.04)

to the first element is observable from of s_2 to s_3. It is of size 10^{-1}. The ratios of the singular values to the first element are given in Table 5.2 Since

s_1/s_1	s_2/s_1	s_3/s_1
1.000	0.528	0.061

Table 5.2. Ratios of singular values of trend part for small model (1991.01–1997.04)

$\frac{1}{\sqrt{T}} = 0.114$, two states should be included in the trend model to capture long-run dynamics. The C–test–statistic for this specification is $C(2) = 90.59$ (d.o.f.=1) indicating that the model order should be augmented (at any error level), but in the case of $n = 3$ the statistic is no longer applicable because of 0 degrees of freedom. Moreover, $n = 3$ resulted in a nonminimal model.

Residual analysis[2] for this first step reveals that the money and interest rate series are specifically well filtered by the trend part of the model: The

	R^2	DW	Q(2)	Q(4)	Q(8)	Q(12)	Q(24)
OMP	0.42	0.81	36.62	45.91	47.26	49.49	68.66
i	0.98	0.82	32.42	45.52	54.29	54.97	93.62
M	0.90	0.54	64.91	89.97	100.90	105.35	118.76

Table 5.3. Residual diagnostics: Trend part of model for subperiod 1991.01–1997.04

residuals from this model are used to construct a model for the transitory part of the joint model. To construct H_p $p = 6$ is chosen. The sequence of singular values and the respective ratios to the first singular value is now: The respective ratios of the singular values to the first element are given in

s_1	s_2	s_3	s_4	s_5	s_6
0.0094	0.0031	0.0014	0.0011	0.0011	0.0008
s_7	s_8	s_9	s_{10}	s_{11}	s_{12}
0.0004	0.0004	0.0004	0.0003	0.0001	0.0001
s_{13}	s_{14}	s_{15}	s_{16}	s_{17}	s_{18}
0.0001	0.0001	0.0001	0.0000	0.0000	0.0000

Table 5.4. Singular values of cyclical part for small model (1991.01–1997.04)

Table 5.4: A jump of the size as nice as in the first step is not observable, the sequence of singular values decreases rather smoothly. Using the preset value as above it is suggested that the number of states to be included in

[2] In the tables showing test statistics for residual diagnostics, DW refers to the Durbin–Watson–statistic as specified to test for serial autocorrelation at lag one and $Q(i)$ to the Box–Pierce statistic to test autocorrelation including lags up until i ($i = 2, 4, 8, 12, 24$). Thereby, the symbol ‡ indicates statistical insignificance of serial correlation at a 5% error level. Significance levels for the DW–statistic are not reported, because its use is only indicative in this context.

s_1/s_1	s_2/s_1	s_3/s_1	s_4/s_1	s_5/s_1	s_6/s_1
1.0000	0.3345	0.1488	0.1133	0.1089	0.0824
s_7/s_1	s_8/s_1	s_9/s_1	s_{10}/s_1	s_{11}/s_1	s_{12}/s_1
0.0477	0.0459	0.0375	0.0276	0.0152	0.0110
s_{13}/s_1	s_{14}/s_1	s_{15}/s_1	s_{16}/s_1	s_{17}/s_1	s_{18}/s_1
0.0072	0.0069	0.0063	0.0030	0.0018	0.0007

Table 5.5. Ratios of singular values of cyclical part for small model (1991.01–1997.04)

the second step of the modelling procedure is three, despite the fact that $C(3) = 441.417$(d.o.f. = 225), indicating at any error level that n should be augmented. (But if n is augmented by 1, the test statistic turns out to be negative.) Hence, specification m(1,2), m*(6,3) is chosen. Residual diagnostics resulting from this specification are given by Table 5.6.

	R^2	DW	Q(2)	Q(4)	Q(8)	Q(12)	Q(24)
OMP	0.65	1.07	0.624‡	1.288‡	3.4308‡	12.675‡	20.268‡
i	0.99	1.89	0.598‡	10.672	17.198	22.405‡	34.087‡
M	0.98	1.96	0.040‡	2.525‡	6.798‡	24.779	43.418

Table 5.6. Residual diagnostics: Joint model for subperiod 1991.01–1997.04

It can be seen that the model is well capable of capturing the dynamics in the multivariate series y_t. Table 5.7 summarises the parameter estimates analogous to (4.74), (4.75):

Inspection of the eigenvalues of transition matrices Λ and J confirms that the dichotomy of the trend and cyclical components as established by the modelling procedure is well reflected in this application: $eig(\Lambda) = (0.973{+}0.020i \quad 0.973{-}0.020i)'$, $eig(J) = (0.759{+}0.210i \quad 0.759{-}0.210i \quad -0.095)'$, whereby the moduli of Λ and J are given by $(0.974 \quad 0.974)'$ and $(0.787 \quad 0.787 \quad -0.095)'$ respectively. Hence, the assumption of unit root components is a reasonable approximation of the underlying stochastic trend. Whether Λ contains unit root components in a statistical sense cannot be answered conclusively on the basis of statistical testing since unit root tests as developed by Dickey and Fuller (1979, 1981) and Fuller (1996) are only applicable if there is no autocorrelation in the residuals or if it is modelled using an autoregressive representation.

In order to derive impulse–responses to orthogonal innovations the variance–covariance matrix Δ of the residual process e_t is decomposed as in (4.31) under the assumption that changes in the supply of open market papers have no contemporaneous effects on the money stock and interest

$$\Lambda = \begin{pmatrix} 0.971 & 0.018 \\ -0.023 & 0.975 \end{pmatrix}, \quad G = \begin{pmatrix} -0.6043 & 2.161 & -2.733 \\ -2.407 & -4.018 & -2.328 \end{pmatrix},$$

$$D = \begin{pmatrix} -0.082 & -0.121 \\ 0.181 & -0.147 \\ -0.205 & -0.081 \end{pmatrix}, J = \begin{pmatrix} 0.639 & -0.210 & 0.024 \\ 0.277 & 0.874 & -0.087 \\ -0.004 & -0.077 & -0.489 \end{pmatrix},$$

$$K = \begin{pmatrix} -8.533 & 1.315 & 15.80 \\ 2.952 & -26.61 & -16.37 \\ 1.447 & 34.76 & 37.47 \end{pmatrix},$$

$$M = \begin{pmatrix} -5.687 & 0.123 & 0.766 \\ 2.600 & 0.135 & 0.788 \\ 3.886 & 1.86 & 0.454 \end{pmatrix} \times 10^2, \quad \Delta = \begin{pmatrix} 38.435 & 0.098 & -0.469 \\ 0.098 & 2.388 & -0.180 \\ -0.469 & -0.180 & 2.698 \end{pmatrix} \times 10^2,$$

Table 5.7. Model parameter estimates (1991.01–1997.04)

rates. Moreover, assuming that money demand shocks will have no contemporaneous effect on the overnight money market rate results in restrictions as reflected in T. Hence, as hypothesised in Section 3.2, Δ is decomposed assuming that the Bundesbank adopts a policy of supplying credit on an elastic basis in order to smooth interest rates in the day–to–day market. However, examining the relative size of diagonal to off-diagonal elements in Δ reveals that changes in the orthogonalisation schemes will have virtually no effect on the shape of impulse–responses. Even if a different operating procedure would be assumed, the sequence of impulse–responses would be the same.

Inspections of impulse–response functions for an 18–month–horizon broadly reflect the specific assumptions made for the money market model under an interest rate rule. They are presented in Figure 5.1. Note that responses are calculated following *innovations* of the size of *one standard error* in the respective variables. The error bounds of the impulse–response functions in this study have been calculated using 1000 bootstrap replications as outlined in Section 4.5.5.

What is indeed most striking, is the fact that changes in the supply of credit through open market operations have no significant effect on the money stock and interest rates. Hence, a liquidity effect is not detectable. Moreover, the observation that reserves have no explanatory power for the money stock is a challenge for those who view the money supply process in the context of a multiplier model. It might be concluded that from January 1991 through April 1997 the Bundesbank has been conducting monetary policy in terms of interest rate targeting. The interaction of variables is analogous to that theoretically derived in Chapter 3 under this regime: the persistence in OMP_t is low compared to that in money and interest rates. There is evidence that the Bundesbank raises interest rates in response to money demand shocks and that the money stock decreases in the case of a tightening of monetary

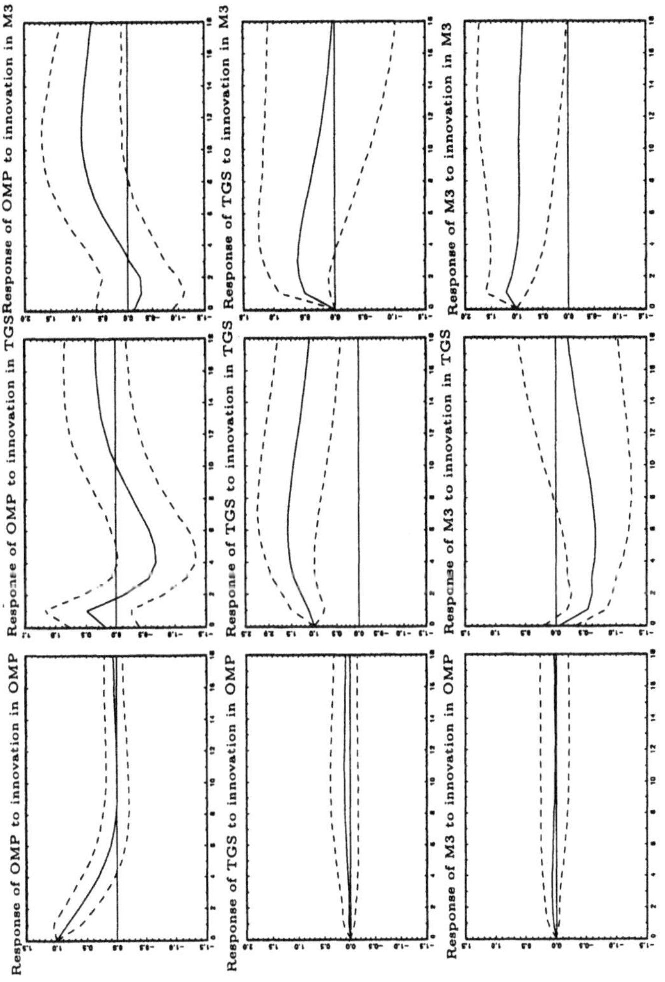

Fig. 5.1. Impulse–responses from money market model: 1991.01–1997.04

policy (i.e. rising interest rates). The reactions of OMP_ts to shocks in money and interest rates are well in accordance with the theoretical considerations made in Chapter 3. Forecast error variance decompositions for an 18–month–horizon derived from the same model specification are presented in Figure 5.2.

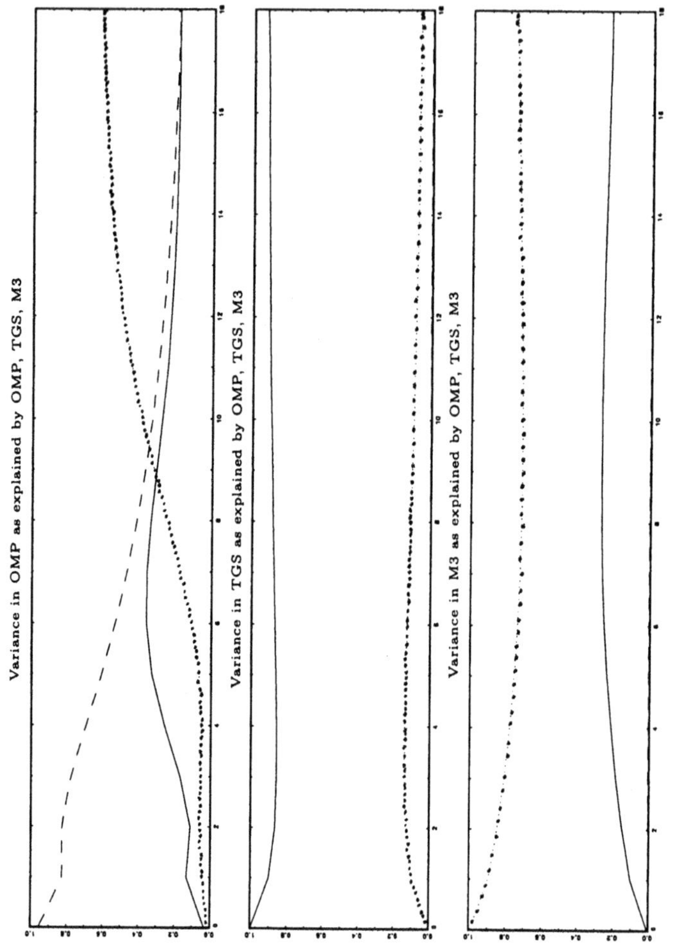

Fig. 5.2. Forecast error variance decomposition from money market model: 1991.01–1997.04. Dotted line: forecast error in a certain variable as explained by errors in M_t. Dashed line: contribution OMP_t. Solid line: contribution of i_t.

It can be seen that the forecast error in OMP_t is dominated by the variance in M_t and i_t. They add to a contribution of 80% at the 18–month–horizon. Furthermore, as already confirmed by the impulse–response sequences, it becomes visible that the supply of open market papers has no explanatory power for the error in the interest rate and the money stock. Reserves supply is therefore endogenous. The error in i_t and M_t is predominantly explained by variations in the variables themselves. The interest rate accounts for roughly 25% of the error in M_t and M_t for roughly 20% of that in i_t. Hence, the evidence that the Bundesbank granted liquidity on an elastic basis in order to smooth interest rates around desired levels is reproduced by the sequences of the forecast error variance decomposition of the respective variables. The theoretical implications derived under an interest rate regime in Section 3.2 are well reflected in this empirical implementation.

Results for 1985.01–1990.05 Re-estimation of the model for Period II (1985/2–1990/5) reveals very similar results. The series y_t is composed as in the first example. In this period model selection has been an especially tricky task with respect to the second step of the modelling procedure. Note that in order to capture money demand effects the monetary aggregate M3 has been employed in the model. This is in contrast to the Bundesbank's policy of targeting money growth using the central bank money stock as practised from 1975–1987. The approach might be justified on the ground that both aggregates developed in much the same way during this time.

In order to construct Hankel matrices for both steps, in the first step $p = 1$ was chosen and in the second step $p = 6$. The Aoki–C–test for $n = 2$ (d.o.f.= 1) is 56.291 suggesting that 3 states should be included to approximate the Hankel matrix for the trend part. For the cyclical part $C(2) = 251.56$ (d.o.f.= 256), so that the H_0 of no significant excluded canonical correlations is to be rejected at any error level for both the cyclical and the trend part. So, the test statistic was not very helpful in model order selection. Specification $m(1,3)$, $m^*(6,2)$ was adopted. Parameter estimates are given in Table 5.8.

$$\Lambda = \begin{pmatrix} 0.951 & 0.062 & 0.015 \\ -0.049 & 0.981 & -0.071 \\ -0.069 & 0.007 & 0.824 \end{pmatrix}, \quad G = \begin{pmatrix} -1.108 & -1.340 & 0.347 \\ -0.035 & 3.021 & -1.806 \\ -2.283 & 2.338 & 10.991 \end{pmatrix},$$

$$D = \begin{pmatrix} -0.604 & -0.018 & -0.019 \\ -0.090 & 0.298 & 0.024 \\ -0.140 & -0.110 & 0.068 \end{pmatrix}, \quad J = \begin{pmatrix} -0.511 & -0.841 \\ 0.835 & -0.473 \end{pmatrix},$$

$$K = \begin{pmatrix} 0.777 & 0.580 & 7.878 \\ 0.815 & 0.067 & -1.449 \end{pmatrix}, \quad M = \begin{pmatrix} 0.049 & -0.087 \\ 0.017 & 0.010 \\ 0.005 & -0.004 \end{pmatrix},$$

$$\Delta = \begin{pmatrix} 34.167 & 0.531 & 0.786 \\ 0.531 & 2.504 & 0.114 \\ 0.786 & 0.114 & 0.283 \end{pmatrix} \times 10^3.$$

Table 5.8. Model parameter estimates (1985.02–1990.05)

The eigenvalues of the transition matrices are $eig(\Lambda) = (0.951 + 0.026i \quad 0.951 - 0.026i \quad 0.854)'$, $eig(J) = (-0.491 + 0.837i \quad -0.491 - 0.837i)'$ and the moduli are $(0.951 \quad 0.951 \quad 0.854)'$ and $(0.971 \quad 0.971)'$ respectively. Hence, with substantial persistence remaining in the cyclical part, the salient features of the decomposition are not reproduced. Moreover, there is still some autocorrelation in the residuals of M3. The residual statistics are given in Table 5.9.

Trend model								
	R^2	DW	Q(2)	Q(4)	Q(8)	Q(12)	Q(24)
OMP	0.87	2.11	1.29‡	6.06‡	8.85‡	29.47	38.21
i	0.95	2.01	1.90‡	2.71‡	7.04‡	7.98‡	18.32‡
M	0.96	1.21	14.06	19.19	31.41	43.99	54.71
Joint model							
	R^2	DW	Q(2)	Q(4)	Q(8)	Q(12)	Q(24)
OMP	0.87	2.09	0.21‡	2.38‡	3.51‡	17.78‡	25.44‡
i	0.97	2.10	2.24‡	3.17‡	7.91‡	9.72‡	20.62‡
M	0.97	1.20	14.01	18.06	31.12	42.34	53.66

Table 5.9. Residual diagnostics for subperiod 1985.02–1990.05

Augmenting the model order p and/or n did not improve this problem. However, since impulse–responses depend crucially on the first step and are barely affected by changes in the specification of the transitory part of the model, one might not worry too much about this lack of efficiency. The same orthogonalisation scheme as above has been used. Inspection of the relative size of off–diagonal elements to diagonal elements in Δ reveals that this orthogonalisation will have no effect on the shape of impulse–responses, but will merely serve to generate impulse–responses to one–standard–innovations in the variables. The bootstrap estimates of dynamic multipliers are depicted in Figure 5.3.

The pattern of interaction is quite the same as in the previous example with the exception that changes in the *Tagesgeldsatz* have a weaker – but yet "significant" – effect on the money stock and, moreover, that the Bundesbank did not increase interest rates due to positive innovations in the money stock.

Forecast error variance decompositions are shown in Figure 5.4. They display quite the same pattern as in the previous case, with the exception that roughly 40% of the forecast–error in the day–to–day rate might be explained by forecast errors in money demand. Again, it might be concluded that from February 1985 through May 1990 the Bundesbank followed an interest rule policy.

Results for 1975.01–1985.01 For Period I (1975.01–1985.01) the vector of observed variables is $y_t = (DL_t \quad i_t \quad M_t)$, where DL_t corresponds to the

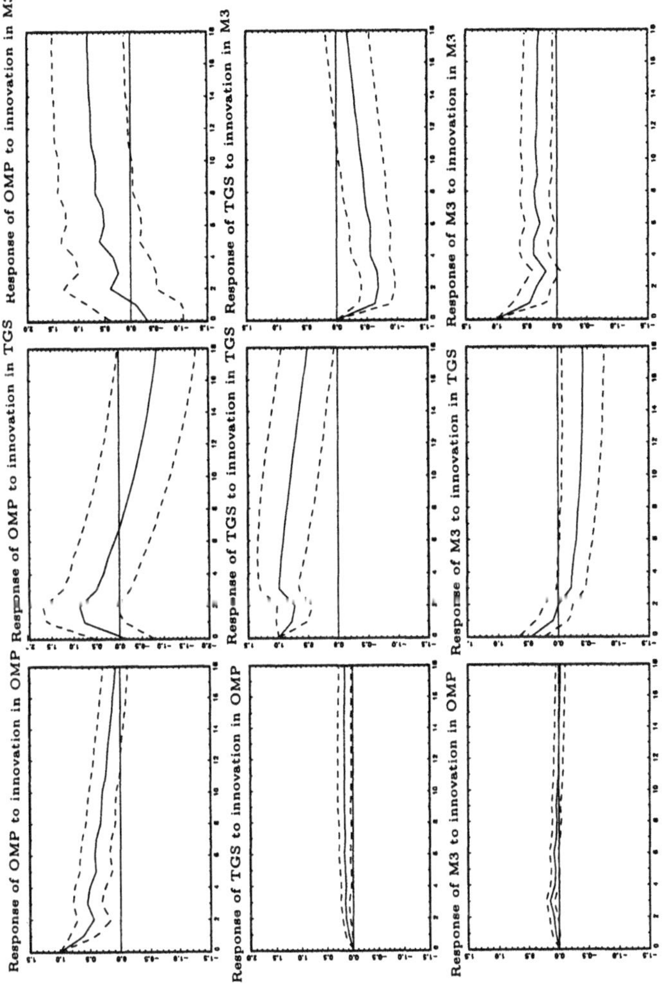

Fig. 5.3. Impulse–responses from money market model: 1985.02–1990.05

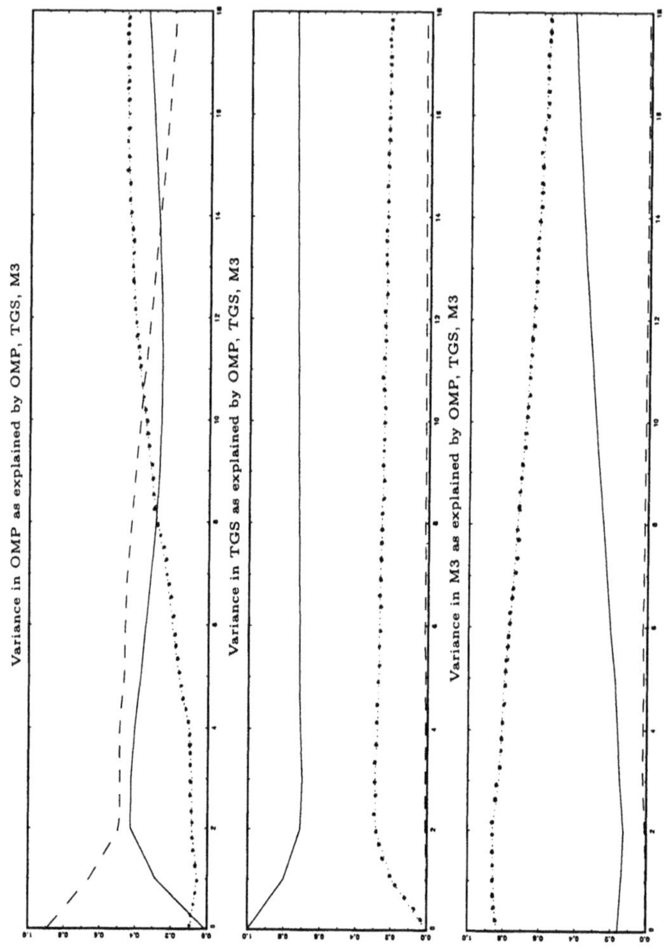

Fig. 5.4. Forecast error variance decomposition from money market model: 1985.01–1990.05. Dotted line: forecast error in a certain variable as explained by errors in M_t. Dashed line: contribution OMP_t. Solid line: contribution of i_t.

sum of credit supply through the discount window and where DL_t and M_t is the log of discount loans and the money stock divided by their initial values and i_t is the mean adjusted series of the *Tagesgeldsatz*.

The model order specification with residuals resembling most closely a white noise sequence is given by m(1,2), m*(4,4). The Aoki–C–Test for the first step is negative for $n = 3$ whereas $C(2) = 186.178$ (d.o.f.= 1), and for the second step $C(4) = 65.66$ (d.o.f.= 64), i.e. only in the second case the null of no significant excluded canonical correlations cannot be rejected at the 5% level. Parameter estimates, eigenvalues and moduli of transition matrices are given in Table 5.10. Residuals in the money stock equation of

$$\Lambda = \begin{pmatrix} 0.9861 & 0.0004 \\ 0.0003 & 0.9785 \end{pmatrix}, \quad G = \begin{pmatrix} -0.507 & 0.253 & -0.726 \\ 0.261 & 1.889 & -0.910 \end{pmatrix},$$

$$D = \begin{pmatrix} -1.177 & 0.020 \\ -0.074066473 & 0.245 \\ -0.47185626 & -0.090 \end{pmatrix}, \quad J = \begin{pmatrix} 0.843 & -0.058 & -0.028 & 0.061 \\ -0.205 & 0.545 & -0.176 & -0.011 \\ 0.082 & 0.087 & -0.879 & -0.131 \\ 0.054 & 0.350 & 0.201 & 0.725 \end{pmatrix},$$

$$K = \begin{pmatrix} -2.770 & 2.758 & 10.57 \\ -2.150 & 2.561 & 26.49 \\ -0.452 & 4.466 & -6.750 \\ 0.780 & 2.749 & 4.793 \end{pmatrix}, \quad M = \begin{pmatrix} -0.536 & -0.378 & -0.400 & 0.531 \\ 0.359 & -0.218 & 0.008 & 0.306 \\ 0.827 & -0.050 & -0.0540 & 0.058 \end{pmatrix} \times 10^1,$$

$$\Delta = \begin{pmatrix} 3.034 & 0.719 & 0.028 \\ 0.719 & 0.699 & -0.016 \\ 0.028 & -0.016 & 0.043 \end{pmatrix} \times 10^2,$$

Eigenvalues: $eig(\Lambda) = (0.986 \quad 0.978)'$, $eig(J) = (\ 0.440 \quad 0.819 + 0.067i \quad 0.819 - 0.067i \quad -0.844)'$ with moduli $(0.986 \quad 0.978)'$ and $(0.440 \quad 0.821 \quad 0.821 \quad -0.844)'$ respectively.

Table 5.10. Model parameter estimates (1975.01–1985.01)

the joint model are plagued by autocorrelation of order 12, a problem that could not be solved even when a deseasonalised series M_t was used. Residual diagnostics are given in Table 5.11.

For the reasons mentioned above we might economically nevertheless rely on this specification. Again, the relative size of diagonal to off–diagonal elements in matrix Δ is large, so that disturbances e_t might be considered to be orthogonal innovations to the different components of the data vector y_t. The shapes of impulse–responses in Figure 5.5 are quite well in accordance with the pattern of interaction derived in the theoretical considerations above in Section 3.4 under an operating procedure serving to supply central bank money through discount and Lombard loans so as to stabilise interest rates. The permanence in M3 and *Tagesgeldsatz*–shocks is very high relative to that in the supply of discount credit. Money and interest rates are independent of the supply of liquidity. DL_t increases in the case of positive innovations in the

Trend model							
	R^2	DW	Q(2)	Q(4)	Q(8)	Q(12)	Q(24)
OMP	0.94	1.62	12.46	12.71	27.63	39.83	45.32
i	0.97	1.61	16.20	23.21	35.11	36.31	45.49
M	0.91	0.29	169.32	270.09	395.83	447.05	529.23
Joint model							
	R^2	DW	Q(2)	Q(4)	Q(8)	Q(12)	Q(24)
OMP	0.94	2.17	$2.80^{\ddagger}$	$4.36^{\ddagger}$	17.56	$20.98^{\ddagger}$	73.70
i	0.90	2.08	$0.88^{\ddagger}$	$0.91^{\ddagger}$	$6.09^{\ddagger}$	$8.72^{\ddagger}$	$19.87^{\ddagger}$
M	0.99	1.90	$4.50^{\ddagger}$	$5.13^{\ddagger}$	22.31	72.70	128.83

Table 5.11. Residual diagnostics for subperiod 1975.01–1985.01

day–to–day rate since in this case it is more profitable to borrow Lombard loans. In addition, it increases in the case of positive innovations in the day–to–day rate, because, in this case, it is more profitable to borrow Lombard loans. Moreover, it increases in the case of money demand shocks.

The Bundesbank raises interest rates in response to money demand shocks. Together with an increase in refinancing needs of the commercial bank DL_t will thus rise. However, it is striking that the response in the money stock to changes in interest rates is weak and not significant as suggested by the error bound. During this period, the Bundesbank's power to target the money stock by means of changes in money market interest rates seemed to be poor.

This evidence is confirmed by inspection of the forecast–error–variance decompositions in Figure 5.6. Errors in the money stock are entirely explained by errors in the money stock itself. On the other hand up to 90% of changes in DL_t may be explained by shocks in the money stock. Forecast erros in the Tagesgeldsatz are due to errors in the money stock (40%), but largely to the Tagesgeldsatz itself. Again the supply of liquidity has no explanatory power for money and interest rates. Hence, M3 and the day–to–day rate are exogenous to the supply of discount and Lombard loans. The Bundesbank seemed to grant loans on an elastic basis so as to smooth interest rates.

Conclusions Given the empirical evidence from estimating a multivariate linear state space model to capture the interaction of reserves supply, the money stock and money market interest rates presented in this section, it might be concluded that throughout the Post–Bretton–Woods era, the Bundesbank conducted monetary policy in terms of smoothing interest rates around desired levels in order to achieve some target in the money stock. The Bundesbank may have raised interest rates in response to positive shocks in money demand. There is no evidence that the monetary authority tried to target bank reserves in order to maintain some projected path in the growth rate of money. Hence, it would be misleading to view the money supply pro-

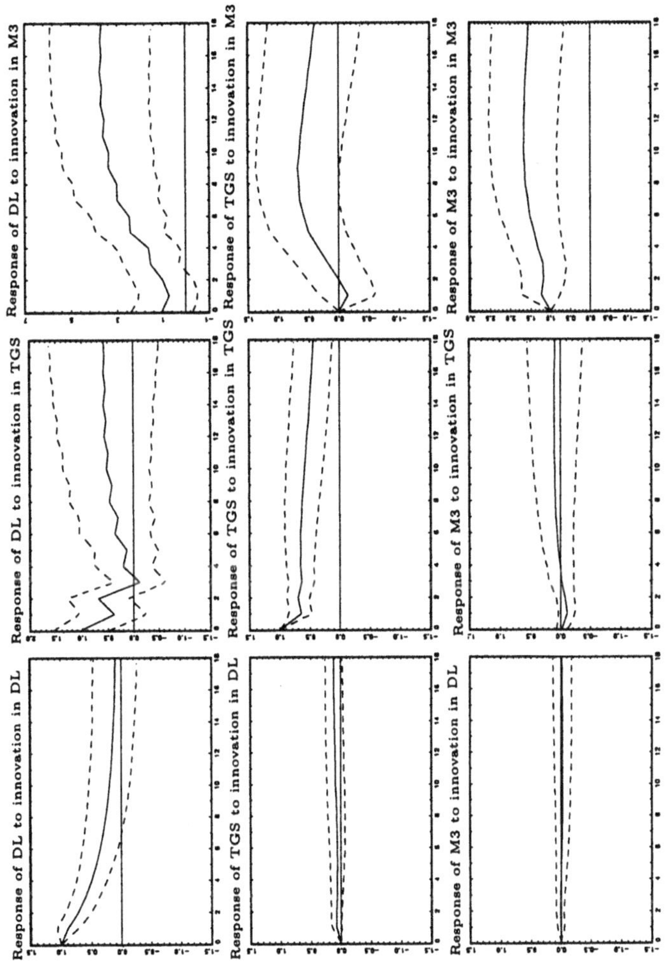

Fig. 5.5. Impulse–responses from money market model: 1975.01–1985.01

cess in terms of a money–multiplier model, since interest rates and money are exogenous to bank reserves and not vice versa. The empirical evidence is overwhelming in this respect.

Finally adopting the expectations theory of the term structure of interest rates, it might be concluded that the Bundesbank exerts influence on interest rates of a longer–term–maturity, because shocks in short–term rates have a

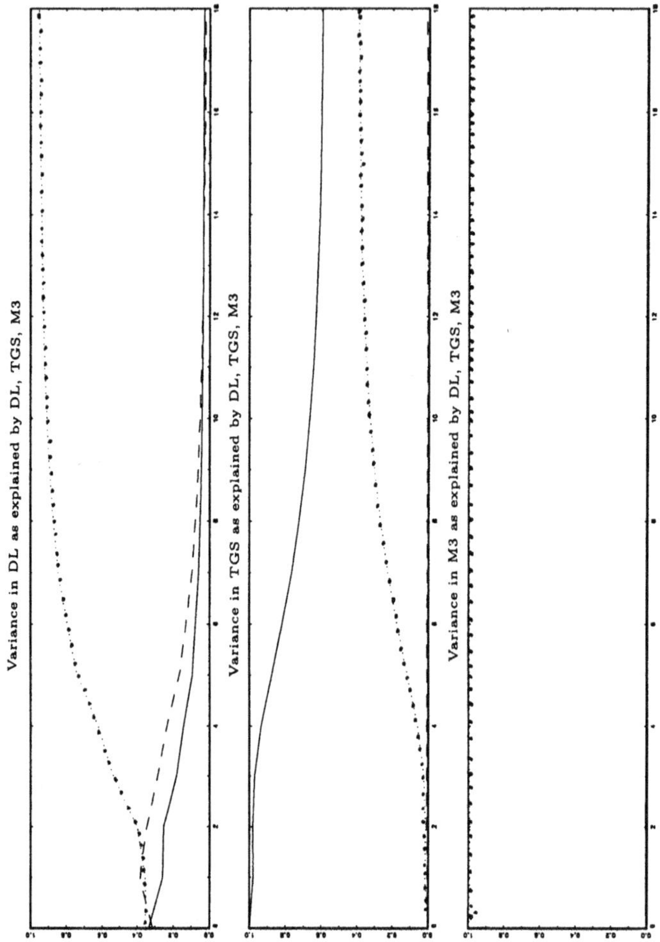

Fig. 5.6. Forecast error variance decomposition from money market model: 1975.01–1985.01. Dotted line: forecast error in a certain variable as explained by errors in M_t. Dashed line: contribution OMP_t. Solid line: contribution of i_t.

high degree of persistence. This conclusion may be drawn even if it is taken into consideration that money demand shocks considerably drive interest rates. However, the model did not comprise long–term interest rates. It would be possible to empirically assess the direction of causation only if an interest rate of a longer–term maturity would additionally be incorporated in the model. Hence, one should be careful with the above interpretation.

5.2 Monetary targeting and the business cycle

In the previous section it has been shown that, in the day–to–day management of its monetary policy, the Bundesbank smoothes the overnight rate in the interbank money market to achieve a goal in a broad monetary aggregate which is officially serving as intermediate variable for its final policy objective. Although that may be so, it is unclear how important monetary targeting was relative to other goals of monetary policy, such as stabilising economic activity or directly influencing the inflation rate. As pointed out in Section 2.5 in their empirical studies on German monetary policy Clarida and Gertler (1996) and Bernanke and Mihov (1997) conclude that the Bundesbank should be described as an inflation targeter rather than a monetary targeter. It is the aim of the following section to assess this issue by augmenting the vector of observed variables y_t in the state space model by variables reflecting economic activity and inflation.

5.2.1 Data

To analyse monetary policy in a broader context empirical results for the most recent subperiod 1990.01–1997.04 and for the subperiod 1975.01–1985.01 are presented. The results for the other subperiod 1985.02–1990.05 are similar.

In order to measure economic activity in Germany a series of monthly GDP is used which is obtained by monthly interpolating quarterly GDP under the assumption that monthly GDP behaves according to the same specific pattern as the German production index[3]. We use GDP instead of the production index because of shifts in the index series in January 1991 due to German unification[4]. As a measure for German inflation the annual time difference of the consumer price index is used (π_t)[5].

The observed variables are scaled by mean–adjusting inflation and the *Tagesgeldsatz* and taking logs of $M3_t$, GDP_t, or Prod_t divided by their respective initial values. GDP, the production index and M3 have been seasonally adjusted using a conventional additive adjustment procedure. The data vector is given by $y_t = (\pi_t \quad GDP_t \quad M_t \quad i_t)'$ and $y_t = (\pi_t \quad \text{Prod}_t \quad M_t \quad i_t)'$

[3] I am grateful to Barbara Jennes for kindly providing this series.

[4] For period 1975.01–1985.01 the same series are used except that economic activity is measured using the production index (Prod_t) as published by the Bundesbank in its monthly reports.

[5] Up until January 1991 the index for Germany (Basis year 1985) is used and recalculated so that 1991.01=100 and that for unified Germany afterwards (basis year is 1991.01). The data are originally taken from the publications of the *Statistisches Bundesamt.*

respectively. Since in the foregoing analysis it was suggested that the Bundesbank granted credit on an elastic basis and conducted its day–to–day policy in terms of smoothing interest rates, the supply of credit has been dropped from the system: As it has been shown, movements in the supply of central bank credit bear no information with respect to interest rates and the money stock.

5.2.2 Results

Results for 1990.06–1997.04 In order to obtain a system of minimal dimension that captures best the dynamic property of the system a model of dimension m(1,3), m*(3,4) was chosen. $C(1) = 286.48$ (d.o.f.= 1)for the trend part (rejecting the null at any error level), for $n \geq 2$ $C(n)$ is negative. Hence $n = 3$ was chosen since the resulting model provided the best fit. For the cyclical part $C(4) = 4.144$ (d.o.f.= 64) indicating (at the 5% level) that the specification is appropriate.

Parameter matrix estimates and resulting eigenvalues of transition matrices are given in Table 5.12.

Note that the decomposition of eigenvalues in the dynamic system into those near (or on) the unit circle and into remainders in the two steps of the modelling algorithm is not achieved in this example. The moduli are given by (0.984 0.984 0.783) for Λ and (0.942 0.870 0.896 0.896) for J, i.e. eigenvalues for the transition matrix J in the (supposedly) stationary part of the model are nearly as large as those of the transition matrix Λ in the (nearly) nonstationary part. Hence, it may be doubted that the common trend part of the model properly reflects the stochastic trend behaviour of the data series. Residual diagnostics are given in the Table 5.13.

Off–diagonal elements of Δ are relatively small compared to diagonal elements, so that structural inference is still relatively robust towards contemporaneous identifying assumptions. As orthogonalisation scheme a usual triangular factorisation of matrix Δ is used, thereby imposing a Wold–ordering scheme on the system as outlined in Section 4.5.2. The day–to–day interest rate which has been identified as the Bundesbank's main policy tool in the previous section is placed first in the ordering succeeded by M_t, Y_t, and the inflation rate π_t.

Responses in the *Tagesgeldsatz* are shown in Figure 5.7. The interest rate seemed to be dominated by own shocks. There are some positive reactions of the day–to–day rate to inflation, output and the money stock, but they are weak and not significant as suggested by the error bounds. Figure 5.8 displays the reaction of money, inflation and economic activity to changes in the stance of monetary policy. Both the money stock and GDP are decreasing in the case of a tightening of monetary policy – however, inflation is rising reflecting what has been dubbed the "price puzzle" (with respect to a specific price index) in the *VAR*–literature. This has often been explained by the failure to identify autonomous monetary policy actions as discussed in Section 2.4 (see

$$\Lambda = \begin{pmatrix} 0.977 & -0.028 & 0.016 \\ 0.019 & 0.9992 & 0.029 \\ -0.012 & -0.007 & 0.781 \end{pmatrix}, G = \begin{pmatrix} -1.465 & -1.522 & 1.549 & -3.412 \\ -2.187 & 0.349 & -4.404 & -3.261 \\ 13.962 & -0.728 & 0.367 & -7.267 \end{pmatrix},$$

$$D = \begin{pmatrix} -0.103 & -0.079 & 0.050 \\ 0.122 & -0.068 & 0.002 \\ 0.194 & 0.120 & -0.004 \\ -0.199 & -0.119 & -0.029 \end{pmatrix}, J = \begin{pmatrix} 0.905 & -0.098 & 0.056 & -0.029 \\ -0.049 & -0.420 & -0.751 & -0.659 \\ -0.014 & 0.814 & -0.474 & 0.050 \\ -0.051 & 0.008 & 0.149 & 0.906 \end{pmatrix},$$

$$K = \begin{pmatrix} -1.378 & -14.629 & -25.366 & -6.611 \\ -7.403 & -8.385 & -25.118 & -1.518 \\ 0.901 & -11.788 & -24.854 & -11.583 \\ -1.204 & -7.966 & 9.4732 & -11.899 \end{pmatrix},$$

$$M = \begin{pmatrix} 0.445 & 0.442 & 0.468 & -0.383 \\ -1.748 & 0.253 & 1.492 & -0.599 \\ -1.293 & -0.663 & -0.290 & 0.160 \\ 0.926 & 0.894 & -0.209 & -0.407 \end{pmatrix} \times 10^2,$$

$$\Delta = \begin{pmatrix} 0.154 & -0.043 & -0.076 & 0.044 \\ -0.043 & 0.156 & 0.105 & -0.096 \\ -0.076 & 0.105 & 0.172 & -0.146 \\ 0.044 & -0.096 & -0.146 & 0.216 \end{pmatrix} \times 10^2,$$

$eig(\Lambda) = (0.984 + 0.022i \;\; 0.988 - 0.022i \;\; 0.738)'$, with moduli $(0.984 \;\; 0.984 \;\; 0.783)'$
$eig(J) = (0.942 \;\; 0.870 \;\; -0.448 + 0.776i \;\; 0.448 - 0.776i)'$ with moduli $(0.942 \;\; 0.870 \;\; 0.896 \;\; 0.896)'$.

Table 5.12. Model parameter estimates (1990.06–1997.04)

Trend model							
	R^2	DW	Q(2)	Q(4)	Q(8)	Q(12)	Q(24)
GDP	0.94	2.09	0.48‡	0.84‡	2.82‡	12.61‡	25.09‡
π	0.85	1.51	9.94	33.67	53.56	59.76	110.58
M	0.98	0.89	40.08	89.93	136.33	158.53	169.05
i	0.99	1.73	2.66‡	12.77	26.66	35.08	41.89
Joint model							
	R^2	DW	Q(2)	Q(4)	Q(8)	Q(12)	Q(24)
GDP	0.94	1.98	0.96‡	0.96‡	5.94‡	19.41‡	34.28‡
π	0.93	1.99	0.09‡	0.88‡	5.97‡	7.05‡	21.94‡
M	0.99	1.70	2.11‡	3.01‡	8.39‡	12.70‡	19.18‡
i	0.99	2.00	0.99‡	3.99‡	9.09‡	11.26‡	17.51‡

Table 5.13. Residual diagnostics for subperiod 1990.06–1997.04

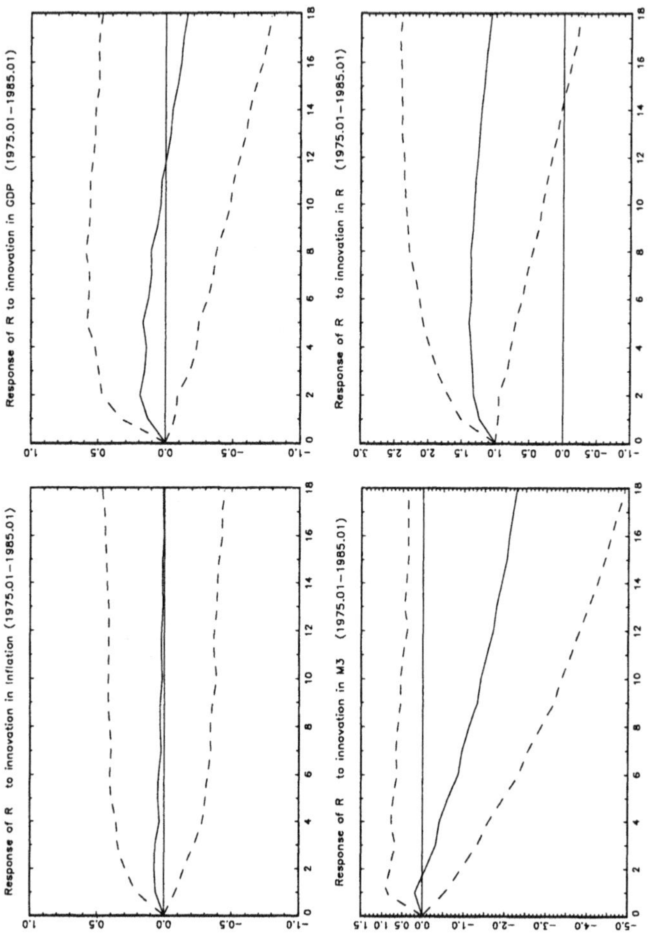

Fig. 5.7. Impulse–responses from general model: 1990.05–1997.04

e.g. Leeper(1996)). It can also be explained on the grounds that the system fails to incorpotate information about the central bank's inflation forecast.

Inspection of some forecast error variance decompositions as in Table 5.14 gives some further evidence on the importance of the variables in the reaction function of the Bundesbank. Clearly, interest rates are dominated by own shocks, since responses to other variables in the system are not significant

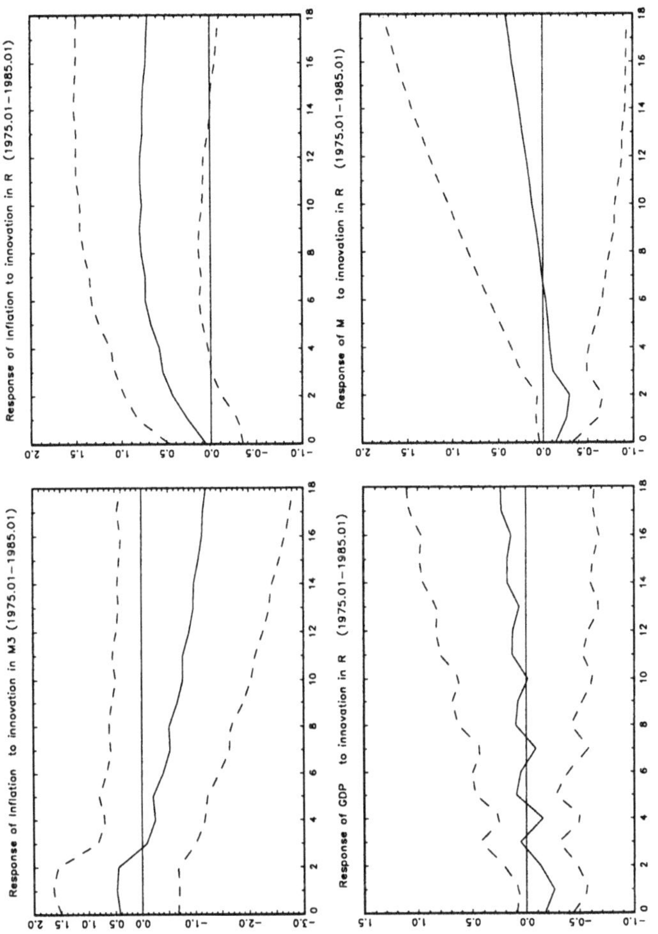

Fig. 5.8. Impulse–responses from general model: 1990.05–1997.04

at any time horizon. Especially a reaction to money demand shocks seems not evident. On the other hand, considering the influence of interest rates on the money stock, GDP and inflation, there is only a significant response of inflation, but it has the wrong sign. A rise in inflation follows positive innovations in the day–to–day rate. This is reflecting the "price–puzzle". Its potential causes have been extensively discussed in section 2.4.1.

Forc. horizon	Forecast error in i_t as accounted for by π	GDP	M	i
0 months	0%	0%	0 %	100%
4 months	7.1%	5.5%	4.5%	82.1%
8 months	6.7%	6.2%	3.9%	83.2%
12 months	5.5%	6.7%	3.3%	84.5%
16 months	4.4%	7.2%	2.6%	85.8%

Forc. horizon	Forecast error in π, GDP, M as accounted for by i: π	GDP	M
0 months	2.8%	13.1%	31.3%
4 months	11.5%	30.2%	36.9%
8 months	23%	31.7%	34.2%
12 months	32.2%	30.1%	30.2%
16 months	41.1%	26.0%	24.6%

Table 5.14. Forecast error decomposition: 1990.06–1997.04

These results are in contrast to those of Bernanke and Mihov (1997) and Clarida and Gertler (1996) who conclude that, in the Bundesbank's reaction function, a low long–term inflation target is paramount, because a reaction of the policy instrument to inflation is not observable.

Results for 1975.01–1985.01 For an implementation for the period 1975–1985 the model specification m(2,3), m*(2,3) was chosen. $C(1) = 482.766$ (d.o.f.= 1)for the trend part, for $n \geq 2$ $C(n)$ is negative. Hence $n = 3$ was chosen since the resulting model provided the best fit. For the cyclical part $C(1) = 143.36$ (d.o.f.= 49), and is negative for $n \geq 2$ $C(n)$. Again, the null of the Aoki-C–tests is to be rejected at any level. The test seems obviously not to be very helpful in constructing the model.

Parameter matrix estimates, the resulting eigenvalues of transition matrices and the residual diagnostics are given in Table 5.15 and 5.16. Figure 5.9 and 5.10 reproduce some impulse–response sequences from an implementation of the model for 1975–1985.

Reactions to inflation and especially to economic activity are much more pronounced. Interest rates were aggressively raised in response to increases in production and inflation, whereas there are no significant reactions to the money stock. What is more, there is no effect from interest rates to the other variables in the system. This evidence is confirmed by inspection of the forecast–error variance decompositions contained in Table 5.17. In this case it is suggested that the Bundesbank sets interest rates predominantly in reaction to innovations in the production index series.

Conclusions. The empirical results in this subsection are dissatisfying in every respect: a multivariate state space model comprising money, production, inflation and interest rates, reveals no clear cut evidence on the Bundesbank's

$$\Lambda = \begin{pmatrix} 0.990 & -0.005 & 0.024 \\ -0.003 & 0.963 & 0.052 \\ 0.004 & 0.038 & 0.947 \end{pmatrix}, G = \begin{pmatrix} -0.007 & -0.331 & -1.915 & -0.112 \\ 3.100 & 3.085 & -0.229 & 1.459 \\ -6.504 & 4.583 & -1.058 & 1.660 \end{pmatrix},$$

$$D = \begin{pmatrix} 0.030 & 0.119 & -0.084 \\ -0.057 & 0.008 & 0.032 \\ -0.496 & -0.015 & -0.005 \\ -0.038 & 0.252 & 0.031 \end{pmatrix}, J = \begin{pmatrix} 0.799 & -0.128 & -0.018 \\ 0.254 & -0.610 & 0.082 \\ 0.011 & 0.160 & 0.955 \end{pmatrix},$$

$$K = \begin{pmatrix} -9.454 & -16.719 & -5.294 & 2.574 \\ 1.297 & -2.484 & -0.232 & -3.700 \\ -3.006 & 0.162 & 27.708 & 0.380 \end{pmatrix},$$

$$M = \begin{pmatrix} -0.005 & -0.001 & -0.005 \\ -0.025 & 0.004 & -0.002 \\ -0.001 & 0.008 & 0.013 \\ 0.027 & 0.024 & 0.003 \end{pmatrix},$$

$$\Delta = \begin{pmatrix} 9.044 & -0.624 & 0.025 & 0.107 \\ -0.625 & 6.039 & 0.256 & 1.514 \\ 0.025 & 0.256 & 0.690 & -0.770 \\ 0.107 & 1.514 & -0.770 & 58.207 \end{pmatrix} \times 10^3,$$

$eig(\Lambda) = (0.0010.005 + 0.045i \quad 0.995 - 0.045i)'$, with Moduli $(0.991 \quad 0.996 \quad 0.996)'$

$eig(J) = (0.781 \quad -0.597 \quad 0.958)'$.

Table 5.15. Model parameter estimates (1975.01–1985.01)

Trend model							
	R^2	DW	Q(2)	Q(4)	Q(8)	Q(12)	Q(24)
Prod	0.95	1.71	$2.93^{\ddagger}$	$4.42^{\ddagger}$	$9.22^{\ddagger}$	33.97	43.82
π	0.74	0.97	73.26	128.70	177.75	190.81	209.13
M	0.99	0.40	151.28	267.08	453.49	560.02	712.34
i	0.91	1.89	$4.78^{\ddagger}$	$5.21^{\ddagger}$	$7.89^{\ddagger}$	$11.96^{\ddagger}$	21.80
Joint model							
	R^2	DW	Q(2)	Q(4)	Q(8)	Q(12)	Q(24)
Prod	0.95	1.88	$0.48^{\ddagger}$	$0.94^{\ddagger}$	$3.24^{\ddagger}$	36.29	46.43
π	0.85	2.35	6.17	10.43	$13.32^{\ddagger}$	22.57	$33.35^{\ddagger}$
M	0.99	1.89	$0.58^{\ddagger}$	$1.23^{\ddagger}$	$6.19^{\ddagger}$	$7.38^{\ddagger}$	$12.29^{\ddagger}$
i	0.99	1.93	$0.18^{\ddagger}$	$0.38^{\ddagger}$	$4.47^{\ddagger}$	$6.43^{\ddagger}$	$18.49^{\ddagger}$

Table 5.16. Residual diagnostics for subperiod 1975.01–1985.01

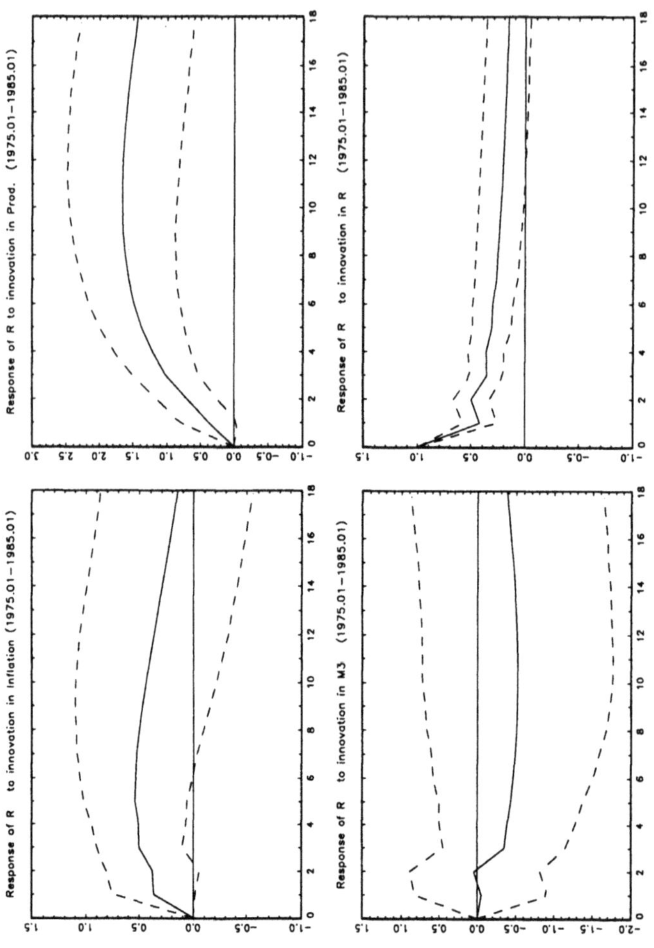

Fig. 5.9. Impulse–responses from general model: 1975.01–1985.01

reaction function. Of course, it would be inappropriate to describe the Bundesbank as a pure monetary targeter. This is not surprising, because it never claimed to achieve its monetary targets at any cost. It always maintained a considerable degree of discretion in the conduct of its policy. The money target has always been derived given a forecast on potential output growth and what might be termed an implicit inflation target, as pointed out in Section

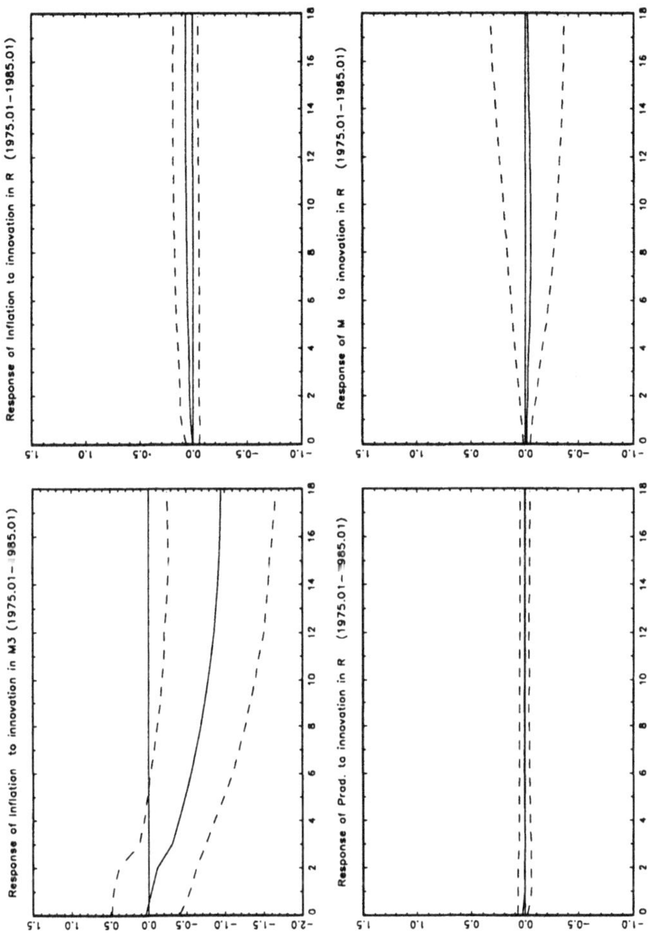

Fig. 5.10. Impulse–responses from general model: 1975.01–1985.01

2.1. It is thus necessary that it doesn't react to deviations from the monetary target alone.

In addition, the analysis is plagued by counterintuitive results. As often encountered in *VAR*–applications for similar data sets, this application also reproduces the "price puzzle". It might be objected that, without additional "structure", it seems impossible to reconcile the debate surrounding

Forc. horizon	Forecast error in i_t as accounted for by π	$Prod$	M	i
0 months	0%	0%	0 %	100%
4 months	10.73%	57.56%	0.03%	31.68%
8 months	7.01%	64.82%	0.22%	27.95%
12 months	5.60%	67.58%	0.56%	26.27%
16 months	6.42%	67.97%	1.2 %	24.41%

Forc. horizon	Forecast error in π, GDP, M as accounted for by i: π	GDP	M
0 months	1.86%	1.11%	0.64%
4 months	3.42%	1.62%	0.39%
8 months	5.14%	1.69%	0.44%
12 months	6.83%	1.66%	0.42%
16 months	8.82%	1.60%	0.30%

Table 5.17. Forecast error decomposition: 1975.01–1985.01

the Bundesbank's reaction function. It seems desirable to develop an empirical framework that accounts for the peculiarities of the implementation of monetary targets in Germany more explicitly. It is the aim of the following section to do so.

5.3 A quantity theory based approach to inflation targeting

5.3.1 Money stock control and inflation targeting

From the more general empirical set–up used in Section 5.2, it might be concluded that the Bundesbank's policy has not been based on pure monetary targeting alone. Apart from reactions to money stock innovations, it also seemed to react directly to movements in inflation and output. This observation should not be surprising: in Section 2.1.1 it has been argued that the monetary target has always been derived given a forecast on potential output growth, the estimated trend in velocity, and what might be termed an inflation target. Therefore, the Bundesbank's policy might be thought of as a strategy of *implicit inflation targeting.* Hence, if there were deviations from projected output growth and the inflation forecast, the Bundesbank should certainly have reacted to this development. It may have focused on the inflationary pressure as derived from the current money stock, given some degree of capacity utilisation. It is the aim of this section to adopt an empirical approach to model this behaviour more explicitly. Apart from that, it will be illustrated how the state space approach fits into "traditional" econometric modelling techniques for nonstationary multiple time series.

If, as argued in Section 2.1, the money stock of M3 is used both to predict and target future inflation as the final policy objective, then the Bundesbank should, of course, ***not*** react to *forecasted* money growth instead of forecasted inflation, as modelled in the VAR approaches of Bernanke and Mihov (1997) and Clarida and Gertler (1996). As pointed out by Svensson (1997, pp. 1127–1130), money growth targeting amounts to inflation targeting, if the money growth is a sufficient statistic for future inflation. Of course, the Bundesbank should have subscribed to this last attitude. Money growth targeting implies money growth *forecast* targeting only in the sense that money growth might react with a lag to the central bank's policy instrument. However, this does naturally not imply that the instrument should be set in reaction to changes in money growth and inflation at the same forecasting horizon, because inflation will itself react with a lag to money stock innovations. Hence, the observation made by Bernanke and Mihov (1997) and Clarida and Gertler (1996) that the Bundesbank reacts to the inflation forecast instead of the money growth forecast, might not necessarily indicate a policy of direct inflation targeting, if the *current* money stock is used to forecast *future* inflation. Considering the Bundesbank's monetarist approach to inflation, this should, of course, be the case.

Hence, whether the Bundesbank should be described more as an inflation targeter or as a monetary targeter seems to depend on the modelling strategy adopted. If the Bundesbank indeed used the money stock as an intermediate variable to achieve its inflation target, its reaction function should amount to exactly what has been measured by the above mentioned authors.

Hence, the purpose of this section is to model the Bundesbank's behaviour towards inflationary pressure as derived from the money stock M3. To do so, we resort to Hallman, Porter and Small's (1991) P^*–model, which has become widely known among monetary macroeconomists. Despite the criticism received by the authors, the approach should be helpful in this context: the implementation of the Bundesbank's monetary targets as well as the model itself explicitly draw on the quantity theory of money[6]:

$$PY = M\bar{V}, \tag{5.1}$$

where P is the price level, Y aggregate real income, M the nominal money stock and $\bar{V}$ its respective velocity which might be assumed to be a stable function of, say, income and interest rates as outlined in Section 2.1.1. Reading (5.1) from the right–hand side to the left, the equation establishes a link between money and nominal income. More specifically, solving (5.1) for P and using time subscripts, the resulting equation

$$P_t = \frac{M_t \bar{V}_t}{Y_t} \tag{5.2}$$

[6] Moreover, note that the Bundesbank officially regards this approach as valuable for forecasting inflation: see Deutsche Bundesbank (1992).

relates the price level at time t to the amount of money and that of commodities circulating during a period of time. The notion of a link between M_t and P_t implicit in (5.2) is that, if $\bar{V}_t$ is rewritten in terms of a money demand function as in Section 2.1.1.2, the price level tends to an equilibrium value largely determined by the domestic money stock. If this is indeed empirically evident, money growth would provide a meaningful measure to control and forecast the price level. This is exactly the way the Deutsche Bundesbank implements its policy of monetary targeting. Of course, the Bundesbank is cautious to interpret the quantity theory as a causal relationship between money and prices in a strict sense. It is quite aware that monetary expansion exerts an influence on the economy with a lag that is long and variable: "The relationship between money and prices does not follow a fixed pattern. Prices respond to changes in the year of monetary expansion with lags that may additionally vary over time."(my translation; see Deutsche Bundesbank (1992, p. 22)). The link depends crucially on influences from money demand and the degree of capacity utilisation. The Bundesbank stresses that in the short run inflation is determined by factors not determined by monetary policy, such as import prices, the exchange rate, wages, value added taxes and fiscal effects (see Deutsche Bundesbank (1992, p. 26)). In the long run inflation is seen as a monetary phenomenon. A rise in inflation can only be reversed if *not* accommodated by money supply. However, this policy bears the risk to induce a severe economic downturn. The Deutsche Bundesbank (1992, p. 26) assumed that monetary expansion was leading inflation with a lag of up to 6 years: after 2 years one third of the effect will have taken effect, after 3 years 50% and only after 6 years will inflation have fully adjusted to excess money supply. In its single equation model for German inflation based on the quantity theory of money, the Deutsche Bundesbank (1992) assumes a long run relationship between money and prices, whereas in the short run inflation itself is determined by own lags and some of the above mentioned short term factors.

5.3.2 The P^* approach

From these quantity theoretic considerations Hallman, Porter and Small (1991) developed the following indicator for long–run inflationary dynamics:

$$P_t^* = \frac{M_t V_t^*}{Y_t^*}. \tag{5.3}$$

Meanwhile, the approach figures prominently as the "P^*–model". It equals the long–term equilibrium price level P_t^* to the money amount per unit of real potential output Y_t^*, multiplied by the long–term equilibrium of velocity V_t^*. Equation (5.3) identifies the price level the current money stock would support, if output and velocity were to settle down to their equilibrium level, i.e. when capacity is fully used and liquidity demand is on its long term average value. It relates money stock to real commodity supply in that it reflects the proposition that an additional amount of money will result in a rising price level if not accommodated by an equivalent growth of the supply of commodities, supposed, again that V_t^* does indeed not change fundamentally. The approach implicitly reflects the assumption of the long run neutrality of money and it cuts through the problems of modelling leads and lags that influence short run price dynamics. Money influences nominal income P_tY_t, but not real potential output Y_t^*:

A monetary expansion exceeding the sum of real potential output growth and the long run decline in velocity will lead to inflation. If not accommodated by economic growth, a rise in the money stock would support P_t^* at a level above P_t and result in what has been termed the *"price gap"*, $P_t - P_t^*$, by the authors: Dividing equation (5.2) by (5.3) and taking logs gives[7]:

$$p_t - p_t^* = (\bar{v}_t - v_t^*) + (y_t^* - y_t). \tag{5.4}$$

Hence, a negative price gap as resulting from excess money would depress v_t below and/or push y_t above their respective long–term equilibrium values. Equation (5.4) relates the price gap to what may be called the ***velocity gap*** and the ***production gap***. The velocity gap indicates excess liquidity i.e. money that may come to the market in terms of commodity demand. The production gap reflects money that has already come to the market in terms of commodity demand. The two gaps will push up p_t^* and, hence, the price gap.

But as velocity and income move back to their long–run values this will reduce the price gap: as v_t rises to v_t^*, shifting aggregate demand to its long–run level consistent with the current money stock, liquidity will transform into commodity demand thereby causing an acceleration in inflation.

For that reason, the price gap $p_t - p_t^*$ should reach only finite values and might be expected to be closed in the long–run. Hence, if both variables are individually non–stationary, in econometric terms, P_t and P_t^* should be cointegrated: they should follow a common non–stationary trend and departures from each other should be stationary. The price gap should therefore negatively account for changes in the inflation rate.

Given the Bundesbank's quantity theoretic approach to inflation, it should not set its policy instruments mechanically in response to deviations from its previously announced money target but rather to inflationary pressure as derived from the output and velocity gap.

5.3.3 Data and results

A state space implementation of the P^* model. In order to implement the model we use quarterly seasonally adjusted series[8] of M3, real and nominal GDP. The sample periods are 1975.I–1990.IV for West–Germany and

[7] Lowercase letters represent logs of their uppercase counterparts.

[8] The data are taken from the *Statistische Beihefte* of the Bundesbank's monthly report: *Saisonbereingte Wirtschaftszahlen.*

1975.I–1997.IV for "unified" Germany respectively. In order to correct for the horizontal shifts in the data series due to German unification, a state space model of dimension m(1, 1), m*(4, 2) has been estimated for each series for 1975–1990, and the 1991.I out of sample forecast was used to measure the shift. The difference between forecasted and actual value was used to subtract it from the data[9] for 1991.I through 1997.IV. In order to obtain real potential output, the degree of capacity utilisation as prepared by the Sachverständigenrat (1998a, 1998b) has been used and smoothed using a 5–quarter–moving–average[10]. Note from Figure 5.11 that real potential output (solid line) is nearly always above real output (dotted line).

Whereas in Hallman, Porter and Small (1991) the construction of the P^* model is based on the assumption that velocity is constant, it becomes apparent from Figure 5.12 that this is rather doubtful in the German case. As evidenced from several empirical studies on German money demand, the income elasticity of $M3$ is greater than one, so that there is a permanent downward trend in velocity (see Deutsche Bundesbank (1992, p. 28)). Hence, it is assumed, that v_t^* follows the linear downward trend as plotted in Figure 5.12. Of course, this is a tremendously restrictive assumption. It may be justified on the ground that there are several empirical studies suggesting that the demand for German $M3$ is stable (see, for example, Wolters, Teräsvirta, Lütkepohl (1996)).

From these considerations, P_t^* can now be derived from these considerations. Together with the GDP deflator it is shown in Figure 5.13. The price level is almost always above P_t^* because GDP is always at a level below y_t^*.

Note that there is a remarkable rise in the gap between P_t and P_t^* due to a considerable decrease in $M3$ in 1994 when investors shifted out of $M3$ and into the newly introduced money market funds. This observation might raise doubts as to whether $M3$ was an appropriate anchor to guide monetary policy.

In order to assess long–run relationships, a state space model of dimension m(1, 1) m*(3, 3) was used to model the observed series

$$y_t = \begin{pmatrix} p_t \\ p_t^* \end{pmatrix}.$$

[9] There are several alternatives of how to deal with the horizontal shift due to German unification. Since data for West–Germany and unified Germany are available throughout 1990 another possibility would be to measure the percentage change occurring due to the shift and use it to correct for the remaining time instances. However, in this case, a deterministic trend would be imposed on the series, implying that the effects of German unification would *never* disappear from the behaviour of the series. An alternative could be to use dummy and step variables which would seriously aggravate the difficulties faced in the context of the estimation algorithm.

[10] The degree of capacity utilisation λ_t is provided on an annual basis, whereby $y_t^* = y_t/\lambda_t$.

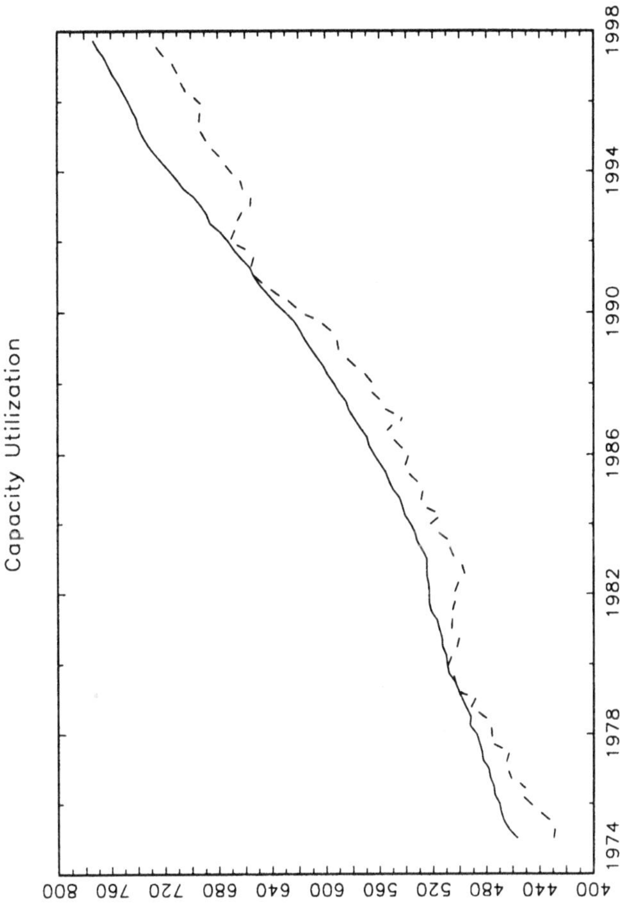

Fig. 5.11. Capacity utilisation: 1975.I–1997.IV.

Note that, as in previous applications, the data series have been divided by their initial values and logs have then been extracted. The model has been estimated for West Germany and for unified Germany. Parameter estimates and residual diagnostics are given in Table 5.18 and 5.19.

The cointegrating vectors resulting from the model are:

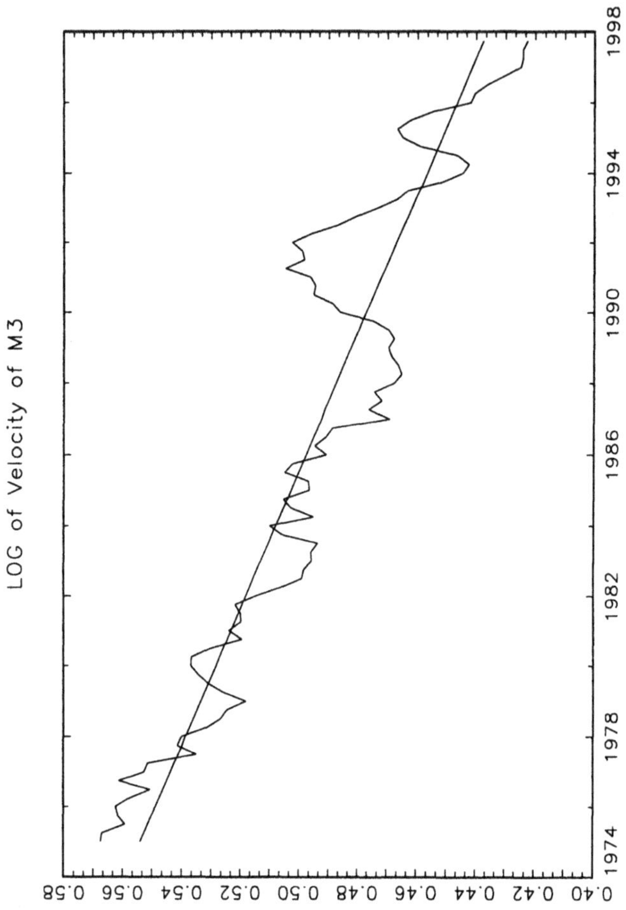

Fig. 5.12. Velocity of German M3: 1975.I–1997.IV.

$$p_t = 1.124 p_t^* \qquad \text{for 1975.I–1990.IV.} \tag{5.5}$$

$$p_t = 1.088 p_t^* \qquad \text{for 1975.I–1997.IV.} \tag{5.6}$$

Inspection of the eigenvalues of the respective transition matrices indicates that the imposition of these long–term relationships easily detrends the

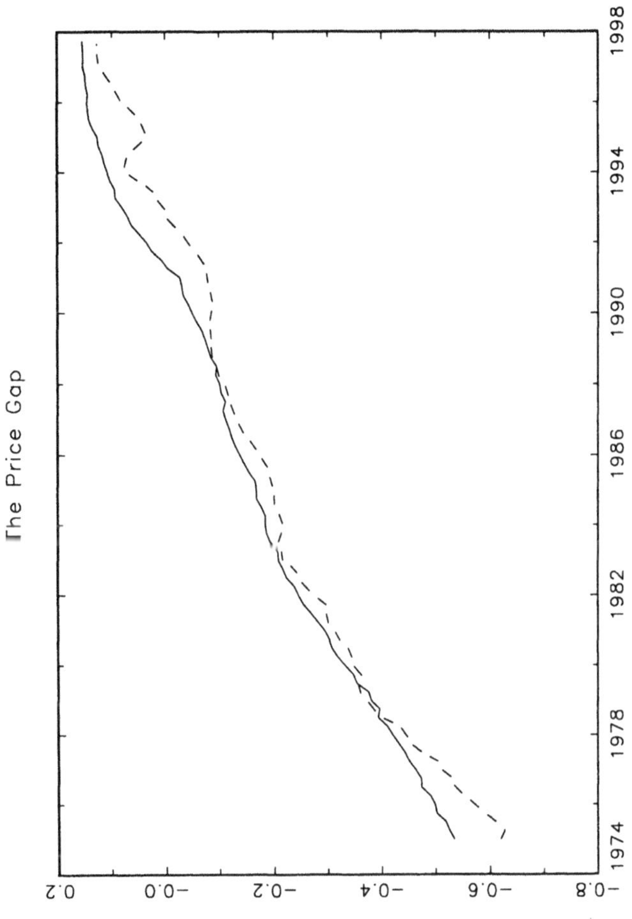

Fig. 5.13. GDP deflator and P^*: 1975.I–1997.IV.

series in the first case, whereas in the second case this is not that clear cut; the dichotomy of the econometric modelling procedure is only reflected for the period 1975–1990. Hence, a long–run positive relationship between p_t^* and p_t might be established from these results at least for this period. It might be concluded that p_t^* serves as an equilibrium for p_t and both variables should converge in the long–run. In addition to this, note that the coefficient of p_t^*

$$\Lambda = \begin{pmatrix} 0.981 \end{pmatrix}, G = \begin{pmatrix} 2.078 & -4.555 \end{pmatrix},$$

$$D = \begin{pmatrix} -0.319 \\ -0.358 \end{pmatrix}, J = \begin{pmatrix} 0.856 & -0.132 & 0.017 \\ 0.007 & -0.242 & 0.353 \\ 0.030 & -0.074 & -0.585 \end{pmatrix},$$

$$K = \begin{pmatrix} -48.80 & 5.618 \\ 142.5 & -126.6 \\ 12.93 & 11.65 \end{pmatrix},$$

$$M = \begin{pmatrix} -1.837 & -0.3850 & 0.1734 \\ -2.000 & -0.4522 & -0.2361 \end{pmatrix} \times 10^2,$$

$$\Delta = \begin{pmatrix} 9.678 & 6.417 \\ 6.417 & 11.45 \end{pmatrix} \times 10^5;$$

$$eig(\Lambda) = (0.981),$$
$$eig(J) = (0.85 \quad -0.34 \quad -0.48)'.$$

	R^2	DW	Q(2)	Q(4)	Q(8)	Q(12)	Q(24)
p_t	0.99	2.052	9.42	16.21	17.94	18.08‡	28.17‡
p_t^*	0.99	2.045	3.40‡	4.78‡	9.58‡	12.32‡	20.51‡

Table 5.18. Parameter estimates and residual diagnostics: State space implementation of P^*–model for West–Germany (1975.I–1990.IV)

is very close to what might be expected from our theoretical considerations. The equilibrium value for the price level as constructed from excess money indicates a one–to–one relationship between money and the price level.

Just note that in both cases there is a positive and persistent effect[11] from p_t^* to p_t. The forecast error variance decomposition from the model corresponding to (5.6) is given Table 5.20. The results for the whole sample period are less pronounced, but it seems evident that excess money as derived from the quantity theoretic approach largely accounts for changes in the price level.

The P^* model from a more traditional econometric perspecitve. In order to compare these long–run relationships with those resulting from more traditional econometric methods, consider the relationship as derived from

[11] Throughout this subsection a usual triangular factorisation of matrix Δ was used when computing forecast–error variance decompositions and impulse–response sequences, with the last variable in y_t placed first in the Wold–ordering. However, as in the previous applications this will barely affect the respective functions: off–diagonal elements in Δ are sufficiently small relative to diagonal elements.

$$\Lambda = \begin{pmatrix} 0.986 \end{pmatrix}, G = \begin{pmatrix} -0.796 & -1.416 \end{pmatrix},$$

$$D = \begin{pmatrix} -0.439 \\ -0.477 \end{pmatrix}, J = \begin{pmatrix} 0.958 & -0.107 & -0.052 \\ 0.013 & -0.403 & 0.467 \\ -0.062 & -0.264 & -0.049 \end{pmatrix},$$

$$K = \begin{pmatrix} -36.44 & -10.77 \\ 132.5 & -56.68 \\ -38.84 & -8.546 \end{pmatrix},$$

$$M = \begin{pmatrix} -1.236 & -0.467 & 0.314 \\ -1.432 & -0.239 & -0.213 \end{pmatrix} \times 10^2,$$

$$\Delta = \begin{pmatrix} 3.68 & 0.946 \\ 0.946 & 6.70 \end{pmatrix} \times 10^5,$$

$eig(\Lambda) = (0.985)$,
$eig(J) = (0.962 \quad -0.2282 + 0.3092i \quad -0.2282 - 0.3092i)'$. with moduli $(0.962 \quad 0.384 \quad 0.384)$

	R^2	DW	Q(2)	Q(4)	Q(8)	Q(12)	Q(24)
p_t	0.99	2.00	$0.55^{\ddagger}$	$3.16^{\ddagger}$	$5.35^{\ddagger}$	$6.06^{\ddagger}$	$16.18^{\ddagger}$
p_t^*	0.99	1.95	$0.25^{\ddagger}$	$0.73^{\ddagger}$	$4.10^{\ddagger}$	$5.79^{\ddagger}$	$13.44^{\ddagger}$

Table 5.19. Parameter estimates and residual diagnostics: State space implementation of P^*–model for unified Germany (1975.I–1997.IV)

Forc. horizon	Forecast error in p_t as accounted for by p_t and p_t^* by p_t	by p_t^*
0 quarters	76.10 %	23.90 %
4 quarters	44.96 %	55.04 %
8 quarters	23.62 %	76.38 %
12 quarters	13.59 %	86.41 %

Table 5.20. Variance decomposition from state space implementation of P^*–model

a cointegrating regression for both variables (with t–statistics for the null of zero coefficients in parantheses)[12]:

$$\begin{array}{lllll} p_t = & 0.041 & + \quad 1.013 & p_t^* & \text{(for 1975.I–1997.IV.)} \\ & (10.43) & \quad (69.84) & & \\ & R^2 = 0.98 & \text{DW} = 0.13 & & \text{S.E.} = 0.028 \end{array} \tag{5.7}$$

Note that, in a statistical sense, the coefficient of p_t^* is not significantly different from one. Applying an augmented Dickey–Fuller test to the residuals including three lagged differences results in a coefficient of -0.119 with a t–value of -3.043 for the lagged level variable. Therefore, the hypothesis that both series are not cointegrated cannot be rejected. Note that, whatever approach is applied, the coefficient of p_t^* in the cointegration relationship remains quite the same.

Given these results, a fixed relation between the price level and an equilibrium level determined by excess money bears some plausible evidence in econometric terms. A combination of $M3$ with the equilibrium level of the velocity of money and that of GDP would provide a meaningful measure for future price movements, at least during the period 1975.I–1990.IV. Possibly, the relationship might have been disturbed by changes in the time series properties of the series caused by German unification and, in the case of the money stock, by financial innovations.

The Bundesbank's reaction function. We next turn to how the Bundesbank sets its policy instrument in response to the inflationary pressure as derived from this quantity theory approach. In order to do so we estimate a state space model of dimension m(1, 2) m*(3, 2) for the series

$$y_t = \begin{pmatrix} u_t \\ i_t \end{pmatrix},$$

where $u_t = p_t - p_t^*$ and i_t denotes the log of the overnight rate. The sample period is 1975.I–1997.IV.

Parameter estimates and residual diagnostics are given in Table 5.21.

Figure 5.14 provides the impulse–response sequences for a 3–year horizon. Evidently, the series are dominated by own dynamics. Nevertheless, a decrease of interest rates due to positive innovations in the price gap (indicating decreasing inflationary pressure) suggest that the Bundesbank significantly increased interest rates in response to excess money. In addition to this, note that positive innovations in its policy instrument seem to have a persistent positive effect on the price gap reducing the inflationary potential.

Admittedly, the Bundesbank's reaction is relatively weak. Forecast–error variance decompositions suggest that, in this context, the interest series is dominated by its own behaviour. Nevertheless, there is a considerable positive feed–back from the money market rates to the price gap.

---

[12] The results for unified Germany are presented here, for the period 1975.I–1990.IV they are quite the same.

$$\Lambda = \begin{pmatrix} 0.967 & -0.012 \\ 0.060 & 0.921 \end{pmatrix}, G = \begin{pmatrix} 11.75 & 21.88 \\ -73.29 & -1.624 \end{pmatrix},$$

$$D = \begin{pmatrix} -0.2754 & -2.306 \\ 5.316 & -0.1195 \end{pmatrix} \times 10^2, J = \begin{pmatrix} -0.641 & 0.440 \\ -0.354 & -0.295 \end{pmatrix},$$

$$K = \begin{pmatrix} 105.9 & 4.510 \\ -133.1 & -6.684 \end{pmatrix},$$

$$M = \begin{pmatrix} -4.164 & -1.547 \\ -4.787 & -2.416 \end{pmatrix} \times 10^3,$$

$$\Delta = \begin{pmatrix} 2.698 & 0.661 \\ 0.661 & 8.370 \end{pmatrix} \times 10^5,$$

$eig(\Lambda) = (0.9445 + 0.01556i \quad 0.9445 - 0.01556i)$, with moduli $(0.945 \quad 0.945)$
$eig(J) = (-0.468 + 0.355i \quad -0.468 - 0.355i)'$. with moduli $(0.588 \quad 0.588)$

	R^2	DW	Q(2)	Q(4)	Q(8)	Q(12)	Q(24)
r_t	0.94	2.06	$0.10^{\ddagger}$	$7.36^{\ddagger}$	$10.14^{\ddagger}$	$12.29^{\ddagger}$	$29.24^{\ddagger}$
u_t^*	0.88	1.97	$0.12^{\ddagger}$	$3.37^{\ddagger}$	$5.46^{\ddagger}$	$7.88^{\ddagger}$	$20.26^{\ddagger}$

Table 5.21. Parameter estimates and residual diagnostics: State space implementation of P^*–model for unified Germany (1975.I–1997.IV)

	Forecast error in i_t as accounted for by i_t and u_t	
Forc. horizon	by i_t	by u_t
0 quarters	99.38 %	0.62 %
4 quarters	98.58 %	1.42 %
8 quarters	97.47 %	2.53 %
12 quarters	96.14 %	3.86 %
	Forecast error in u_t as accounted for by i_t and u_t	
Forc. horizon	by i_t	by u_t
0 quarters	0.0 %	100.00 %
4 quarters	33.75 %	66.25 %
8 quarters	41.43 %	58.57 %
12 quarters	45.64 %	54.36 %

Table 5.22. Variance decomposition from Bundesbank-reaction-function.

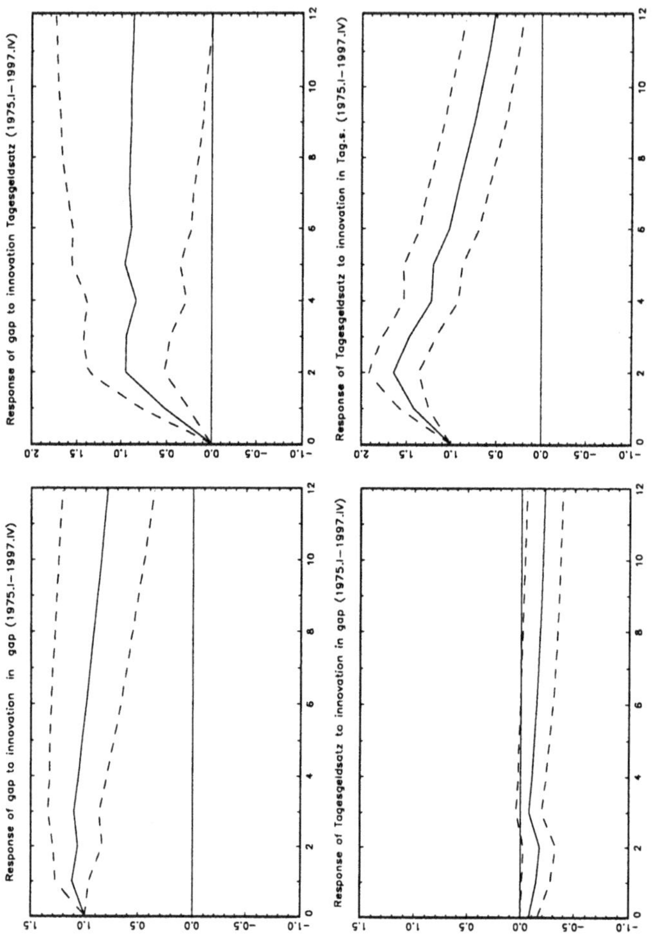

Fig. 5.14. Impulse-responses for price gap and overnight rate from state space representation: 1975.I–1997.IV.

A comparison with results from a *VAR* model. We illustrate whether these findings may be reproduced using as conventional *VAR* approach. A *VAR(4)* has been found capable of producing white noise residuals. We do not present parameter estimates, because they are not relevant for structural analysis. The impulse–response sequences resulting from the specification are

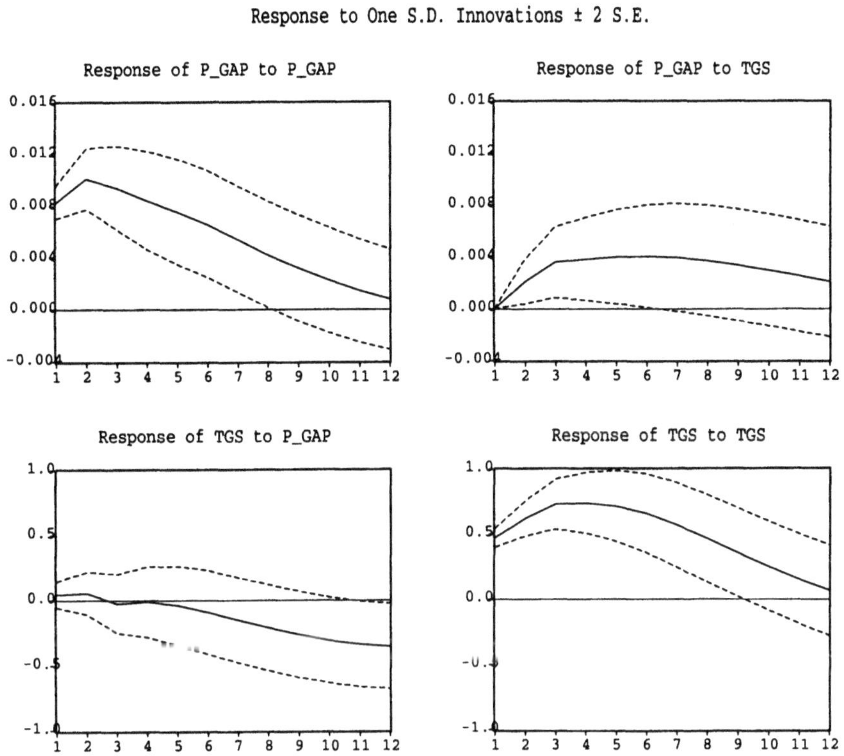

Fig. 5.15. Impulse-responses for price gap and overnight rate from VAR representation: 1975.I–1997.IV.

given in Figure 5.15. The error bounds have again been calculated using 1000 bootstrap replications of the impulse–responses. The multipliers reveal the same pattern of reaction; the Bundesbank significantly tightens monetary policy in reaction to excess liquidity as measured by the price gap. The reaction is similarly weak as suggested by a state space model of the series.

From an econometric perspective it is interesting to compare the width of the error bounds as resulting either from the *VAR* or from the state space model. This width is somewhat smaller in the state space model suggesting that, in this case, the modelling technique is a bit more efficient than a *VAR*. Above all, the similarity of the results from both approaches is quite striking.

6. Conclusions

6.1 Methodological remarks

This is predominantly an empirical study and before turning to its potential political implications it should be worthwhile to briefly highlight the salient features, powers and limitations of the econometric method adopted therein.

The state space modelling approach fits well into the range of economically largely unrestricted multiple time series models now generally accepted for macroeconomic analysis. At the same time it represents an attractive generalisation of the common practice of using *VAR*s and *VECM*s. It allows for a more efficient and parsimonious representation of time series, a feature that is especially desirable when only short sub periods are investigated, as it was the case in this study.

It has been shown in Section 4.7.3 that the concept of "cointegration" as involved in the system theoretic approach is not restricted to stationary relationships among contemporaneous components of the data series. It involves non-contemporaneous components as well. The direct and explicit representation of the evolution of unobserved common stochastic trends is an especially appealing and very innovative feature of this method. And finally, as illustrated in Section 4.7.2, the approach allows to model nonstationary time series without imposing unit roots. In order to implement cointegration relationships the practitioner is therefore not restricted to the use of unit root test that have been widely criticised for their weak power.

Diebold (1989) expressed reservations about the state space modelling procedure because of its lack of statistical foundation. We tried to base the model specification more on formal statistical testing. However, as illustrated in the empirical part of this study, the tests suggested by Aoki (1990, pp. 157–159) and Dorfman (1991) were not always helpful, especially when applied to the nonstationary part of the model. In practice, model selection turns out to require substantial proficiency. The promise is not redeemed that model specification is easier than in the case of *VAR*s and more specifically that it might be conducted on an automatic basis using the tests given a pre–set "significance"–level. Using these criteria might either produce nonminimal or nonstable models or models that turn out to fit the data very poorly. For that reasons it seems improbable that in near future the state space modelling approach in the spirit of Aoki (1990) might receive a higher degree of acceptance.

As to the general modelling philosophy the approach is similar to the well–known *VARs* and *VECMs*. The emergence of the approach lead to a rivalry between economically largely unrestricted multiple time series models and large–scale macroeconomic models. Given the resilience of the puzzles encountered both in this study and generally in *VAR* analysis, especially when applied to monetary policy issues, econometricians should not feel too comfortable with the technique. At least the conclusions seems inappropriate that large–scale macroeconomic models are now dead, as Diebold (1998) puts it. A further drawback of time series models lies in the fact that they are only applicable to a limited set of economic problems: the approach results in modelling small sub–systems such as, for example, "money demand systems" instead of fully articulated macroeconomic systems. The assessment of policy effects on a large set of variables of a country or even a certain number of countries is far beyond the scope of multiple time series analysis. Whereas on the one hand time series methods seem to be specifically tailored at describing the data most accurately at the cost of losing potential for structural inference, the identifying assumptions imposed on structural models often lack statistical foundation. Hence, it seems desirable to develop macroeconomic modelling techniques incorporating both an accurate description of the statistical data basis and a clearly articulated structure including decision rules for economic agents.

6.2 Money stock control and the day–to–day conduct of monetary policy

In this study a model of the German money market has been presented serving to separate money demand and supply shocks in order to assess the Bundesbank's monetary policy in the post Bretton Woods era. With respect to different subperiods a measure for bank liquidity was used to analyse whether monetary policy has been conducted more in terms of interest rate targeting or of targeting banks' reserves.

It has been shown that, throughout the past decades, the Bundesbank may well be described as a pure interest rate targeter, or to put it more precisely, that it conducted monetary targeting in terms of interest rate targeting. Its behaviour did not seem to be subject to frequent changes in monetary policy – except perhaps with the exception of some very short periods of monetary tightening. Within the policy period the Bundesbank fully accommodated money demand shocks through an elastic supply of reserves so as to meet its interest target. This is a challenge to money multiplier models for Germany. Multiplier models using bank reserves as explanatory variables are inadequate. They fail the underlying exogeneity assumption and are thus to be excluded from the right hand side of an econometric equation explaining the money supply.

The results of this study may be relevant for those who work on money demand specifications. Several empirical studies suggest that the demand for M3 in Germany is a stable function (see, for example, Wolters, Teräsvirta and Lütkepohl (1996)). That indication is confirmed considering the results in this study that the Bundesbank's day–to–day policy regime has not been subject to changes throughout the past decades. A regime shift from interest rate targeting to reserves targeting and vice versa is not observable for Germany.

After all, this study might serve to shed some more light on the relationship of monetary policy instruments with intermediate variables for monetary policy. This is especially useful with respect to shaping the policy of the future European Central Bank: The ECB took the decision to conduct its day–to–day operations on the basis of *REPO* operations as carried out by the Bundesbank. In addition to this the ECB will apply a minimum reserve ratio applicable to deposits and securities so as to induce stability in reserves demand.

6.3 Money stock control and inflation targeting in Germany

In the more general empirical set–up adopted in Section 5.2 and on a tentative basis, it might be concluded, that – apart from monetary targeting – the Bundesbank might have set interest rates following a regime of "good news on output and bad news on inflation". Hence, it would be inappropriate to describe the Bundesbank as a pure monetary targeter. However, the result is not that surprising. Even when following its official statements the Bundesbank seemed to be never willing to achieve its monetary targets at any cost. It always maintained a considerable degree of discretion in the conduct of its policy. The money target has always been derived given a forecast on potential output growth and what might be termed an implicit inflation target. Hence, it should, of course, not be surprising that it allowed the money growth to overshoot its target level if output was not on target.

In order to assess the Bundesbank's behaviour more appropriately, it is necessary to investigate whether at all it followed a monetarist policy where the money stock plays a significant role. It would therefore appear too crude to study what importance deviations in the pre–announced growth rate in M3 has in its reaction function. In order to assess whether the Bundesbank followed a monetarist policy it is instead necessary to study its reaction to *inflationary pressure* as derived from *excess money*. That approach has been adopted in section 5.3 and it has been shown that the Bundesbank sets its policy instrument in response to inflationary pressure as derived from quantity theory considerations.

6.4 Prospects for the ECB's monetary policy strategy

As discussed above, in recent years, a significant number of central banks in industrial countries has been adopting a policy of direct inflation targeting. The adoption of the strategies seems to have been inevitable because monetary aggregates became disturbed by financial innovations and currency substitution. For several inflation prone countries a strategy of direct inflation targeting seemed to be an appropriate tool to gain and maintain a higher degree of credibility. With respect to the British case, Bowen (1995, pp. 56–57) states:

> "The decision to set up an inflation target reflected the conclusion that there were no appropriate intermediate targets for other variables which could be relied upon to steer monetary policy in the correct direction in all circumstances. It is still thought that the monetary aggregates and the exchange rate contain useful information about inflationary trends, but so do other variables, too, including survey data on price expectations and real variables such as the unemployment rate." [...] "The most appropriate guide to monetary policy is the best obtainable forecast of the probability distribution for inflation, over a time horizon defined by how long it takes for a change in monetary policy to affect inflation. Such a forecast must use information from a wide variety of sources. It can be thought of as an intermediate target: monetary policy is to be adjusted to maximise the probability forecast at the time of the policy adjustment–of inflation falling within the target range by the time the adjustment has taken effect."

There are reasons, why central banks might not feel too comfortable with the new framework: In his presidential address delivered at the Annual Meeting of the American Economic Association in 1967, Milton Friedman (1968, pp. 14–15) asked the question:

> "How Should Monetary Policy Be Conducted?"

One of his answers was:

> "The first requirement is that the monetary authority should guide itself by magnitudes that it can control, not by ones that it cannot control. ... Of the various alternative magnitudes that it can control, the most appealing guides for policy are exchange rates, the price level as defined by some index, and the quantity of a monetary total—currency plus adjusted demand deposits, or this total plus commercial bank time deposits, or a still broader total."

From a monetarist viewpoint monetary aggregates are especially appropriate as an intermediate target for price stabilisation because they are considered to be controllable by the central bank. In the context of a strategy of direct inflation targeting, it is instead the central bank's *inflation forecast* serving as intermediate target. Svensson (1997) shows that inflation targeting implies inflation *forecast* targeting. Inflation targeting as practised by several industrial countries implies publishing inflation forecasts as derived from structural econometric models or *VARs* for exchange rates, import prices, productivity, wages and profit margins (see, for example, Fischer (1995, p. 41)) and even *real* variables as mentioned in Bowen (1995, p. 57). It goes without saying that – at least from a quantity theoretic perspective – with the exception of the exchange rate all these variables are *not* controllable by the central bank. In addition, from a monetarist point of view it might be argued that the exchange rate should serve as an anchor for monetary policy only for short term periods of disinflation and monetary stabilisation. How, then, should the central bank be able to target the inflation forecast? If the inflation forecast is derived from indicators not subject to influence by the central bank then its policy would rest on a rather weak basis and the credibility gains from that policy would be marginal.

In addition to this, at least on theoretical grounds it becomes more difficult to understand how the use of monetary policy instruments is transmitted to the economy and what effect that will have on inflation. Does the approach reflect the jettisoning of the theoretical reasoning that inflation is always a monetary phenomenon? In contrast to the quantity theory approach, the strategy of direct inflation targeting does not rest on a fully articulated theory of the short and long term effects of monetary policy. It is obviously a rather pragmatic approach and some central banks seem to have been adopting an eclectic view on that issue. This appears to be dissatisfying on theoretical grounds.

On October, 13th 1998, the governing council of the European Central Bank took the decision to use a two pillar strategy to pursue price stability. In the context of its first pillar, money is assigned a prominent role, the second pillar represents a broad assessment of the outlook for price stability[1]. Both pillars cannot directly be viewed as intermediate targets. The concept rather reflects that monitoring developments in money constitutes an indispensable element of a stability oriented monetary policy as soon as it is acknowledged that inflation is ultimately a monetary phenomenon. Monetary policy will be based on a "reference value" for monetary growth. But this is *not* taken as *target* growth. Duisenberg, the President of the ECB, stated: "However, the concept of a reference value does not imply a commitment on the part of the ESCB to mechanistically correct deviations of monetary growth from the reference value over the short term."

In the light of the research undertaken in this study, it might be concluded that the ECB's policy will not differ so much from what the Bundesbank has

[1] See ECB Press Conference as of 13 October 1998, Monthly Bulletin of January 1999 and the FINANCIAL TIMES from 14 October 1998 as indicated in the Bibliography.

been pragmatically practicing since 1974. The economic indicators observed by the ECB are quite the same as those used by the Bundesbank to implement its policy, as demonstrated in Section 5.3. Hence, the ECB's strategy will grant continuity. A further reason why the ECB's policy will resemble more that of the Bundesbank rather than that of, say, the Bank of England is related to its way of revealing information about its policy decisions. The minutes of the governing council's meeting as well as the central bank's own inflation forecast will not be made publicly available. The Bank of England chose to do so in order to gain more credibility and independence from the government. In order to gain credibility and to induce accountability, public monitoring of the inflation target is seen as a key feature underlying a policy of inflation targeting (see Svensson (1997)). The Bank of England is also publishing the minutes of the meetings of the Monetary Policy Committee including voting records. In contrast to that, given a central bank's independence, the Bundesbank's record demonstrates that credibility might also be gained without these tools. Publication of inflation forecasts does not necessarily strengthen transparency and accountability. It might put political pressure on the central bank when pursuing its objectives and influence inflation expectations in an undesirable way. The ECB's governing council has so far vetoed the publication of minutes and voting records on grounds that individual council members might then come under political pressure from their governments.

In the light of this study it is evident that the ECB's strategy is neither that of a monetary targeter nor of an inflation targeter. It reflects the need that in an environment of uncertainty, it is unwise to rely on a single indicator variable that can be thought of as comprising all necessary information. Hence, the ECB has chosen a strategy to structure the complex information necessary for the conduct of monetary policy from two perspectives, as reflected in the two pillars. These two pillars do not constitute targets, but rather complementary perspectives for the assessment of the outlook for price stability.

List of Figures

2.1 Inflation and the development of the German overnight money market rate ... 13
2.2 Development of M3 (monthly: 1974.01 – 1997.04) ... 14
2.3 Development of West German GDP – (quarterly, in prices of 1991, 1974.01 – 1990.04) ... 15
2.4 Development of GDP for unified Germany – (quarterly, in prices of 1991, 1991.01–1998.01) ... 16
2.5 Interest rates for different refinancing facilities ... 21
2.6 Refinancing sources of commercial banks ... 24

4.1 Graphical representation of model (4.3)–(4.4) ... 58
4.2 Graphical representation of system (4.10), (4.11) in innovation form. 59
4.3 The Kalman filter ... 69

5.1 Impulse–responses from money market model: 1991.01–1997.04 ... 107
5.2 Forecast error variance decomposition from money market model: 1991.01–1997.04 ... 108
5.3 Impulse–responses from money market model: 1985.02–1990.05 ... 111
5.4 Forecast error variance decomposition from money market model: 1985.01–1990.05 ... 112
5.5 Impulse–responses from money market model: 1975.01–1985.01 ... 115
5.6 Forecast error variance decomposition from money market model: 1975.01–1985.01 ... 116
5.7 Impulse–responses from general model: 1990.05–1997.04 ... 120
5.8 Impulse–responses from general model: 1990.05–1997.04 ... 121
5.9 Impulse–responses from general model: 1975.01–1985.01 ... 124
5.10 Impulse–responses from general model: 1975.01–1985.01 ... 125
5.11 Capacity utilisation: 1975.I–1997.IV ... 131
5.12 Velocity of German M3: 1975.I–1997.IV ... 132
5.13 GDP deflator and P^*: 1975.I–1997.IV ... 133
5.14 Impulse-responses for price gap and overnight rate from state space representation: 1975.I–1997.IV ... 138
5.15 Impulse-responses for price gap and overnight rate from VAR representation: 1975.I–1997.IV ... 139

List of Tables

2.1 Monetary targets of the Deutsche Bundesbank 11

3.1 Interaction among the variables under an interest rate rule 49
3.2 Interaction among the variables under a reserves targeting procedure 51
3.3 Interaction among the variables under the discount borrowing rule 52

5.1 Singular values of trend part for small model (1991.01–1997.04) .. 103
5.2 Ratios of singular values of trend part for small model (1991.01–1997.04) 104
5.3 Residual diagnostics: Trend part of model for subperiod 1991.01–1997.04 104
5.4 Singular values of cyclical part for small model (1991.01–1997.04) . 104
5.5 Ratios of singular values of cyclical part for small model (1991.01–1997.04) 105
5.6 Residual diagnostics: Joint model for subperiod 1991.01–1997.04 .. 105
5.7 Model parameter estimates (1991.01–1997.04) 106
5.8 Model parameter estimates (1985.02–1990.05) 109
5.9 Residual diagnostics for subperiod 1985.02–1990.05 110
5.10 Model parameter estimates (1975.01–1985.01) 113
5.11 Residual diagnostics for subperiod 1975.01–1985.01 114
5.12 Model parameter estimates (1990.06–1997.04) 119
5.13 Residual diagnostics for subperiod 1990.06–1997.04 119
5.14 Forecast error decomposition: 1990.06–1997.04 122
5.15 Model parameter estimates (1975.01–1985.01) 123
5.16 Residual diagnostics for subperiod 1975.01–1985.01 123
5.17 Forecast error decomposition: 1975.01–1985.01 126
5.18 Parameter estimates and residual diagnostics: State space implementation of P^*–model for West–Germany (1975.I–1990.IV) 134
5.19 Parameter estimates and residual diagnostics: State space implementation of P^*–model for unified Germany (1975.I–1997.IV) 135
5.20 Variance decomposition from state space implementation of P^*–model 135
5.21 Parameter estimates and residual diagnostics: State space implementation of P^*–model for unified Germany (1975.I–1997.IV) 137
5.22 Variance decomposition from Bundesbank-reaction-function. 137

Bibliography

Anderson, B.D.O. and J.B. Moore, 1976, *Optimal filtering*, Prentice–Hall Electrical Engineering Series, New Jersey.

Aoki, M., 1976, *Optimal control and systems theory in dynamic economic analysis*, North–Holland Publishing Company, Amsterdam.

Aoki, M., 1988a, Cointegration, error correction, and aggregation in dynamic models: a comment. *Oxford Bulleting of Economics and Statistics*, Vol. 50, No.1, pp. 89–95.

Aoki, M., 1988b, On alternative state space representations of time series models, *Journal of Economic Dynamics and Control*, 12, pp. 595–607.

Aoki, M., 1990a, State space approach to modeling cointegrated time series, *Advances in Econometrics*, Vol. 8, pp. 203–224.

Aoki, M., 1990b, *State Space Modeling of Time Series*, Springer Verlag, Berlin.

Aoki, M., 1991, A state space time series modelling method without individual detrending, *Journal of Time Series Analysis*, Vol. 12, No. 1, pp. 1–26.

Aoki, M., 1994a, Modelling economic time series by forward and backward state–space innovation models and IV estimators, *European Journal of Operational Research*, Vol. 73, No. 2, pp. 265–278.

Aoki, M., 1994b, Two complementary representations of multiple time series in state–space innovation forms, *Journal of Forecasting*, Vol. 13, pp. 69–90.

Aoki, M. and A. Havenner, 1991, State Space Modeling of Multiple Time Series, *Econometric Reviews*, Vol. 10, No. 1, pp. 1–59.

Assenmacher, W., 1998, *Trend und Zyklus im Bruttoinlandsprodukt der Bundesrepublik Deutschland*, Jahrbücher für Nationalökonomie und Statistik, Vol. 217, No. 5.

Barnett, W.A., D. Fisher, and A. Serletis, 1992, Consumer theory and the demand for money, *Journal of Economic Literature*, Vol. 30, pp. 2086–2116.

Barro, R.J., 1978, Unanticipated money, output, and the price level in the United States, *Journal of Political Economy*, 86, pp. 549–580.

Bartlett, M.S., 1939, A note on tests of significance in multivariate analysis, *Proceedings of the Cambridge Philosophical Society*, No. 35, pp. 180–185.

Bernanke, B.S., and A.S.Blinder, 1992, The Federal Funds rate and the channels of monetary transmission, *American Economic Review*, Vol. 82, No. 4, pp. 901–921.

Bernanke, B.S., and I. Mihov, 1995, *Measuring monetary policy*, NBER Working Paper, No. 5145, June 1995.

Bernanke, B. S., and I. Mihov, 1997, What does the Bundesbank target?, *European Economic Review*, Vol. 41, No. 6, July 1997, pp. 1025–1054.

Bernanke, B. S., and F. Mishkin, 1992, *Central bank behavior and the strategy of monetary policy: observations from six industrial countries* NBER Working Paper, No. 4082.

Beveridge, S., and Nelson Ch.R., 1981, A new approach to decomposition of economic time series into permanent and transitory components with particular attention to measurement of the 'Business Cycle', *Journal of Monetary Economics*, 7, pp. 151–174.

Blinder, A.S., 1998, *Central banking in theory and practice*, MIT Press, Cambridge, Massachusetts.

Bomhoff, E.J., 1977, Predicting the money multiplier – a case study for the U.S. and the Netherlands, *Journal of Monetary Economics*, 3, pp. 325–345.

Bowen, A., 1995, British experience with inflation targetry. In: L. Leiderman and L.E.O. Svensson, eds., *Inflation targets*, Center of Economic Policy Research, London pp. 53–68.

Bradley, M.D., and D.W. Jansen, 1986, Federal Reserve operating procedures in the Eighties. *Journal of Money, Credit and Banking*, Vol. 13, No. 3, August.

Brocket, R., 1970, *Finite dimensional linear systems*, John Wiley and Sons, N.Y..

Brunner, K., 1961, A schema for the supply theory of money, *International Economic Review*, January, pp. 76–109.

Brunner, K., and A. Meltzer, 1964, Some further investigations of demand and supply functions for money, *Journal of Finance*, May, pp. 240–283.

Christiano, L.J., and M. Eichenbaum, 1992, Identification and the liquidity effect of a monetary shock. In: A. Cukierman, L.Z. Hercowitz, and L. Leiderman, eds., *Political economy, growth and business cycles*, MIT Press, Cambridge MA.

Clarida, R., and M. Gertler, 1996, *How does the Bundesbank conduct monetary policy?*, NBER Working Paper, No. 5581.

Cooley, Th.F. and St.F. LeRoy, 1981, Identification and estimation of money demand, *The American Economic Review*, Vol. 71, No. 5, pp. 825–844.

Cuthbertson, K., S.G. Hall and M.P. Taylor, 1992, *Applied Econometric Techniques*, Philip Alan, Hertfordshire, UK.

Deutsche Bundesbank, 1985, *Die deutsche Bundesbank. Geldpolitische Aufgaben und Instrumente.*

Deutsche Bundesbank 1992, Zum Zusammenhang zwischen Geldmengen- und Preisentwicklung in der Bundesrepublik Deutschland, *Deutsche Bundesbank. Monatsbericht November 1992*, pp. 20–29.

Deutsche Bundesbank, 1994, Die Geldmarktsteuerung der Deutschen Bundesbank, *Deutsche Bundesbank. Monatsbericht Mai 1994*, pp. 61–75.

Deutsche Bundesbank, 1995, *Die Geldpolitik der Bundesbank.*

Dickey, D.A., and W.A. Fuller, 1979, Distribution of estimates for autoregressive times series with a unit root, *Journal of the American Statistical Association*, 74, pp. 427–431.

Dickey, D.A., and W.A. Fuller, 1981, Likelihood ratio statistics for autoregressive time series with a unit root, *Econometrica*, pp. 1057–1072.

Diebold, F.X., 1989, State space modeling of time series – a review essy, *Journal of Economic Dynamics and Control*, 13, pp. 597–612.

Diebold, F.X., 1998, The past, present, and future of macroeconomic forecasting, *Journal of Economic Perspectives*, Vol. 12, No. 2, pp. 175–192.

Dorfman, J.H , 1991, Comment: a model specification test for state space models, *Econometric Reviews*, Vol. 10, No. 1, pp. 67–73.

Dorfman, J.H., and A. Havenner, 1992, A Bayesian approach to state space multivariate time series modelling, *Journal of Econometrics*, 52, pp. 315–346.

Dorfman, J.H., and A. Havenner, 1995, Model specification tests for balanced representation of state space models, *Communications in Statistics: Theory and Methods*, Vol. 24, No. 1, pp. 97–119.

Efron, B., and R. Tibshirani, 1986, Bootstrap methods for standard errors, confidence intervals, and other measures of statistical accuracy, *Statistical Science*, Vol. 1, No. 1, pp. 54–77.

Efron, B., and R. Tibshirani, 1993, *An Introduction to the Bootstrap*, Chapman & Hall, New York.

Eichenbaum, M., 1992, Comment on 'Interpreting the macroeconomic time series facts: the effects of monetary policy' by Christopher Sims, *European Economic Review*, 36, pp.1001–1011.

Engle, R.F. and C.W.J. Granger, 1987, Cointegration and error correction: representation, estimation and testing. *Econometrica*, 55, pp.251–276.

Ericsson, N.R., 1992, Cointegration, exogeneity, and policy analysis: an overview, *Journal of Policy Modelling*, Vol. 14, No. 3, pp. 251–280.

Estrella, A., and F.S. Mishkin, 1996, *Is there a role for monetary aggregates in the conduct of monetary policy?* NBER Working Paper, No. 5845, Cambridge, MA, November 1996.

Estrella, A., and F.S. Mishkin, 1997, The predictive power of the term structure of interest rates in Europe and the United States: implications for the European Central Bank. *European Economic Review*, Vol. 41, No. 7, July, pp.1375–1402.

European Central Bank, 13 October 1998, *Press Conference – Tuesday, 13 October 1998 – The President's Introductory Statement*, `http://www.ecb.de/key/st981013.htm`.

European Central Bank, 1 December 1998, *Press Conference – Tuesday, 1 December 1998 – The President's Introductory Statement*, `http://www.ecb.de/key/st981201.htm`.

European Central Bank, 14 December 1998, *Press Release 14 December 1998*, `http://www.ecb.de/key/st981214.htm`.

European Central Bank, , 1999, *The stability-oriented monetary policy strategy of the Eurosystem*, ECB Monthly Bulletin, January 1999, pp. 39-50.

FINANCIAL TIMES, 14 October 1998, p. 2: *Transperancy debate reopens as Duisenberg keeps the lid on*, by Wolfgang Münchau.

Fischer, A., 1995, New Zealand's experience with inflation targets. In: L. Leiderman and L.E.O. Svensson, eds., *Inflation targets*, Center of Economic Policy Research, London pp. 32–52.

Fisher, I., 1930, *The theory of interest*, Macmillan, New York.

Friedman, M., 1956, A quantity theory of money – A restatement. In: Friedman, M., *Studies in the quantity theory of money*, Chicago, Chicago Press.

Friedman, M., 1968, The role of monetary policy, *American Economic Review*, Vol. 58, No. 1, pp.1–17.

Friedman, M., and A.J. Schwartz, 1971, *A monetary history of the United States 1867–1960*, 3rd edition, Princeton University Press.

Fuller, W.A., 1996, *Introduction to statistical time series*, Second Edition, John Wiley and Sons, New York.

Gaab, W. , 1996, On the Demand for Divisia and Simple-Sum M3 in Germany. In: Mullineux, Andrew, ed., *Financial innovation, banking and monetary aggregates*, Cheltenham, U.K., Elgar, 1996, pp. 160-86.

Gordon, D.B., and E.M. Leeper, 1992, In search of the liquidity effect, *Journal of Monetary Economics*, 29, June, pp. 341–369.

Gordon, R.J., 1984, The short–run demand for money: a Reconsideration, *Journal of Money, Credit, and Banking*, Vol. 16, No. 4, pp. 825–844.

Hallman, J.J., R.D. Porter and D.H. Small, 1991, Is the price level tied to the M2 monetary aggregate in the long run? *American Economic Review*, Vol. 81, No. 4, pp. 841–858.

Hamilton, J.D., 1987, Monetary factors in the great depression, *Journal of monetary economics*, 19, pp. 145–169.

Hamilton, J.D., 1994, *Time Series Analysis*, Princeton University Press, Princeton.

Harvey, A.C., 1989, *Forecasting, structural time series models and the Kalman filter*, Cambridge University Press, Cambridge.

Harvey, A.C., 1993, *Time series models*, Harvester Wheatsheaf, Hertfordshire, UK.

Heuser, H., 1986, *Lehrbuch der Analysis*, 3rd and revised edition, Teubner, Stuttgart, Germany.

Hodrick, R.J., and E.C. Prescott, 1997, Post–war U.S. business cycles: an empirical investigation, *Journal of Money, Credit, and Banking*, Vol. 29, No. 1, pp. 1–16.

Householder, A.S., 1964, *The Theory of Matrices in Numerical Analysis*, Dover Publications, New York.

Hume, D., 1752, *Of money*. In: Eugene Rotwein, 1955, ed., David Hume – Writings on Economics, London.

Johansen, S., and K. Juselius, 1990, Maximum likelihood estimation and inference on cointegration – With applications to the demand for money, *Oxford Bulletin of Economics and Statistics*, 52, pp. 169–210.

Kasman, B., 1992, A Comparison of Monetary Policy Operating Procedures in Six Industrial Countries, *Federal Reserve Bank of New York Quarterly Review*, 17, No. 2, September.

King, R.G., and Ch.I. Plosser, 1984, Money, credit and prices in a real business cycle *American Economic Review*. Vol. 74, No. 3, pp. 363–380.

Kitagawa, G., 1981, A nonstationary time series model and its fitting by a recursive filter, *Journal of time series analysis*, Vol. 2, No. 2, pp.103–116.

Kneeshaw, J.T. and P. Van den Bergh, 1989, *Changes in central bank money market operating procedures in the 1980s*. BIS economic papers, No. 23, Bank of International Settlements, Basle, January.

Kmenta, J., 1990, *Elements of Econometrics*, 2nd edition, Macmillan Publishing Company, New York.

Kydland, F.E., and E.C. Prescott, 1982, Time to build and aggregate fluctuations, *Econometrica*, Vol. 50, No. 6, pp.1345–1370.

Laidler, D.E.W., 1977, *The demand for money: theories and evidence*, 2nd edition, Harper and Row, New York.

Laidler, D.E.W., 1980, *The demand for money: theories and evidence*, 3rd edition, Harper and Row, New York.

Leiderman, L., and L.E.O. Svensson, 1995, eds., *Inflation targets*, Center of Economic Policy Research, London.

Leeper, E.M., 1996, *Narrative and VAR approaches to monetary policy: common identification problems*. Indiana University, Monetary Economics Working Paper Series, Vol. 2, No. 3, Febr. 10.

Litterman, R.B., and L. Weiss, 1985, Money, real interest rates, and output: a reinterpretation of postwar U.S. data, *Econometrica*, 53, January, pp. 129–156.

Lucas, R.E.,Jr., 1973, Some international evidence on the output–inflation tradeoffs, *American Economic Review* 63, pp. 1113–1144.

Lütkepohl, H., 1993, *Introduction to multiple time series analysis*, 2nd edition, Springer Verlag, Berlin.

Lutz, F.A., 1940, The structure of interest rates, *Quarterly Journal of Economics*, No. 55, pp. 36–63.

Mittnik, St., 1987, *Alternative Methods for Multivariate Time Series Analysis with Application to U.S. Money-Output Data*, PhD–Thesis, Saint Louis, Missouri.

Mittnik, S., 1981, State space modeling of multiple time series: a comment. *Econometric Reviews*, Vol. 10, No. 1, pp. 75–90.

Nelson, Ch.R., and Ch.J. Plosser, 1982, Trends and random walks in economic time series, *Journal of Monetary Economics*, 10, pp. 135–162.

Nichols, D.A., D.H. Small and Ch.E. Webster, Jr., 1993, Why interest rates rise when an unexpected large money stock is announced, *The American Economic Review*, Vol. 73, No. 3, pp.383–388.

Pecchi, L. 1992, Time series evidence on the money supply process in the USA, *Economic Modeling*, Vol. 10 ,Nr. 3, July, pp. 187–200.

Roley, V.V, 1987, The effects of money announcements under alternative monetary control procedures. *Journal of Money, Credit and Banking*, Vol. 19, No.3, August, pp. 292–307.

Roley, V.V. and C.E. Walsh, 1985, Monetary policy regimes, expected inflation, and the response of interest rates to money announcements, *The Quarterly Journal of Economics*, Vol. 100, Supplement, pp. 1011–1039.

Romer, Ch.D., and D.H. Romer, 1989, Does monetary policy matter? A new test in the spirit of Friedman and Schwartz. In: O.J. Blanchard and S. Fischer, eds., *NBER Maroeconomics Annual*, 1989, MIT–Press, Cambridge, MA, pp. 121–183.

Runkle, D.E., 1987, Vector autoregressions and reality, *Journal of Business and Economic Statistics*, Vol. 5, No. 4, October, pp. 437–442.

Sachverständigenrat, 1998a, *Produktionspotential,Bruttoinlandsprodukt und Auslastungsgrad*, http://www.sachverstaendigenrat-wirtschaft.de/pm/tab_pp.htm.

Sachverständigenrat, 1998b, *Zur Bestimmung des gesamtwirtschaftlichen Produktionopotentials (Sachkapazitäten) für das frühere Bundesgebiet*, http://www.sachverstaendigenrat-wirtschaft.de/pm/pp.htm.

Shapiro, M.D., 1994, Federal Reserve policy: causes and effect. In: N.G. Mankiw, ed., *Monetary policy*, pp. 307–334, University of Chicago Press, Chicago.

Sims, Ch.A., 1980, Macroeconomics and Reality, *Econometrica*, Vol. 48, No. 1, pp.1–48.

Sims, Ch.A., 1992, Interpreting the macroeconomic time series facts, *European Economic Review*, 36, pp. 975–1000.

Stock, J.H. and M.W. Watson, 1988, Testing for Common Trends, *Journal of the American Statistical Association*, December, Vol. 83, No. 404, pp. 1097–1107.

Strongin, S., 1995, The identification of monetary policy disturbances. Explaining the liquidity puzzle, *Journal of monetary economics*, No. 35, pp. 463–497.

Svensson, L.E.O., 1997, Inflation forecast targeting: implementing and monitoring inflation targets, *European Economic Review*, Vol. 41, No. 6, pp. 1111–1146.

Trehan, B., 1989, The practice of monetary targeting: a case study of the West German experience, *Federal Reserve Bank of San Francisco, Economic Review*, Spring, pp. 30–34.

Vinod, H.D. and P. Basu, 1995, Forecasting consumption, income and real interest rates from alternative state–space models, *International Journal of Forecasting*, Vol. 11, No. 2, pp. 217–231.

von Hagen, J., 1995, Inflation and monetary targeting in Germany. In: L. Leiderman and L.E.O. Svensson, eds., *Inflation targets*, Center of Economic Policy Research, London pp. 107–121.

von Hagen, J., 1989, Monetary targeting with exchange rate constraints: the Bundesbank in the 1980s, *Federal Reserve Bank of St. Louis, Review*, 71, No. 5, pp. 53–69.

Wolters, J., T. Teräsvirta and H. Lütkepohl, 1996, *Modelling the Demand for M3 in the Unified Germany*, Discussion Paper 24, Sonderforschungsbereich 373, Humboldt Universität zu Berlin.

A. GAUSS–programs

A.1 Estimation of balanced state space model

The following algorithm represents estimation of model coefficients applying an iterative solution of the Ricatti – Equation.

```
/*
**
** ESTIMATION of the balanced State Space Model
**
**          x_{t+1} = A*x_t+B*e_t
**          y_t     = C*x_t+e_t
**                        with
**                        DELTA=E[e_t*e_t']
**                        P    =E[x_t*x_t']
**
**
** according to Aoki's (1990) Method of Stochastic
** Realisation based on autocovariances.
**
** Parameter estimates are obtained via an iterative
** solution algorithm for the Ricatti-equation.
** Note, that this works  only if the system is
** minimal, i.e. observable and controllable.
**
** Data must me arranged columnwise in y.
**
** USAGE: {A,B,C,delta,P}=aoki_it(y,lags,norm,state);
**
**
** lags: order of the underlying data generating process
** norm: if norm is 1 data are scaled by first observations,
**       if norm is 2 data are mean-adjusted,
**       if norm is 0 data are not scaled at all.
**       norm=1 should be chosen only if nonstationarity
**       of the data is expected.
** state:Selection of the number of states
**       (the Kronecker index, ki) in the modeling procedure.
**       if state=0, ki is selected automatically according to
**                  a given criterion,
**       if state=1, ki may be set to any value by the user:
```

```
**                this might be appropriate if a minimal
**                representation cannot be selected
**                automatically by the algorithm.
**                In this case the user will be asked to
**                choose KI during the estimation procedure
**
**                        Copyright by Claus Brand, June 1997
*/
proc(5)=aoki_it(y,lags,norm,state);
        local t,m,i,y_min,y_plus,row,ACOV,H,HA,
              H_M,H_C,U,S,V,UA,SA,ki,
              a,b,c,delta,p,
              diagS,SRatios,VA,MAT,la_0,PSI,Q,D,
              PHI,W_21,W_11,PM1,F,EPSILON,n,W;

        t=rows(y);        @ number of observations    @
        m=cols(y);        @ number of variables incl. @

        if norm==1;
            "SCALING DATA BY FIRST OBSERVATIONS...";
            y=y-y[1,.];
        elseif norm==2;
            "MEAN-ADJUSTING DATA...";
            y=y-meanc(y)';
        endif;

        @ Computation of Hankel Matrices               *@
                                                      @*@
            y=y';                                     @*@
            @ ------ Computation of Y_{-} ------ @   @*@
            i=1;                                      @*@
            Y_min=y[.,1:(t-1)];                       @*@
            do while rows(y_min) < (lags+1)*m;        @*@
                row=zeros(m,i)~y[.,1:(t-(i+1))];      @*@
                Y_min=Y_min|row;                      @*@
                i=i+1;                                @*@
            endo;                                     @*@
            @ ------ Computation of Y_{+} ------ @   @*@
            i=1;                                      @*@
            Y_plus=y[.,2:t];                          @*@
            do while rows(y_plus) <  (lags+1)*m;      @*@
                row=y[.,2+i:t]~zeros(m,i);            @*@
                Y_plus=Y_plus|row;                    @*@
                i=i+1;                                @*@
            endo;                                     @*@
            y=y';                                     @*@
                                                      @*@
            ACOV=((y_plus*y_min')./(t));              @*@
              /*
              **   ACOV is an auxiliary  matrix to facilitate
              **   computation of the shifted Hankel matrix
              */
        H=ACOV[1:m*lags,1:m*lags];
```

```
        HA=ACOV[m+1:m*lags+m,1:m*lags];

        H_m=H[.,1:m];     @ Extract first column block from H @
        H_c=H[1:m,.];     @ Extract first row block from H @

            @ Singular Value Decomposition of H: @

            {U,S,V}= svd1(H);             @ APPROXIMATION @
            {UA,SA,VA}=svd1(HA);                 @ " @
                                                 @ " @

        diagS=diag(S);
             /* Computation of ratios of singular values
             ** to the first singular value
             */
        SRatios=diagS./diagS[1:1];
cls;
"";
"**********************************************************";
"Singular Values of Hankel Matrix:";
diagS';
"**********************************************************";
"Ratios to the first element:";
SRatios';
"**********************************************************";
"";
"States that produce ratios up to";;1/sqrt(T);;"should be";
"included.";
    ki=sumc(SRatios.ge 1/sqrt(T));
    format /rd 1,0;
if state==0;
    "==> SUGESTED NUMBER OF STATES TO BE INCLUDED IS ";;ki;
    wait;
    "PRESS ANY KEY TO CONTINUE...";
elseif state==1;
    "==> SUGESTED NUMBER OF STATES TO BE INCLUDED IS ";;ki;
    "INSERT NUMBER OF STATES:";
    ki=con(1,1);
endif;
        format /rd 16,8;
        /* Implementation of lower order approximation */
                                                 @ " @
        S=S[1:ki,1:ki];                          @ " @
        U=U[.,1:ki];                             @ " @
        V=V[.,1:ki];                             @ " @
        SA=SA[1:ki,1:ki];                        @ " @
        UA=UA[.,1:ki];                           @ " @
        VA=VA[.,1:ki];                           @ " @
                                                 @ " @
        H=U*S*V';                                @ " @
        HA=UA*SA*VA';                            @ " @
```

```
        /* Computation of system matrices A and C */

       A=inv(S^(.5))*U'*HA*V*inv(S^(.5));
       Mat=inv(S^(.5))*U'*H_m;
       C=H_C*V*inv(S^(.5));
       "";
       "A=";;A;
       "C=";;C;
       "";
       la_0=(y'*y)./(t);

           /*
           **
           **  Solution of the Ricatti equation
           **     X=AXA'+(M-AXC')*(La_0-CXC')^(-1)*(M-AXC')'
           */

             PM1=zeros(rows(a),rows(a));
             P=A*PM1*A'+(MAT-A*PM1*C')
               *inv(La_0-C*PM1*C')*(MAT-A*PM1*C')';
             cls;
"";
"";
"*********************************************************";
"        ITERATIVE SOLUTION  OF RICATTI EQUATION          ";
"*********************************************************";
             format /rd 1,0;
             "Iteration Step 1";
             format /ros 16,8;
             "";
             "P=";;P;
"*********************************************************";
             i=2;
           @do while i < 100;@
             EPSILON=1e-2;
           do while sumc(sumc(abs(abs(p)-abs(pm1))))>1e-10;
             PM1=P;
                     @ non-stepwise search @
             P=A*PM1*A'+(MAT-A*PM1*C')
               *inv(La_0-C*PM1*C')*(MAT-A*PM1*C')';
                     @ stepwise search     @
             /* F=A*PM1*A'+(MAT-A*PM1*C')
               *inv(La_0-C*PM1*C')*(MAT-A*PM1*C')';
             P=PM1+EPSILON*(F-PM1);    */
             cls;

"";
"";
"*********************************************************";
"        ITERATIVE SOLUTION  OF RICATTI EQUATION          ";
"*********************************************************";
             format /rd 1,0;
             "Iteration Step ";;i;
```

```
              format /ros 16,8;
              "";
              "P=";;P;@wait; @
"*********************************************************";
              i=i+1;
            endo;

format /rd 1,0;
"";
"Convergence of Ricatti-Equation after ";;i-1;;"iterations";
format /ros 16,8;

          /* Computation of system matrices B and DELTA */

        delta=la_0-c*p*c';
        B=(Mat-A*p*c')*inv(delta);

                                @ Print model coefficients:@

"";
"";
"";
"*********************************************************";
"************** Model coefficients: **********************";
"*********************************************************";
"";
"---------------------------------------------------------";
"A=";;A;
"---------------------------------------------------------";
"";
"---------------------------------------------------------";
"B=";;B;
"---------------------------------------------------------";
"";
"---------------------------------------------------------";
"C=";;C;
"---------------------------------------------------------";
"";
"---------------------------------------------------------";
"DELTA=";;DELTA;
"---------------------------------------------------------";
"";
"---------------------------------------------------------";
"PI=";;P;
"---------------------------------------------------------";
"";

        retp(A,B,C,Delta,P);
endp;
```

The following algorithm represents estimation of model coefficients based on the solution of the Ricatti–equation using symplectic matrices.

```
/*
```

```
**
** ESTIMATION of the balanced State Space Model
**
**       x_{t+1} = A*x_t+B*e_t
**       y_t     = C*x_t+e_t
**                  with
**                  DELTA=E[e_t*e_t']
**                  P    =E[x_t*x_t']
**
**
** according to Aoki's (1990) Method of Stochastic
** Realization based on autocovariances.
** Parameter estimates are obtained via solution
** of the Ricatti-equation using symplectic matrices.
**
** Note, that - as in the case of the iterative solution
** algorithm - this works if and only if the system is
** minimal, i.e. observable and controllable.
**
** Data must me arranged columnwise in y.
**
** USAGE: {A,B,C,delta,P}=aoki_sym(y,lags,norm,state);
**
**
** lags: order of the underlying data generating process
** norm: if norm is 1 data are scaled by first observations,
**       if norm is 2 data are mean-adjusted,
**       if norm is 0 data are not scaled at all.
**       norm=1 should be chosen only if nonstationarity
**       of the data is expected.
** state:Selection of the number of states
**       (the Kronecker index, ki) in the modeling procedure.
**       if state=0, ki is selected automatically according to
**                 a given criterion,
**       if state=1, ki may be set to any value by the user:
**               this might be appropriate if a minimal
**               representation cannot be selected
**               automatically by the algorithm.
**               In this case the user will be asked to
**               choose KI during the estimation procedure
**
**                 Copyright by Claus Brand, June 1997
*/
proc(5)=aoki_sym(y,lags,norm,state);
       local t,m,i,y_min,y_plus,row,ACOV,H,HA,
             a,b,c,delta,p,
             H_M,H_C,U,S,V,UA,SA,VA,
             diagS,SRatios,ki,
             MAT,la_0,PSI,Q,D,
             PHI,W_21,W_11,n,W,J;

       t=rows(y);          @ number of observations    @
       m=cols(y);          @ number of variables incl. @
```

```
if norm==1;
    "SCALING DATA BY FIRST OBSERVATIONS...";
    y=y-y[1,.];
elseif norm==2;
    "MEAN-ADJUSTING DATA...";
    y=y-meanc(y)';
endif;

@ Computation of Hankel Matrices                        *@
                                                        @*@
    y=y';                                               @*@
    @ ------ Computation of Y_{-} ------ @              @*@
    i=1;                                                @*@
    Y_min=y[.,1:(t-1)];                                 @*@
    do while rows(y_min) < (lags+1)*m;                  @*@
        row=zeros(m,i)~y[.,1:(t-(i+1))];                @*@
        Y_min=Y_min|row;                                @*@
        i=i+1;                                          @*@
    endo;                                               @*@
    @ ------ Computation of Y_{+} ------ @              @*@
    i=1;                                                @*@
    Y_plus=y[.,2:t];                                    @*@
    do while rows(y_plus) <  (lags+1)*m;                @*@
        row=y[.,2+i:t]~zeros(m,i);                      @*@
        Y_plus=Y_plus|row;                              @*@
        i=i+1;                                          @*@
    endo;                                               @*@
    y=y';                                               @*@
                                                        @*@
    ACOV=((y_plus*y_min')./(t));                        @*@

/* ACOV: Auxiliary matrix to facilitate computation
** of shifted Hankel matrix
*/

H=ACOV[1:m*lags,1:m*lags];
HA=ACOV[m+1:m*lags+m,1:m*lags];

H_m=H[.,1:m];   @ Extract first column block from H @
H_c=H[1:m,.];   @ Extract first row block from H @

    @ Singular Value Decomposition of H: @

    {U,S,V}= svd1(H);           @ APPROXIMATION @
    {UA,SA,VA}=svd1(HA);                @ " @

diagS=diag(S);
     /* Computation of ratios of singular values
     ** to the first singular value
     */
SRatios=diagS./diagS[1:1];
cls;
```

```
"";
"**********************************************************";
"Singular Values of Hankel Matrix:";
diagS';
"**********************************************************";
"Ratios to the first element:";
SRatios';
"**********************************************************";
"";
"States that produce ratios up to";;1/sqrt(T);;"should be";
"included.";
    ki=sumc(SRatios.ge 1/sqrt(T));
    format /rd 1,0;
if state==0;
    "==> SUGESTED NUMBER OF STATES TO BE INCLUDED IS ";;ki;
    wait;
    "PRESS ANY KEY TO CONTINUE...";
elseif state==1;
    "==> SUGESTED NUMBER OF STATES TO BE INCLUDED IS ";;ki;
    "INSERT NUMBER OF STATES:";
    ki=con(1,1);
endif;
        format /rd 16,8;
        /* Implementation of lower order approximation */
                                                      @ " @
                                                      @ " @
        S=S[1:ki,1:ki];                               @ " @
        U=U[.,1:ki];                                  @ " @
        V=V[.,1:ki];                                  @ " @
        SA=SA[1:ki,1:ki];                             @ " @
        UA=UA[.,1:ki];                                @ " @
        VA=VA[.,1:ki];                                @ " @
                                                      @ " @
        H=U*S*V';                                     @ " @
        HA=UA*SA*VA';                                 @ " @

         /* Computation of system matrices A and C */

        A=inv(S^(.5))*U'*HA*V*inv(S^(.5));
        Mat=inv(S^(.5))*U'*H_m;
        C=H_C*V*inv(S^(.5));
        "";
        "A=";;A;
        "C=";;C;
        "";

        la_0=(y'*y)./(t);

/*
**
**  Solution of the Ricatti equation
**    X=AXA'+(M-AXC')*(La_0-CXC')^(-1)*(M-AXC')'
**  using symplectic matrices
```

```
*/

/*
** Auxiliary Matrices
*/

    PSI=A'-C'*inv(La_0)*MAT';
    Q=C'*inv(La_0)*C;
    D=MAT*inv(La_0)*MAT';

/*
** Construction of symplectic matrix PHI
*/

    PHI=((PSI-Q*((inv(PSI))')*D)~(Q*((inv(PSI))')))|
        ((-((inv(PSI))')*D)~(((inv(PSI))')));

/*
** SCHUR decomposition of PHI
*/

    {s,w}=schur(PHI);

    n=rows(PSI);

/*
** PARTIONING OF W, DERIVATION OF SOLUTION
*/

    W_21=W[n+1:2*n,1:n];
    W_11=W[1:n,1:n];

    P=W_21*inv(W_11);

          /* Computation of system matrices DELTA and B */

        delta=la_0-c*p*c';
        B=(Mat-A*p*c')*inv(delta);

                        @     Print model coefficients    @
"";
"";
"";
"*********************************************************";
"************** Model coefficients: *********************";
"*********************************************************";
"";
"--------------------------------------------------------";
"A=";;A;
"--------------------------------------------------------";
"";
"--------------------------------------------------------";
"B=";;B;
```

```
"-------------------------------------------------------";
"";
"-------------------------------------------------------";
"C=";;C;
"-------------------------------------------------------";
"";
"-------------------------------------------------------";
"DELTA=";;DELTA;
"-------------------------------------------------------";
"";
"-------------------------------------------------------";
"PI=";;P;
"-------------------------------------------------------";
"";
        retp(A,B,C,Delta,P);
endp;
```

A.2 Obtaining in–sample forecasts using the Kalman filter

```
/* -------------------------------------------------
**   Kalman-Filter for Balanced State Space Model:
**
**      x_{t+1} = A*x_t+B*e_t
**      y_t     = C*x_t+e_t
**                   with
**                   Delta=E[e_t*e_t']
**                   P    =E[x_t*x_t']
**
**       Each series is to be stored
**                 columnwise in y_t
**
**
**   Usage: {y_hat}=kal_BSSM(y,A,B,C,Delta,p);
**
**
**                        Copyright by Claus Brand
**                             July 1997
** -------------------------------------------------
*/
proc(1)=kal_BSSM(y,A,B,C,DELTA,p);
        local t,F,Q,H,R,xi_tm1_tm1,
              K_t,
              xi_t_t,P_t_t,xi_t_tm1,P_t_tm1,y_t_tm1,
              x_t,i,p_tm1_tm1,y_hat;
```

```
        t=rows(y);



        F=A;
        Q=B*Delta*B';
        H=C';
        R=Delta;

@--- Following the Notation in             @
@   Luetkepohl 1993 pp.428-432 ------------@

    xi_tm1_tm1 =  zeros(cols(A),1);
    p_tm1_tm1  =  p;


    i=1;


    do while i <= rows(y);

        @ ---- Prediction step -------- @

        xi_t_tm1     =    F*xi_tm1_tm1;
        p_t_tm1      =    F*p_tm1_tm1*F'+Q;
        y_t_tm1      =    H'*xi_t_tm1;

        @ ---- Correction step -------- @

                          @ Kalman gain: @
        K_t          =    p_t_tm1*H*inv(H'*p_t_tm1*H+R);
        xi_t_t       =    xi_t_tm1
                         +K_t*((y[i,.])'-y_t_tm1);
        p_t_t        =    p_t_tm1
                         -K_t*(H'*P_t_tm1*H+R)*K_t';

        @ -- Redefinition of variables -- @

        xi_tm1_tm1=xi_t_t;
        p_tm1_tm1=p_t_t;

        @ Store the Filtration Output @
        if i==1;
               y_hat=(y_t_tm1)';
         else;
               y_hat=y_hat|(y_t_tm1)';
         endif;
         i=i+1;
    endo;
    retp(y_hat);
endp;
```

A.3 Calculation of impulse–responses

```
/*
** Impulse Response Analysis  of the State Space Model
**
**      x_{t+1} = A*x_t+B*e_t
**      y_t     = C*x_t+e_t
**                   with
**                   Delta=E[e_t*e_t']
**                   P    =E[x_t*x_t']
**
**
**       Each series is to be stored
**                 columnwise in y
**
**
**   Usage: {response}=imp_res(A,B,C,Delta,T,lags);
**   In order to use imp_res.prc, first decompose
**   matrix DELTA subjecto to a specific identification scheme
**   so that T*D*T'=DELTA.
**
**                                Copyright by Claus Brand
**                                              04/07/1997
**
*/
proc(1)=imp_res(A,B,C,Delta,T,lags);

        local APot,k;

        k=0;
        do while k le lags;
                if k==0;
                        RESPONSE=T;
                elseif k==1;
                        RESPONSE=RESPONSE|C*B*T;
                elseif k==2;
                        APot=A;
                        RESPONSE=RESPONSE|C*APot*B*T;
                else;
                        APot=APot*A;
                        RESPONSE=RESPONSE|C*APot*B*T;
                endif;
        k=k+1;
        endo;
        retp(response);
endp;
```

A.4 Calculation of forecast–error variance decompositions

```
/*
**  Forecast Error Variance Decomposition for the State Space Model
**
**      x_{t+1} = A*x_t+B*e_t
**      y_t     = C*x_t+e_t
**                    with
**                    Delta=E[e_t*e_t']
**                    P    =E[x_t*x_t']
**
**
**       Each series is to be stored
**                 columnwise in y
**
**
**   Usage: {ratios}=forc_dec(A,B,C,Delta,lags);
**
**
**                                                  April, 1998
**                                      Copyright by Claus Brand
**
** If the dimension of y_t is k, FORC_DEC will be of dimension
** (lag*k x k). Each (k x k)-block will be constituted as follows:
** The j-i-th element in this block is equivalent to the portion
** of the j-th variable's forecast error as accounted for by the
** i-th variable in the system.  Therefore, row elements in
** FORC_DEC will add up to one.
**
*/
proc(1)=FORC_DEC(A,B,C,Delta,T,lags);

        local APot,k,sum_num,sum_den,Ratios;

        k=0;
        do while k le lags;
                if k==0;
                        RESPONSE=T;
                        SUM_NUM=(RESPONSE^2);       @ numerator @
                        SUM_DEN=diag(RESPONSE*RESPONSE');
                                                    @ denominator @
                        RATIOS=SUM_NUM./SUM_DEN;
                elseif k==1;
                        RESPONSE=C*B*T;
                        SUM_NUM=SUM_NUM+(RESPONSE^2);
                        SUM_DEN=SUM_DEN+diag(RESPONSE*RESPONSE');
                        RATIOS=RATIOS|SUM_NUM./SUM_DEN;
                elseif k==2;
                        APot=A;
                        RESPONSE=C*APot*B*T;
                        SUM_NUM=SUM_NUM+(RESPONSE^2);
                        SUM_DEN=SUM_DEN+diag(RESPONSE*RESPONSE');
```

```
                    RATIOS=RATIOS|SUM_NUM./SUM_DEN;
                else;
                    APot=APot*A;
                    RESPONSE=C*APot*B*T;
                    SUM_NUM=SUM_NUM+(RESPONSE^2);
                    SUM_DEN=SUM_DEN+diag(RESPONSE*RESPONSE');
                    RATIOS=RATIOS|SUM_NUM./SUM_DEN;
                endif;
        k=k+1;
        endo;

        retp(ratios);
endp;
```

A.5 Decomposition of Error Variance–Covariance-Matrix Δ

```
/*
**
**  DECOMP.PRC
**
**  Computes decomposition of an error variance-covariance matrix
**  DELTA from a multivariate time series model in order
**  to compute impulse-responses and forecast-error variance
**  decompositions for orthogonalized innovations, so that
**
**                      DELTA =  T * D * T'
**
**  where D is a diagonal matrix of orthogonalized innovations.
**
**  Matrix MASK is to be defined by the user subject to specific
**  identification schemes: Hereby, MASK is a zero matrix containing
**  ones on positions where offdiagonal elements in T are assumed
**  to be nonzero.
**
**  USAGE:      {T,D}=DECOMP(DELTA,MASK);
**
*/

proc(2)=decomp(DELTA,MASK);
        local T,Tp1,D,i,n;

        n=rows(MASK);
        D=eye(n);
        T=zeros(n,n);
        Tp1=eye(n);
        i=1;
                do while sumc(sumc(abs(abs(DELTA)
                        -abs(Tp1*D*Tp1'))))>10^(-10);
                    T=Tp1;
                    D=inv(T)*DELTA*inv(T');
```

```
                        D=D.*eye(n);
                        T=(inv(D)*inv(T)*DELTA)';
                        Tp1=(T-(eye(n).*diag(T))).*mask+eye(n);
                          /*cls; delta;
                          **"i=";;i;;Tp1;T;
                          ** ((DELTA)-(Tp1*D*Tp1'))*1000;
                          ** wait;cls; */
                        if i==999;
                           goto ERROR;
                        else;
                        endif;
                i=i+1;
                endo;
                format /rd 3,0;
        ERROR:
        if i le 999;
                "**********************************************";
                " CONVERGENCE REACHED AFTER ";;i;;" ITERATIONS   ";
                "**********************************************";
                format /rd 16,8;
        elseif i==1000;
                "**********************************************";
                "* NO CONVERGENCE REACHED AFTER 1000 ITERATIONS *";
                "* ENSURE IDENTIFICATION OF PARAMETERS IN T !!  *";
                "**********************************************";
                format /rd 16,8;
        endif;
     retp(Tp1,D);
endp;
```

A.6 Aoki C-Test for model specification

In the code below the `toepl`–procedure that comes along with Dorfman and Havenner's `SSATS 2.0` module is used to compute the Toeplitz matrix R in (4.62).

```
/*
**
**  Aoki's (1990) error covariance test for model specification
**
**  USAGE: {ci,dof}=bartlett(y,lags,ki);
**
**                       y   : multivariate time series
**                       lags: order of autocovariances to construct
**                             Hankel matrix
**                       ki  : Kronecker index of the system
**
**                       CI  : Aoki-C test statistic
**                       dof : Degrees of freedom
**
```

```
**                               Claus Brand, 08/18/1998
*/

proc(2)=bartlett(y,lags,ki);
        local t,m,i,y_min,y_plus,row,ACOV,H,
              U,S,V,UPROX,SPROX,VPROX,HPROX,R,
              Lambda,CI,dof;

        t=rows(y);          @ number of observations    @
        m=cols(y);          @ number of variables incl. @


        @ Computation of Hankel Matrices                 *@
                                                        @*@
            y=y';                                       @*@
            @ ------ Computation of Y_{-} ------ @      @*@
            i=1;                                        @*@
            Y_min=y[.,1:(t-1)];                         @*@
            do while rows(y_min) < (lags+1)*m;          @*@
                row=zeros(m,i)~y[.,1:(t-(i+1))];        @*@
                Y_min=Y_min|row;                        @*@
                i=i+1;                                  @*@
            endo;                                       @*@
            @ ------ Computation of Y_{+} ------ @      @*@
            i=1;                                        @*@
            Y_plus=y[.,2:t];                            @*@
            do while rows(y_plus) <  (lags+1)*m;        @*@
                row=y[.,2+i:t]~zeros(m,i);              @*@
                Y_plus=Y_plus|row;                      @*@
                i=i+1;                                  @*@
            endo;                                       @*@
            y=y';                                       @*@
                                                        @*@
            ACOV=((y_plus*y_min')./(t));                @*@

        H=ACOV[1:m*lags,1:m*lags];

        @ Singular Value Decomposition of H: @

        {U,S,V}= svd1(H);                      @ APPROXIMATION @
                                                     @ " @


        format /rd 16,8;
                                                        @ " @
        SPROX=S[1:ki,1:ki];                             @ " @
        UPROX=U[.,1:ki];                                @ " @
        VPROX=V[.,1:ki];                                @ " @
                                                        @ " @
        HPROX=UPROX*SPROX*VPROX';                       @ " @
        @HPROX=U*SPROX*V;       @

        R=toepl(y,lags);
```

```
        Lambda=det(R-(H')*inv(R)*(H'))/
                 det(R-(HPROX)*inv(R)*(HPROX'));

        CI=-(T-ki-0.5*(m*lags+1))*ln(Lambda);
        retp(CI);

        dof = ((cols(y)*lags)-ki)^2;
endp;
```

GPSR Compliance

The European Union's (EU) General Product Safety Regulation (GPSR) is a set of rules that requires consumer products to be safe and our obligations to ensure this.

If you have any concerns about our products, you can contact us on ProductSafety@springernature.com

In case Publisher is established outside the EU, the EU authorized representative is:

Springer Nature Customer Service Center GmbH
Europaplatz 3
69115 Heidelberg, Germany

Batch number: 10725973

Printed by Printforce, the Netherlands